Political manipulation and administrative power

A comparative study

Eva Etzioni-Halevy

Routledge & Kegan Paul
London, Boston and Henley

First published in 1979
by Routledge & Kegan Paul Ltd
39 Store Street, London WC1E 7DD,
Broadway House, Newtown Road,
Henley-on-Thames, Oxon RG9 1EN and
9 Park Street, Boston, Mass. 02108, USA
Photoset in 10 on 11 Times by
Kelly Typesetting, Bradford-on-Avon, Wiltshire
and printed in Great Britain by
Unwin Brothers Ltd, The Gresham Press,
Old Woking, Surrey
A member of the Staples Printing Group

British Library Cataloguing in Publication Data

Etzioni-Halevy, Eva

Political manipulation and administrative power.
– (International library of sociology).
1. Democracy 2. State, The
3. Power (Social sciences)
4. Elite (Social sciences)
I. Title II. Series
301.5'92   JC423   79–40869

ISBN 0 7100 0352 8

To Ethan, my eldest
with love and gratitude
for his compassion and understanding

Contents

Bureaucracy

CONTENTS

Acknowledgments

A large part of this study was carried out while I was on a visiting fellowship at the Department of Sociology, the Research School of Social Sciences, the Australian National University. I am greatly indebted to the department for the opportunity it afforded me to devote myself full-time to this project. Other parts of the project were carried out at the Department of Sociology, Tel-Aviv University, and at the Department of Sociology, Faculty of Arts, the Australian National University. I wish to express my gratitude to both departments for their generous support and assistance. I would like to express special thanks to the heads of the three departments, Professor F. Lancaster Jones, Dr Yochanan Peres and Professor Jerzy Zubrzycki, for their personal encouragement.

Several Australian scholars devoted generously of their time to discussions of Australian politics and history, from which this study greatly benefited. I am especially grateful to Ms Eileen Price and Dr Bruce Mitchell of the University of New England; to Dr Colin Hughes, Dr Peter Loveday and Dr Don Rawson of the Australian National University; and to Dr Malcolm MacKerras of Duntroon College. I have made extensive use of the ideas they suggested but they are not to be held responsible for whatever misinterpretations may have found their way into these ideas as they were incorporated into the study.

I am also greatly indebted to Professor Leonard Broom, Dr John Higley, Professor F. Lancaster Jones, Mr Klaus Loewald, Dr Bruce Mitchell, Professor John Nalson, Ms Eileen Price and Dr William Rubinstein for reading parts of the manuscript at various stages of its preparation and for their most valuable and helpful comments. The revisions undertaken after each round of such comments greatly improved the manuscript, but I must claim sole responsibility for whatever shortcomings remain.

ACKNOWLEDGMENTS

I would like to express my deepest gratitude to Mr Lew Golan for his outstanding work in editing the manuscript and for turning a foreigner's cumbersome style into intelligible English. Thanks are also due to Ms Sandra Kruck and Ms Ettie Oakman for their invaluable help in patiently typing and retyping the manuscript more times than I care to remember. Finally I wish to thank my son Oren for his most helpful and intelligent research assistance and for his cheerful encouragement.

I should like to thank the following authors, publishers and authorities for permission to quote short extracts: W. L. Guttsman, *The British Political Elite*; the Mitchell Library, Sydney, for brief quotation from three manuscript letters; Oxford University Press for C. O'Leary, *The Elimination of Corrupt Practices in British Elections*; Prentice-Hall, Inc., Englewood Cliffs, New Jersey, for Robert D. Putnam, *The Comparative Study of Political Elites*, 1976; Yale University Press for S. Kuznets, *Modern Economic Growth*.

Introduction: political manipulation and the role of elites

It is widely recognized in the literature that elites tend to entrench themselves in power through the manipulation of the rank-and-file public. But although this manipulation has been frequently alluded to, it has been much less frequently analysed and documented. This book examines in detail certain types of such manipulation; the socio-cultural conditions under which they have thrived and the structural and normative developments that have led to their partial decline in recent years. Seen differently, this is a study of how political and administrative elites in Western-style democracies have tried to obtain or keep power by methods which run counter to the spirit (and the letter) of democracy yet without overtly disrupting the democratic system. It is a study of how the elites have exploited the democratic process for the purpose of domination – and of the normative codes of propriety developed by these same elites which (in some countries more than in others) have eventually curbed this usage.

Political manipulation, theories of domination and normative restraints

Two basic models have evolved for the study of social domination. One focuses on social classes in the tradition of Marx, the other concetrates on elites in the tradition of Pareto, Mosca and Michels (see Aron, 1950; Field and Higley, 1973). The basic assumption of Marxist class analysis is that capitalist societies are divided by a conflict of interest based on economic expropriation of surplus, and that classes are rooted in that antagonism. One class (the dominant class) wields economic power by virtue of its ownership and control of the means of production; consequently it expropriates the surplus of the production process, or at least benefits from such expropriation. The other class (the dominated class), having no control over the means of production, is exploited by the process of expropriation.

The elite model, too, sees society (any society) as divided by a conflict of interests – but this cleavage is political rather than economic. Society is divided into a minority (the ruling elite), that holds the key positions in the governmental structures and thus wields political power, and a majority, the public (or the 'masses'), that is subject to this power. By virtue of its position, the elite can use coercive or manipulative practices that serve its own interests – especially to keep itself in power, enhance its power and maximize the rewards of power. When a ruling elite is none the less replaced, the new ruling elite engages in basically the same practices as did its predecessor.

Both models thus see society as divided into those who wield power and those who are subject to it; but the class model focuses on economic power, the elite model on political power. Both models include a ruling group; but they address themselves to different phenomena. The elite model's 'ruling class' (Mosca) or 'ruling elite' (Pareto) includes those who wield power because they hold the key positions in a political structure and make the key decisions in it. In the class model the holders of key positions (the 'state apparatus') do not have primary importance; their decisions merely serve to solidify a certain economic system. Therefore, the class model's ruling class goes far beyond the small number of decision-makers themselves, and includes those who benefit from this economic system.[1] Both models focus on the means by which the ruling group solidifies its position – but in the class model it is economic exploitation, while in the elite model it is political manipulation that counts.

The strange thing is that class analyses, which are concerned with economic power and exploitation, are considered progressive and radical – but elite analyses, which are concerned with political power and manipulation (a different, but by no means less crucial form of domination), have not been awarded such laudatory epitaphs. The view that the ruling elite exercise power only in a formal sense, while actually reflecting the interests of a wider group of people, is considered *avant-garde* and therefore is 'in'. But the view that the ruling elite is a separate entity which promotes its own interests (particularly the retention of power) is considered *status-quo*-oriented and therefore is 'out'.[2]

At the risk of lagging sadly behind the times, I nevertheless work on the assumption that political power is no less essential than economic power for several reasons. Not only are political power and economic power closely interconnected but governing elites have a large degree of control over the allocation of economic resources, and political power may thus serve as a source of economic power (rather than its handmaiden). Furthermore, political power is a major resource and reward in its own right. Therefore, I propose that rather than serving the interests of an economic stratum in every case, the political elite may well utilize such a stratum to serve its own interests.[3] And since political power is no less crucial than economic power, political manipulation geared to solidify this power is no less worthy of analysis than is economic exploitation – which in any event has been so brilliantly exposed so many times[4] that little new is left to be added. Indeed, given so many impressive recent analyses of economic class exploitation, perhaps the time has arrived for the pendulum to swing toward a renewed emphasis on elite analysis (as exemplified, for instance, by Higley, Field and Grøholt, 1976).

Although I advocate a re-orientation toward the elite model of society, this does not imply that the model must necessarily be adopted as an all encompassing, exclusive point of view. On the risk of falling even further out of step with the times, I also suggest that evolving codes of ethics and emerging normative traditions have successively curtailed (and in some countries even eliminated) certain manipulatory practices previously engaged in by political and administrative elites in their struggle for power.

Several elite-model analysts (as well as adherents of the more broadly defined 'power and conflict school' such as Dahrendorf and Rex), if they addressed themselves to norms and values at all, generally viewed them in Mills's words as 'master symbols of legitimation'.[5] The central argument of this essay, however, is that norms and values – especially those of elites – have a role that goes far beyond merely legitimizing power structures and counter structures. Political and administrative elites are seen as oriented basically towards their own self-interest (the principle of 'what's in it for me'), especially self-entrenchment. At the same time, it will be shown that values and codes of ethics influence both the elites' perceptions of their interests and the means by which they feel free to pursue those interests.

Are the members of the elites themselves committed to those codes of ethics? Or do they fear that their defiance of such codes could be used by their adversaries to discredit them? Or do they accept these codes as rules of the game because they ensure that their pursuit of their interests will not be unduly hindered by their rivals' pursuit of *their* interests? These are moot questions. What is crucial is that once institutionalized, the codes set effective limits to the manner in which elites can entrench themselves in power, and thus have a distinct, independent effect on power structures and

3

political regimes. In a way, then, this study is an attempt to bring norms and values back into the analysis of elites and power.

While the analysis thus diverges in some respects from the elite model and the 'power and conflict' school (both of which tend to minimize the importance of values), it also differs in some respects from the structural-functional school – which has tended to maximize that importance. Parsons and other sociologists of the latter tradition tended to analyse norms and values as abstract categories – almost as tantamount to social structure itself. However, it seems that a more fruitful approach is to specify the groups of people whose norms and values are held to be of such crucial importance. I try to show that the most important values – those that have the clearest impact on a socio-political structure – are the values developed and adhered to by political and administrative ruling elites.

This analysis thus draws on (and sometimes adapts) the tenets of disparate sociological traditions. From the elite and power schools it takes the emphasis on interests, on political power as a crucial resource in its own right (rather than as subordinate to economic power), and on ruling elites as the key groups that wield such power. From the structural-functional school comes the emphasis on values and norms (albeit especially those of the elites). Far from seeing those themes as contradictory, I assume that power interests and values are so intimately interrelated that one can hardly be analysed without serious consideration of the other; and that the political elites are the agents that link the two.

All of the schools virtually disregard political democracy as a mitigating factor in the structure of social domination and subjugation. Marx and most of his followers did not perceive political democracy as a remedy for class exploitation, just as Pareto, Mosca, Michels and most of their followers have not regarded democracy as a remedy for elite domination. As for the structural-functional school, it has had little to contribute to the study of power in any case; although it presumably has a favourable orientation toward democracy, it does not have much to say about it.

While this study is not an analysis of democracy *per se*, it is confined to electoral manipulation in Western-style democracies. This limitation is based on the assumption that electoral manipulation is more significant where elections give the public at least the potential for some participation in the political arena (and, thus, for checking the power of the elites). It may be argued that democracy itself is the outgrowth of self-imposed limitations by elites, and that only where elites impose such restraints on themselves can elections be meaningful in further mitigating the elites' power. Hence, it is not surprising that electoral manipulation of the type dealt with in this study is much more widespread in non-Western countries – where democratic restraints are partly or completely absent in any case, where the opposition is banned or restricted, where electoral results are periodically voided by military coups and the like, and where the electoral process is thus questionable to begin with. But it is precisely for this very reason that electoral manipulation holds less interest in these countries: if unsuccessful, it can always be supplemented or supplanted by one or more of the above devices. Manipulation is worthy of being studied only where it is the sole method of distorting elections and only where its decline is thus synonymous with an increase in the significance of public political participation.

Political manipulation and theories of political participation

This, in turn, brings up the subject of the public's political participation in Western-style democracies. Since so much stress has been put on the importance of ruling elites and their values in shaping a socio-political system, does this imply that the public, even in a Western democracy, has little or no influence in shaping that system? This is the very question that originally aroused my interest in the study of political manipulation.

The elite model of society from Pareto onward (C. Wright Mills included) has usually attributed to the elites alone, the major driving and initiating force in society; it sees the public (the 'masses') as basically a passive object of elite action, even in democratic societies. The analyses by Field and Higley (1973, 1978) corroborate and extend this view by showing that unity among elites is the most crucial factor in the stability of a socio-political regime; the attitude of the public has little bearing on it. The class model of society, on the other hand, has viewed the dominated class as capable of taking its destiny into its own hands and transforming the socio-political system, even if it has seldom actually used this potential.

Recently, the controversy between the elite tradition and the class tradition of sociological analysis has been duplicated in a different context. An apparently incomprehensible cleavage of opinion has developed among political scientists on the question of political participation. Observers working within the elite tradition claim that in contemporary societies, political power is being increasingly concentrated at the elite level, while the masses are becoming increasingly apathetic and politically impotent. Other political observers (although not necessarily influenced by the class model of society) claim the opposite: that the public is becoming increasingly involved politically, and is having a growing influence on the political centre.

For instance, Mills (1959, p. 324), referring to the masses, writes: 'in many countries . . . they lose their will for rationally considered decision and action; they lose their sense of political belonging because they do not belong; they lose their political will because they see no way to realize it' (see also Marcuse, 1964).

On the other hand, Eisenstadt (1966, pp. 15–16), maintains (and see also Almond and Verba, 1965, and Huntington, 1968):

> The broader strata of society tend more and more to impinge on its central institutions, not only in making various demands on it but also in the sense of developing the aspirations to participate in the very crystallization of the center, its symbols and institutional contours . . . The growing participation of broader strata in the center of society and in the civil order can be seen as two basic attributes of modern nation building, of the establishment of new, broader political entities.

It is intriguing that such antithetical conceptions have been applied to characterize the same reality, and that they co-exist peacefully in modern sociology. Ostensibly, the optimistic conception is the correct one, at least as far as Western democracies are concerned. In the last few centuries the principle of the sovereignty of the people and of government based on consent by the people has been widely if not universally accepted. Further, this principle has found expression in the development of popular elections, in the extension of the voting franchise to wider and lower social strata, and in the increasing tendency of people to use this franchise. Institutions designed to mobilize and organize popular participation or to represent popular interests in the political arena – such as political parties and parliaments – have developed in all Western countries. With the introduction and proliferation of the media of mass communication, increasing weight has accrued to public opinion in the political process.

On the face of it, then, it looks as if the elitist, or the pessimistic view has little to go on – except for one thing: the manipulation of the public by elites to elicit political support or consent in order to entrench themselves in power. In Mills's words (1959, p. 310), 'the public has become the object of intensive efforts to control, manage, manipulate'.

The idea of popular sovereignty that was developed in the West in the last few centuries implied that the people exercise that sovereignty by extending their consent to the government, which thereby becomes authorized to act in their name.[6] Lately, however, another view has become prominent. The claim made by the elite theorists and other observers is that it is actually the ruling elite – or the political and bureaucratic establishment – which moulds the people's consent to itself and its policies, thereby ensuring its own rule. According to this view, consent comes down from the top, rather than ascending from the bottom. For instance, Walter Lippman (1961, p. 248) writes:

> That the manufacture of consent is capable of great refinement, no-one, I think, denies . . . the opportunities open to anyone who understands the process are plain enough. The creation of consent is not a new art . . . It has . . . improved enormously in technic because it is now based on analysis . . . Within the life of the generation now in control of affairs, persuasion has become a self-conscious art and a regular organ of popular government.

More recently, it has been argued that the establishment may promote consent by distributing information selectively (Partridge, 1971, p. 41); by emitting symbolic cues which define or interpret states of affairs for the public (Edelman, 1971); and by means of ritualistic and evocative rhetoric and emotionally laden linguistic symbols which, in themselves, contain predefinitions of the situation (Mueller, 1973).

These various conceptions emphasize symbolic means for the manufacturing of consent. In addition, it is evident that a variety of non-symbolic manipulative devices can be and have been employed by political establishments.[7] Michels (1949) asserted that – internal elections notwithstanding – party leaders frequently use manipulative devices such as co-optation, financial dependence of their followers and monopoly over professional skills to keep themselves in power – and thus minimize the impact of the rank-and-file on the political process.

Further, Mills (1959, p. 310) claimed that voluntary associations which once had been a major vehicle for public influence have largely been turned into passive instruments of manipulation by the elites, or have withered from lack of use. Such associations, Mills maintained, are being replaced by centralized mass organizations in which the rank-and-file's opinions no longer carry substantial weight.

Therefore, it may be argued, although there are now more avenues for popular participation than there were in the past, and although the public (at least in Western-style societies) has increasingly availed itself of these avenues, this increasing participation may not really be meaningful. This is because growing political participation *by* the public has been offset by growing (or more effective) political manipulation *of* the public by the ruling elites.

Instead of enabling the public to exert more influence, it can be

7

claimed that this increasing participation has merely been utlized by the elites to put and keep themselves in power. The avenues of increasing democratic participation, instead of being instruments in the service of the public, have mainly been devices in the service of the elite. The extension of democratic rights merely implies that the political elites have had to modify the devices of the struggle for power to include, to a greater extent than before, the manipulation of public opinion. In sum, it may be argued, that political manipulation has counterbalanced the democratizing processes which have taken place in Western-type democracies.

The present analysis, although derived from the elite model of society, steers a middle course on this issue. The major thesis is that the public's participation in the political process in Western-style democracies has not only increased throughout the last century or so but has also become more meaningful as certain types of non-symbolic manipulation have unquestionably diminished throughout these years. At the same time it will be demonstrated that – paradoxically – this decrease in non-symbolic manipulation and the concomitant increase in the significance of the public's political participation (which in some countries has been more pronounced than in others) is primarily the result of growing self-restraints introduced at the level of the elites and the political-administrative establishments they head. Socio-cultural developments at the level of the public itself may have marginally contributed to these changes but were not their major initiating or driving force. The extent that the public has been able to increase the significance of its participation in the political process is thus due to the initiative of elites considerably more than to its own exertions.

Non-symbolic manipulation: the handing out of material inducements

In what follows, this thesis is substantiated by an analysis of non-symbolic manipulation and its decline or partial decline in some Western-style democracies. The analysis is confined to non-symbolic manipulation not from lack of awareness of the pervasiveness of symbolic manipulation. Rather, it focuses on non-symbolic manipulation because it is held that the latter poses a greater threat to democracy than the former. For one thing, symbolic manipulation – if carried out within certain restraints – is usually lawful; some major types of non-symbolic manipulation run counter to the rules of the democratic game, have been gradually outlawed in Western societies and thus fall under the heading of political corruption.

In the second place, symbolic manipulation by ruling elites in Western democratic societies is usually counteracted by similar manipulation by counter elites. It has been claimed (perhaps with a large degree of validity) that the ruling elite may have at its disposal more extensive means of symbolic manipulation than a counter elite. It has also been claimed that in capitalist society the mass media are motivated by commercial interests to emphasize a conservative rather than a radical stand and this, even if it does not work explicitly in favour of one party rather than another, generally serves to perpetuate the political *status quo*. It has further been claimed that the media – especially television – by extolling the virtues of material goods (e.g., in commercials), strengthen the definition of what is desirable as embedded in the existing sociopolitical system. Additionally, it has been claimed that the entertainment content, especially of television, while ostensibly non-political, does have a political impact in that it deflects attention from politics and furthers receptive, passive, apathetic rather than active, critical tendencies amongst the audience. Thus, it is claimed, media tend to buttress prevailing institutions.

At the same time there is certainly a limit to the biasing and pacifying effect of the media. It is precisely the media that see to it that there is much that the ruling elite cannot get away with. Moreover, there are some channels and devices through which the opposition can make its view known to the public – for instance according equal broadcasting time to government and opposition views, political assemblies and rallies, or informal communication.

Therefore, if the ruling elite predefines the situation for the public, as Edelman and Mueller assert, there is a limit to the efficacy of such definitions. Some situations simply cannot be defined away or defined into existence, especially as the public is likely to be exposed (albeit not as forcefully and as frequently) to a contradictory definition of the situation from the opposition. While these definitions may not be so well balanced as to neutralize each other, they still detract from each other. The public is thus afforded enough leeway to develop a certain sophistication and a considerable degree of independence of judgment in forming its own opinion.

But while symbolic manipulative devices administered by opposing parties detract from each other, non-symbolic manipulative devices administered by opposing parties do nothing of the sort; on the contrary; they are additive. The more political bodies that are engaged in such manipulation, the greater the number of people subject to it.[8] Non-symbolic manipulation thus poses more of a menace to the democratic process than does symbolic manipulation, because it is more difficult to neutralize.

Another reason for confining the analysis to non-symbolic manipulation is, that symbolic manipulation is as widespread as elections, democracies or even governments themselves. It is difficult to imagine a ruling elite in any political regime or at any time that has not used or will not use symbolic persuasion (i.e., progaganda) – and who is to tell where symbolic 'persuasion' ends and symbolic 'manipulation' begins?

But the case with non-symbolic manipulation is different. While some forms of non-symbolic manipulation occur wherever citizens vote, others do not. Societies may thus be compared in the extensiveness of such practices and their development over time. Some informed guesses (or even tentative conclusions) may therefore be reached on the extent to which these devices may have offset the democratic process in various societies at various periods, and the extent to which they have recently declined.

The most significant form of non-symbolic electoral manipulation is undoubtedly the giving of material inducements in return for votes. For one thing, this device has been (and in some societies still is) extensively employed. Also, it springs from one of the most basic features of political power itself: the fact that it is closely connected to and frequently serves as a basis of economic power (or, as a basis of control over the allocation of material resources). Finally, it is of special interest because it is – as I will try to show – cleary related to certain features by which elites in different societies differ, and can thus be largely explained by these features. Hence, it is chiefly with this device, its development and partial decline, and the elite-traits which explain these trends, that the present analysis is concerned.

Conditions for the decline of material inducements: administrative power and elites' codes of ethics

Material inducements in the political process may be ordered on a continuum from the national level to the local and even individual level. On the macro level, this device concerns the creation of overall national – especially economic – policies (e.g., tax cuts), in accordance with the perceived wishes of the electorate. On the intermediate level, it concerns the moulding of policies in line with the demands of various country-wide interest groups. On the micro level, it entails benefits to various communities, sub-communities or interest groups within communities or, finally, to families and individuals. As one moves from the macro to the micro level, this device turns into an explicit exchange of benefits for votes. This exchange is the topic of the present analysis.

Such an exchange may take the form of outright bribery of voters. It may take the form of treating – that is, offering various kinds of refreshments (especially alcoholic beverages) in return for votes. It may also take more subtle forms such as giving voters jobs or

apartments or preferential treatment by authorities well in advance
of election day; the assumption being that the voters will then feel a
moral obligation (or find it in their interest) to support the donors at
the polls – or even to be active on behalf of the donating party.

While the use of material benefits by the political establishment is
considered legitimate and even desirable on the macro level, it is
perceived as increasingly illegitimate as one moves down to the
micro level – until finally, at the level of families or individual
voters, it falls under the heading of 'political corruption' or the
'political machine'.[9] While the use of material benefits is prevalent
at all times in all societies at the macro and intermediary levels
(what government – democratic or otherwise – can afford to be
impervious to the pressures of powerful interest groups?) there has
been an evident decline (at least in Western-style democracies) in
its application on the micro level. Moreover, present-day societies
differ significantly in the extent to which they still retain this practice
or remnants of it. Several theories have been advanced to explain
both the general decline of material inducements in the western-
style political processes and the differences between various countries in this respect.

It has been argued (for instance by Scott, 1973) that material
inducements flourish where the electorate or parts of it lack strong
ideological commitments; or where there is social disorganization
(by which is meant the presence of large numbers of immigrants
who are as yet disoriented in the new society) and poverty. Conversely, material inducements decline where such conditions
diminish or disappear. Although this theory sounds plausible, the
analysis will show that it explains neither the general decline in
material inducements nor the differences between the countries in
this respect. Following the Marxist model, it may be argued that
material inducements flourish and are most resilient where they
serve the economically dominant classes' interests. The analysis will
show that this perspective cannot explain the differences between
the countries any more than the previous one. It will be seen that
what makes the difference is not so much the tendencies found in
the rank-and-file public or among various social classes, but rather
the tendencies found among the elites.

But, if so, what tendencies among the elites account for these
processes? It has been claimed, for instance, that elites in democratic countries seek to limit, by an ever tighter application of the
law, the giving of material inducements because unless it is tightly
regulated, the great power of centralized governments would
enable that section of the political elite that currently controls the
government to perpetuate its control indefinitely. In other words,
the increasing aggregation of power represented by the modern

11

state requires, if important sections of the elites are not to be denied access (or re-access) to power, a successively more rigorous set of controls on the way that this power aggregation may be utilized. The analysis will show, however, that plausible as it is, this theory cannot furnish an explanation for the differences between the countries, either.

This is not to say that consideration of their own interests in ensuring their share in power have not weighed heavily with the elites or that the consideration of their own interests has not influenced their decisions as far as the restriction of material inducements is concerned. But it appears that such considerations of self-interest have been intertwined with structural and normative developments in a much more complex manner, as will be shown below.

Another theory has to do with relative strength of a country's administrative elites compared with its political elites, or the relative strength of a country's central administrative system compared with its political bodies. For instance, Heidenheimer (1970) maintains that electoral corruption (including the offering of material inducements) occurs where electoral assemblies and political parties were powerful prior to the development of a strong, bureaucratized civil service and does not occur where the opposite was the case. But whatever merits this theory may have in explaining the initial development of the practice, it will be seen that it cannot explain its decline or partial decline or contemporary differences between countries.

What, then, may explain such diminution and such differences? I do not propose to offer a general theory, but merely an explanation of the differences among the specific countries analysed here. In this, I follow the same pattern as did Brinton (1959) for instance, who expounded the conditions preceding and explaining four major revolutions – but did not claim that the same conditions must necessarily precede all revolutions.

Contrary to Scott's thesis, my argument is that what counts is not so much the tendencies found in the rank-and-file public, but rather the tendencies of the elites – especially as embodied in the public administration. But contrary to Heidenheimer's thesis, my argument is that (on the contemporary scene) what counts is not when the public administration developed or how much power it has, but the degree of its political involvement.

Two major types of public administration have been distinguished: a politically neutral one and a politically involved one. In the first, the selection, appointment and advancement of personnel are overwhelmingly by objective criteria of merit in an open, competitive system; public servants generally refrain from major party political activity; and policies (to the extent that they are shaped by the bureaucracy itself) are guided largely by non-partisan considerations. This type approaches Weber's ideal-type model of bureaucracy, incorporating neutrality, impersonality and emphasis on objective criteria; it has also been referred to as 'meritocracy'.

In the second type, a significant proportion of the officials are appointed by party-political criteria rather than (or in addition to) merit criteria; since they owe allegiance to a political party, they frequently engage in major partisan activity. As a result, the administration's actions are shaped to a much greater extent by partisan considerations. This type of administration has also been referred to as 'politocracy'.

Initially, all Western democracies included in this study had a politicized public administration and electoral processes pervaded by material inducements. But it will be shown that where the public administration has subsequently approached the first type, or the Weberian model of bureaucracy, electoral corruption has ceased to offset the democratic process to any considerable extent. Conversely, where the administrative structure has persistently approached the second type and has continuously deviated from the Weberian model, material inducements have continued to bias the electoral process to a far greater extent and have continued to render it at least partly invalid.

Bureaucracy that approaches the Weberian model has been critized as being rigid and even ritualistic (see Merton, 1957b). Conversely, a politically committed public administration has been perceived as being more favourably disposed to implement the policies of the politically committed minister. However, the other side of the coin is that even with all its drawbacks, an objective, neutral bureaucracy seems to be essential for an uncorrupted Western-style democracy – while a politically involved administration, whatever its advantages, has frequently served as a basis for manipulative practices that must be considered incompatible with democracy.

It is interesting to note that the communist regimes of Eastern Europe have, in fact, developed politically committed rather than politically neutral bureaucracies, and that these have served as a major tool in the perpetuation of the one-party system. While Weber saw bureaucracy as being characteristic of modern societies in general, anything approaching his model of bureaucracy is actually characteristic of only some capitalist, Western-style democracies.

Within the latter type of country – it has been argued (Sorauf, 1960) – the political involvement of the bureaucracy is itself the outgrowth of large-scale immigration and poverty. In contrast, my argument is that it is the outgrowth of codes of ethics or notions of propriety adopted by political and administrative elites. The development of these traditions antecedes, and hence has little to do with, the present conditions of immigration or poverty among the rank-and-file public.

The development of such codes of ethics among the elites, in turn, is related to the overall differentiation between the politically committed (partisan) and politically neutral (non-partisan) organs of government. In most Western countries, Huntington (1968, p. 109) notes, modernization was characterized among other things, by the emergence of more specialized governmental institutions and bodies. 'Administrative, legal, judicial, military institutions developed as semi-autonomous but subordinate bodies in one way or another responsible to the political bodies . . . which exercised sovereignty.'

But in some Western countries, this differentiation has not been fully effected – and party-political bodies have remained inter-meshed to a considerable extent with other governmental bodies. In such countries, there has been no clear separation between party-political and non-partisan considerations in the shaping and imple-mentation of social policy.

As Medding (1972, p. 222) points out, few major areas of institu-tional life are detached from political processes or are not affected by political decisions in the widest sense of the term. This includes policy formation, which involves conceptions about the right kind of society and the means of obtaining it. But while much of society has some relation to the political realm, not all of it is necessarily permeated by *partisan* political criteria.[10] Some societies have safeguards embedded in the ethos which is adhered to by their elites; these impede the penetration of such partisan considerations into other institutional spheres. In societies without such built-in safeguards, party politics have pervaded ostensibly neutral struc-tures such as the judiciary and the police. In some of these countries party-political considerations have even branched out into the economy, the health services or education.

In countries such as these, where differentiation between the political and non-political organs of government has not greatly advanced, where partisan considerations have been pervasive and where there has been considerable intermeshing of party-political and non-political criteria of action, the public administration and the public service have formed part of this pattern of politicization – and the roles of public servants have been defined accordingly. This in turn has served as the basis for the continuous exchange of material benefits for votes.

The same argument may be couched in more general terms,

14

following Parsons's distinction between universalist and particularist criteria of action. With some oversimplification, the former may be defined as objective criteria of merit, while the latter are based on personal relations or common membership in a particular group within a wider society. While universalism and particularlism may be viewed as two poles on a continuum (or as black and white with varying shades of grey in between), activities or institutions may yet be classified by their proximity to one or other of the poles.

In pre-modern society, particularism predominates in the activities of governmental elites and in most institutional spheres; with modernization, elites become increasingly oriented to universalist criteria of action, several institutional spheres gain autonomy from particularist considerations and universalism thus comes to predominate. Nevertheless some pockets of particularism legitimately remain. While the criteria that rule the bureaucracy in its ideal-type form are universalist, the criteria that rule partisan politics are particularist, (i.e., based on belonging to a particular social body – the party).

In countries where the politicization of the bureaucracy and the penetration of partisan considerations into the economy, the judiciary, the military, education, health services and the like, persist, this may be viewed as an imperfect differentiation between institutional spheres in which universalism rules and those in which particularism predominates. This in turn is related to an imperfect orientation to universalism by the ruling elites. It thus implies the existence or the persistence of particularism in areas which, by modern standards (and usually by modern laws and regulations as well) universalist criteria alone are thought to be relevant. It is in such countries that particularist criteria for the allocation of material benefits tend to persist in the electoral process as well.

Method

The study is based on a secondary analysis of a variety of historical and contemporary data including documents collected and presented by historians, historical analyses, empirical research projects and newspaper reports. The contribution of this study thus does not lie in primary historical or empirical research as such. It lies rather in the uncovering of remote and little-known data; in bringing together material from a large number of sources; in integrating seemingly unrelated data so as to create a general overview of developments; in the conceptualization of these developments and in relating them to a theoretical framework of analysis.

Most of the material that could be uncovered is of a qualitative rather than a quantitative nature. This is not surprising, since electoral manipulation of the kind studied is a topic that hardly lends itself to quantification. Most of the processes usually take place in privacy if not in secrecy, and only the tip of the iceberg usually becomes publicly visible. Nevertheless, some quantitative material has been uncovered, relating mainly to electoral petitions, numbers of political appointments and, in one case, to results of an ingeniously worded questionnaire which made it possible to quantify reported manipulative practices as such.

Much of the existent data (qualitative as well as quantitative) were fragmentary rather than systematic. While some countries in some periods are fairly well covered by systematic historical analyses, others are not, so the fragmentary information had to be pieced together in the manner of a jigsaw puzzle. When this operation was performed, some general, clear-cut trends of development did emerge and some fairly well grounded conclusions could be reached for practically all countries and periods studied.

However, as it turned out, the material on which these conclusions were based was difficult to find, especially where some countries in some periods (such as nineteenth-century Australia) are concerned. Quite a lot of work went into the grinding and pedestrian task of collecting the data. Consequently, I had to scale down my ambitions as the work went along. I originally intended to analyse all Western-style democracies, but I soon realized that this was an impossible task. I thus decided to concentrate my efforts on four countries: Britain, the United States, Australia and Israel.

The reasons for this choice are partly objective and partly personal. All four countries have stable bi-party or multi-party systems, universal suffrage, secret elections and free speech. None has had its democratic processes disrupted by encroaching regulations, *coups d'état* or military juntas. All four countries in a sense emerged from the British system of government and thus have a common political background; it is therefore of special interest to see how differently they have branched out from it. At one time, material inducements were employed in all four, but two of the countries have retained the practice to a much greater extent than have their counterparts; this division presents a special advantage that facilitates the analysis.

Finally, I have some personal acquaintance with three of the four countries – having resided in all except Britain. Where material was more difficult to come by, especially in Australia, I really needed to collect the data myself in the country, while a personal acquaintance with contemporary political processes and personal conversations with local scholars could hardly have been dispensed with. The choice of Britain itself, whose system gave birth to the others, was a natural one.

16

As the work proceeded, I became increasingly entranced by each country's colourful political scene. I can only hope that some of the local flavour will come across to the reader.

Plan of the book

Chapter 1 presents a general overview of the growing political participation by the public in Western-style democracies as reflected in elections – with special emphasis on the four countries that are the focus of this analysis. The next four chapters trace political manipulation of the public by elites in each of the four countries as reflected in the extending of material inducements. These chapters explore the degree to which such manipulations have counteracted the growing public participation in politics, the relationship between such manipulation and class interests and the (differential) extent to which these manipulations have declined in the various countries in recent years. Chapter 6 endeavours to demonstrate that the differences among the countries in this decline cannot be accounted for by socio-economic attributes, class interests or ideological awareness of the rank-and-file public, and presents my own explanation of the differences.

This explanation is substantiated in the next four chapters; these analyse the four countries' patterns of public administration, the elites' codes of ethics and the wider structural patterns in which they are embedded and demonstrate how these factors are related to the political manipulation of material inducements. The Conclusion draws together the lines of the analysis and relates it back to the theoretical concerns with which the discussion began.

1 Background: the development of elections[1]

The two contradictory views of public participation in politics (see Introduction) have based their arguments to a considerable extent on the development of the electoral process. The optimists, who say that public political participation has been expanding over the last centuries, point (among other things) to the extension of the right to vote and the growing tendency to exercise that right by all strata of the population. The pessimists, who claim that the public has become more impotent and apathetic in the political arena, point (among other things) to electoral manipulation which – they say – has rendered increasing electoral participation meaningless. By tracing the development of the electoral process (in this chapter) and by analysing some of the manipulations which have beset it (in the following four chapters), we can test the validity of the opposing conceptions.

Elections hold such an important place in both theories because they are the central process of democratic political participation. When open, free and competitive, they are the only channel of political participation in which all citizens have an equal voice,[2] and they are the most strategic democratic mechanism by which the power of a ruling elite can be countervailed. Those who belittle the importance of elections argue that they occur only periodically; that most political decisions are made between elections; that the most crucial decisions are based on information that is either secret or too complex to be readily available to voters; and that most voters take little interest in such complex issues anyway. Nevertheless, voting is still the only channel of participation in which no citizen has an advantage over any other – as opposed to such channels as voluntary associations' activities, lobbying or 'direct action' (protest), where a powerful, active or militant minority may outweigh a moderate, silent majority.

18

Some scholars argue that excessive public participation is not only unnecessary for democracy, but actually harmful; a low level of public involvement in political decision-making enables the government to function more smoothly. If day-to-day political activity is delegated to the most interested and the most competent, then decisions would be made by experts, and citizens would be freed to pursue their own vocations.[3] However, this line of reasoning assumes absolute justice in the allocation of resources controlled by ruling elites and absolute benevolence by such elites. Obviously, these utopian assumptions are far removed from reality.

Consequently, it is very much in the interests of the various groups, sections and strata of society to press for the greatest possible share of resources – in other words, to try to influence policy-making. Moreover, even if day-to-day decisions are left in the hands of the ruling elite, elections still serve as the basic mechanism for selecting the elite, and for checking its power once selected, by holding it accountable for its performance in office and by periodical replacement or threat thereof. Indeed, it is precisely for this very reason that elites have invested such major efforts in manipulating elections.

However, a distinction should be made between the form and substance of elections. The great majority of the world's 150-plus nations hold elections. But many of these have one-party systems in which the act of voting is no more than a ritual designed to legitimize the leaders' rule.[4] Others have unstable systems in which elections are interspersed with *coups d'état* or other methods of annulling electoral results. It is thus only in a handful of countries that stable, bi-party or multi-party electoral systems have made it possible for the public to curb the power of elites, and it is only in these that such countervailing power of the public has been threatened by electoral manipulation (see Introduction). It is with the development of the electoral process in the latter type of country – commonly referred to as 'Western-style democracies' – that the present analysis is concerned.

Early developments

The development of elections in these countries may be seen as part of their modernization. Some elections took place in ancient times – for instance, in Greek and Roman assemblies. During the Middle Ages, in Europe, some kinds of elections apparently survived at the local level and in regional assemblies. However, the medieval, hierarchical, feudal structures were not congenial to elections; in practice, most official positions were passed along by inheritance. Moreover, the age of absolutism in the sixteenth and seventeenth centuries (except in England and Sweden) interrupted the evolution of whatever feeble electoral mechanisms might have existed until then. It was only from the seventeenth century onward that elections in the modern sense developed. Three features characterized these modern-style elections: they became the basis for the selection of parliamentary assemblies, they focused on the individual as the electoral unit to be counted, and they came to be considered as the mechanism of establishing the consent of the governed to those who govern them.

Parliamentary assemblies antedated modern elections; they developed in Western Europe in the late medieval period. Indeed, at first, they were not connected with such elections. A parliament had judicial functions and served as a consultative link between the king and his subjects. It enabled him to raise larger revenues and armies than he could hope to raise merely by exacting the customary feudal dues; in exchange, he had to make some concessions to popular demands – as mediated by the parliament – in matters of justice and policy. Thus, parliamentary assemblies took part in a bargaining process on behalf of their communities.

Although in this sense the assemblies represented the communities, this did not involve electoral representation. Membership in the assemblies was considered a burden to be shunned, rather than a privilege to be sought. Consequently, there were no elections in the modern sense, with competing candidates standing for office. Only when the parliaments gained more political importance (as in Western Europe during the fourteenth and fifteenth centuries), and membership in them became worth competing for, did election of candidates develop.

But a century later, the existing parliamentary regimes succumbed to absolutism. At the beginning of the seventeenth century all Western European countries had assemblies of estates, but by the end of the century, most had been eliminated or reduced in power. In France, the last Estates General before the revolution met in 1615. In the kingdom of Naples, parliamentary proceedings ended in 1642. The Danish Crown became hereditary in 1665, and towards the end of the century absolute rule was re-established in Sweden. Authority was centralized in England as well; although the machinery of parliament was retained for a time, and even enlarged, it served mainly as a tool in the hands of the ruling despots (Huntington, 1968, p. 103).

Eventually, however, the process was reversed; once again, power shifted from monarchical rulers to popular assemblies. Where medieval assemblies survived the age of absolutism, according to Huntington, the royal powers were gradually limited as power was transferred in stages to the parliaments. But in countries where assemblies or estates did not survive absolutism, the transition was harder and more abrupt; sometimes the monarchy had to be overthrown by revolution so that an elected assembly could be installed in its stead.

In England, the power of parliament *vis-à-vis* the king reasserted itself after the revolution of 1688. Until that time there had been a dual system in which parliament and the king had shared the responsibility of government. The revolution abolished this dualism; parliament became the dominant institution. On the Continent, the French revolution started a similar process: the monarch (who had embodied the state) was eventually supplanted by parliamentary government.

In the Australian colonies, legislative assemblies originally were appointed by the colonial governors and had very limited powers; towards the middle of the nineteenth century they gradually came to be based on elections and their powers increased to resemble those of their British counterpart. Only in America, according to Huntington, was there no place for either absolute monarchy or parliamentary supremacy; the authority continued to be divided between the executive and the legislative. Even so, Congress came to be a powerful part of the governmental process.

Although parliamentary power greatly gained in importance in Europe and America, the exercise of that power was still vested in a minority of the population. In eighteenth-century Britain, for instance, the parliamentary oligarchy represented a much smaller proportion of the people than did parliaments before the revolution. Only the extension of the franchise in the nineteenth and twentieth centuries brought about the final convergence between parliamentary government and popular representation.

When parliamentary power had been mainly a matter of bargaining with the Crown about how royal prerogatives were to be exercised, members of the assembly were regarded as the agents of communities, local bodies, special interests and estates – while the king supposedly represented the state as a whole. From the seventeenth century onward, holds Huntington, parliament greatly reduced its representation of localities and took on a function as the collective representative of the nation on the one hand, and as the representative of individual rights on the other.

In America, the president continued to represent the nation as a whole, while senators and congressmen owed their primary loyalties to their constituencies. But even there, although localism was retained, individual representation was not neglected: members of the legislature represented not only their constituencies, but their individual constituents as well.

Thus, while the medieval conception of representation was

holistic, the modern conception is individualistic. It was only when this individualistic conception developed that free elections by independent individuals seemed to make sense. Yet even afterwards, for some time, it was still customary for powerful patrons (such as landowners and employers) to tell their dependants how to vote – and for these dependants to accept such directives (a practice known as deferential voting). Consequently, the principle of individual representation was not immediately realized since many candidates still directly represented large-scale vested interests. Only when deferential voting was abolished (see chapter 2), did the principle assert itself in practice.

In modern times, individual representation is closely related to the basic democratic doctrine – that the right to govern derives from the consent of the governed. The parliamentary institutions of the late medieval periods were based on the rudiments of the consent principle, as well as on expediency: the government apparatus was too inefficient to assert the monarchy's authority over distant areas without the consent of its subjects. However, the medieval, rudimentary principle of consent was superseded during the period of absolutism by the doctrine that the king derived his right to rule from divine grace. With the decline of absolutism, the doctrine of government by consent of the governed reasserted itself and found expression in popular elections.

This however still left the problem of deciding specifically whose consent was necessary to legitimize a government. In principle, the democratic answer was universal adult suffrage. But in practice, the electorate was originally very limited; in most Western countries, the gradual extension of the franchise was a protracted process. But eventually, with the attainment of universal suffrage (see below) the three principles of parliamentary government, individual representation and consent of the governed came to be firmly interlinked.

The secret ballot

This in itself, would not have held much significance were it not for another landmark in the development of the electoral process: the introduction of the secret ballot. The previous open voting system encouraged pressure, harassment, intimidation and bribery of voters. In Australia, Britain, the United States and elsewhere, the supporters of many candidates used intimidation and violence to prevent supporters of the other side from voting; in some cases, voters were even frightened into voting a certain way. The purpose of those who advocated the secret ballot was to eliminate these malpractices, and thus to ensure truly free elections.

Before the introduction of the secret ballot, the prevalent form of open voting was oral. This gradually gave way to a system of voting by ballot which supposedly was secret – but which actually was not. Ballots were printed by parties or candidates, and were sometimes in different colours or otherwise recognizable by observers at the polls. Various measures for ensuring secrecy under this system were ineffective. Finally, those who wanted a truly secret vote turned to what became known as the Australian ballot.

This method used a standardized, government-printed ballot paper, containing the names of all parties or candidates. These ballots were distributed only by the election officers at the polling place, and were to be marked on the spot. Voting booths and other physical arrangements were designed to keep the entire voting procedure private.

The secret ballot was advocated in Britain as early as 1780, and especially from 1830 onward; however, the principle was invariably rejected by the House of Lords. In Australia the system was first advocated in the late 1840s and early 1850s by an organization known as the Ballot Association – but here, too, the proposal encountered strong opposition. Politicians (whose interests were evidently served by open voting) rejected the ballot on the ground that it was unconstitutional as well as un-British for people to be secretive about their political leanings.

Despite this opposition, the ballot was pioneered in Victoria in 1856. The other Australian States rapidly followed suit; almost all of them had adopted it by the late 1850s.[5] Britain introduced the ballot in 1872, and most Western European countries did so towards the end of the nineteenth century. Most of the American States kept pace with this trend. Kentucky was first to introduce the ballot (in 1880), and by 1900, the majority of them had adopted the new system. But some States lagged behind and adopted it only during the first half of the twentieth century, and the last one did not fall into line until 1950. Even then, according to Key (1964, pp. 638–40), some States in America retained proceedings under which the secrecy of the ballot could be violated.[6]

Backers of the secret ballot had high hopes for its effectiveness in eliminating electoral malpractices – but, as it turned out, it was only partly successful. The ballot was more effective in ending intimidation and violence than it was in doing away with bribery and more subtle electoral manipulations. However, since it did hinder the more blatant abuses, it came to be regarded as an essential component of modern elections and as a *sine qua non* of Western-style democracy. It is generally agreed that despite its limitations the

23

secret ballot gave the extension of the franchise whatever significance it has; without the ballot, universal suffrage would have remained an empty ritual.

The extension of the franchise

The basic democratic doctrine of government by consent of the governed clearly calls for universal adult suffrage. But this ran counter to powerful vested interests – especially those of the upper classes and the political establishments, who feared that extending the franchise to the propertyless, the uneducated and the young would jeopardize the existing social order (and with it, their own privileges).

Accordingly, participation in eighteenth-century elections was limited to a small group – mainly the aristocracy – and regulated by local customs. After the French revolution, all citizens were declared formally equal, but the franchise remained a power possessed by few; various qualifications (especially property) were still attached to the right to vote. Like the secret ballot, the extension of the franchise at times encountered severe opposition and entailed major struggles against prevailing vested interests. In America the attainment of white male suffrage did not occasion major conflicts; but in Europe, universal male suffrage was preceded by the establishment of active workingmen's associations; for women, gaining the suffrage depended on the organization of the suffragettes as an active movement, and the attainment of the vote for blacks in America involved major struggles as well.

Step by step, these struggles bore fruit. Financial qualifications were made less stringent, and later abolished. The franchise was gradually extended from aristocracy, to upper bourgeoisie, to lower bourgeoisie, to peasantry, and finally to the working class. By the beginning of the twentieth century most Western countries had universal suffrage for men; women attained the vote in most countries in the first decades of the twentieth century, especially after the First World War.

Yet, some groups continued to be over-represented in the electoral system while others continued to be disadvantaged. In some countries, plural voting (i.e. voting on the basis of more than one qualification) for the well-to-do and the educated persisted. In others (notably the United States), racial minorities were still effectively barred from voting. Both practices were abolished not long ago. Only recently have all Western countries achieved the goal of one man (or woman) one vote – without which universal suffrage has little validity. But while Western-style democracies have all reached this point by now, they did not set out from the same starting-point, travel the same road or reach the finish at the same time.

Britain

The British electoral system dates from the thirteenth century; its modern history, however, begins with the Reform Bill of 1832 – the first in a series of Acts which have gradually brought about universal suffrage. Before that the franchise had been limited to 40-shilling freeholders in the counties while various unequal franchises prevailed in the boroughs. In 1832 a £10-occupation franchise replaced the traditional franchises in the boroughs – thereby expanding the electorate from 5 to 7 per cent of the adult population. Plural voting was retained, as was the 40-shilling freehold qualification in the counties.

In 1867–8, household suffrage and a lodger franchise were introduced into English and Scottish boroughs. A new occupation franchise was established in the counties, and the existing qualifications were reduced. This increased the electorate to 16 per cent of all adults.

In 1884 a uniform household franchise, a uniform lodger franchise and a uniform occupation franchise were established throughout the United Kingdom, giving a vote to every man over twenty-one who had a home; this comprised 28 per cent of all adults. In 1918, property qualifications in counties were abolished; qualifications now were either six months' residence or the occupation of £10-business premises. This reform enfranchised virtually all men, as well as women over the age of thirty who were householders or the wives of householders – a total of 74 per cent of the adult population. Plural voting for university graduates and the holders of business premises was retained, but was restricted to two votes.

In 1928 the voting age for women was reduced to twenty-one – introducing universal adult suffrage. However, the fact that all adults now had a vote did not mean that all had an equal vote, since plural voting and university constituencies were still preserved. Not until 1948 were these privileges abolished, thus establishing the principle of one man (or woman) one vote (Leonard, 1968, p. 10).

The United States

America assumed a pioneering role in expanding the suffrage, except where the voting of blacks was concerned. In the eighteenth century, the franchise was restricted to freeholders or real property owners; the restrictions differed widely among the colonies (and, after the revolution, among the States). The pre-revolution requirement in New York, for instance, was ownership of real estate worth £40. Some States required ownership of a specific acreage. Ownership of specified amounts of personal property sometimes was an alternative to the real property requirements. These restrictions, however, were less severe than is often supposed. In Massachussetts, for instance, the property qualifications disfranchised few men, because economic opportunities and inexpensive land created almost universal property ownership. In some areas, the property requirements were largely ignored (Key, 1964, p. 600).

After the revolution, the economic qualifications (which in many States had not disfranchised large numbers of men in any event) quickly withered away. First, property qualifications were replaced by even more lenient tax-paying requirements;[7] these were often nominal. In some States, the tax standards were not rigorous, and, whatever they were, their administration was frequently loose. In any event, these qualifications were soon abolished altogether.[8]

As new States were admitted to the Union, they generally came in with no economic restrictions on the suffrage. By 1845, property restrictions were almost extinct; by the end of the Civil War, only four States[9] retained the more moderate tax requirements. Thus, universal suffrage for white men had become the norm in most States.

The extension of the suffrage thus occurred earlier in America than in Britain and most European countries. Moreover, the United States pioneered not only increasing the number of people who could vote for public officials, but also increasing the number of public officials who could be voted for by the people. In Europe, the suffrage was normally limited to the lower house and to local councils; in the United States, on the other hand, a large number of national, State and local officials were subject to election (governors, both houses of the State legislatures, many State administrative offices and boards, and in many States the judiciary).

However, suffrage for women was introduced more slowly in America. In some States [10] women had the vote by the 1890s – but it was not until 1910 that other (mainly western) States enfranchised women, and only in 1920 was the matter settled on a national basis by the 19th Amendment, which gave all American women the vote.

The extension of the vote to blacks took even longer. Formally, the Reconstruction Act of 1867 imposed black suffrage on the former Confederate States, and the 15th Amendment (adopted in 1870) forbade the State to deny the vote to anyone on account of race or colour. In practice, however, southern blacks were frequently discouraged or even barred from voting. This practice became more, rather than less, frequent, and by the turn of the century the southern States had effectively (although not formally) disfranchised the blacks.

This was accomplished through State laws that were ostensibly non-discriminatory but actually discriminated against blacks. Literacy requirements were introduced at a time when most blacks were still illiterate. Citizens were required to interpret the Constitution – which made it easy for election officials to discriminate by asking simple questions of white voters and difficult questions of black voters.[11] The laws were supplemented by social pressures, persuasion, fraud, intimidation and even violence; these persisted throughout the south for more than half a century.

Another means of disfranchising blacks became prominent at the beginning of the twentieth century; this was the white Democratic primary. Blacks were barred from voting in the primaries on the ground that the Democratic Party was a voluntary organization and, hence, was not subject to the anti-discriminatory laws which ruled general elections. Since the Democratic nominees were certain of election to almost any public office in the solid south, blacks were effectively excluded from participation in the election of public officials.

The process of attaining the vote for blacks gained momentum towards the middle of the twentieth century. In 1944 the Supreme Court outlawed the white primary. The situation was further improved by civil rights legislation in 1957, 1960, 1964 and 1965, and by the large-scale voter education project conducted by the Southern Regional Council.

The proportion of southern black adults registered to vote rose from less than 5 per cent in 1940 to over 60 per cent in 1968. This approached the share expected of a population with a comparable level of education under 'normal' circumstances, and the trend is clearly towards full political equality. As Converse (1972, p. 303) points out, this belated advance in *de facto* black suffrage represents almost the last mobilization of a major population group into the national electorate of a Western democratic country.[12] The United States was thus among the first Western countries to achieve universal white manhood suffrage – but among the last to achieve universal suffrage.

Australia

Responsible government came to Australia in the middle of the nineteenth century.[13] However, it was not achieved by a unified country, but by the various colonies separately. Like their American counterparts, the Australian colonies (later States) varied in their electoral practices. Some adopted so-called

27

'universal' manhood suffrage[14] – that is suffrage for all men except for Aborigines – fairly early, while others trailed behind. Even after the attainment of such suffrage, however, plural voting (except for the South Australian lower house) still affected the value of votes, and such inequalities were added to by enrolment or registration procedures which made it difficult for electors to get their names onto the rolls. These inequalities remained in the electoral system up to and beyond 1850.

In New South Wales, Australia's largest colony, popular representation was introduced in 1842. At that time a restricted franchise allowed owners of freeholds worth £200 and householders paying £20 to elect two-thirds of the Legislative Council; the other third was still appointed by the governor. These property qualifications were somewhat lowered in 1850 so that about one-quarter of the adult male population had the vote by 1851.

In 1856, with the advent of responsible government, a new constitution gave the vote to a little more than half of the State's adult males. The Act of 1858 extended the franchise to men with miners' rights, and to men who had lived in the colony for twelve months and in the electorate for six months. However, the Act retained plural voting, for which about 15 per cent of the voters were eligible. By 1880 about 85 per cent of British men had the vote; by 1893, as property qualifications were abolished, so-called universal suffrage was obtained and plural voting was abolished as well.

The other States followed their own patterns: property qualifications were abolished and 'universal' male suffrage was introduced in Victoria, Queensland and South Australia by 1859, and in Western Australia in 1899. Tasmania retained a £10 household franchise (which gave the vote to only 70 per cent of the men) between 1856 and 1870; it finally gave 'universal' suffrage to men in 1900.

Thus, when the Australian Commonwealth was established in 1901, all the States had universal suffrage for non-Aboriginal adult males – which applied to Commonwealth elections from the beginning. Australian women attained the vote in 1902. At that time the franchise attained its present form, except for Aborigines who did not begin voting until the 1960s. It was then that true universal suffrage was established in Australia.

Israel

Like America and Australia, Israel developed its electoral system while under British rule.[15] Unlike the other two countries, however, Israel had universal suffrage for its citizens from the beginning. The pre-state Jewish community (commonly referred to as the Yishuv[16], created a semi-autonomous self-government and held its first elections in 1920; the system was formally recognized by the British Mandatory Government in 1927. Since the Yishuv was a latecomer to the political scene, its electoral system emerged when those of the other Western countries had more or less reached their present stage. So Israel did not undergo the same gradual extension of the franchise as the others; the Yishuv adopted the modern Western electoral system ready-made,[17] and the system was continued when the state was established in 1948.

The pre-state self-government of the Jewish community did not include Arabs, who were at liberty to set up their own governmental institutions. With the establishment of the state, however, all Arabs living within its boundaries (both men and women) were automatically enfranchised. After the 1967 Six-Day War, East Jerusalem was annexed to the state of Israel and all Arabs living in the city were given the vote. The other occupied territories, presumably held on a temporary basis, were not annexed and their Arab inhabitants were not granted the right to vote for the Israeli parliament, but they have participated in municipal elections.

Whatever the course of development – early or late, gradual or abrupt – all Western-style democracies eventually ended up with universal adult suffrage.[18] But the legal right to vote does not guarantee that this right will be exercised. Even when the suffrage is not simply an empty formality (as was the case with American blacks for many years) but a *de facto* right, participation in elections is not automatic, but depends on several social factors as well. The extension of voting participation thus followed, but did not stand in a one-to-one relationship with the extension of the franchise.

The extension of voting participation

Voting participation may be measured as a percentage of the population (or the adult population) or as a percentage of those entitled to vote, the electorate (voting turnout). These two measures have not always followed the same trends; and have differed in various countries. For instance, participation in the United Kingdom and the United States is compared in Tables 1.1 and 1.2.

In both countries, voting eligibility as a percentage of the population has increased steadily with only small setbacks, while participation as a percentage of the electorate has decreased more significantly at certain times. But beyond this, the two countries have differed from each other in each of the two measures. From 1886 until the First World War, the United States was ahead of Britain in the first measure of participation, but after the war Britain caught up with the United States and gradually overtook it; the difference became especially conspicuous after the Second World

War. Since the 1950s over 50 per cent of the population of the United Kingdom have participated in elections, compared with only 35–39 per cent of the American population.

TABLE 1.1   *Voting participation in the United Kingdom 1885–1974*

Year	Voters as percentage of population	Voters as percentage of electorate[a] (turnout)	Year	Voters as percentage of population	Voters as percentage of electorate (turnout)
1885	12·9	81·2	1931	47·0	76·4
1886	8·1	74·2	1935	47·0	71·1
1896	12·1	77·4	1945	51·0	72·8
1899	9·5	78·4	1950	56·8	83·9
1900	8·6	75·1	1951	56·9	82·6
1906	13·0	83·2	1955	52·5	76·8
1910 (June)	14·8	86·8	1959	53·6	78·7
1910 (Feb.)	11·7	81·6	1964	51·3	77·1
1918	25·0	57·0	1966	50·0	75·8
1922	32·5	73·0	1970	51·1	72·0
1923.	32·6	71·1	1974 (Feb.)	55·9	78·8
1924	37·0	77·0	1974 (Oct.)	52·2	72·8
1929	49·6	76·3			

Sources: Compiled and computed from: Great Britain Central Statistical Office, *Annual Abstract*, nos 47–8 (1885–1900), Table 107; no. 67 (1906–20), Table 106; no. 70 (1911–25), Table 5; no. 82 (1913, 1924–37), Table 5; no. 113 (1976), Table 2.1; no. 114 (1977), Table 2.1; Craig (1976), Table 1.28.

[a] The figure for voting turnout makes allowance prior to 1950, for the two-member seats. Only the actual number (or an estimated figure in a few cases where details were not available) of electors voting in these seats have been counted. In calculating the percentage of votes, each vote in a two member seat has been counted as a half vote. See Craig (1976), Introductory Notes.

No data for the period prior to 1885 have been presented because, according to authorities on this subject, it was not possible to calculate the percentage of voting turnout with any degree of accuracy for that period. Due to the system of registration, it was common for some electors to have their names recorded more than once in the same electoral register. They were, however, entitled to vote only once in the same constituency and many of the official returns published during the period gave no indication as to the number of duplicates. In some constituencies (especially in Scotland) the registers published in the 1930s and 1840s were not subject to revision and contained a large number of names of electors who had died or moved from the constituency; see Craig (1977), Introductory Notes.

The two countries have further differed in the second measure of participation. In both countries voting turnout slumped at the beginning of the twentieth century and especially after the First World War; both countries eventually recovered; but in Britain the

TABLE 1.2   *Voting participation in the United States (presidential elections) 1824–1976*

19th century Year	Voters as percentage of population	Voters as percentage of electorate (turnout)[a]	20th century Year	Voters as percentage of population	Voters as percentage of electorate (turnout)
1824	3·8	26·9	1904	16·5	65·2
1828	11·3	57·6	1908	16·8	65·4
1832	10·4	55·4	1912	15·8	58·8
1836	11·6	57·8	1916	18·2	61·6
1840	16·5	80·2	1920	25·1	49·2
1844	15·8	78·9	1924	25·4	48·9
1848	15·8	72·7	1928	30·6	56·9
1852	14·5	69·6	1932	31·9	56·9
1856	16·7	78·9	1936	35·6	61·0
1860	17·0	81·2	1940	37·8	62·5
1864	b	73·8	1944	34·7	55·9
1868	b	78·1	1948	33·3	53·0
1872	15·4	71·3	1952	39·2	63·3
1876	18·3	81·8	1956	36·9	60·6
1880	18·3	79·4	1960	38·1	64·0
1884	19·0	77·5	1964	36·8	61·7
1888	18·8	79·3	1968	36·5	60·6
1892	18·5	74·7	1972	37·2	55·7
1896	19·5	79·3	1976	37·9	59·2
1900	18·4	73·2			

Sources: Compiled and computed from: Lane (1952), Table 2.1; U.S. Bureau of the Census (1975), Tables 27–8; U.S. Bureau of the Census (1977), Table 788.

[a] Establishing voting turnout in the United States presents a difficult problem because no reliable figures are available on the numbers of persons entitled to vote. The voting lists usually include only the name of those who have registered rather than those who meet the requirements of the suffrage (the electorate). Hence the percentages of voting turnout are based on estimates only. Most variations among such estimates derive from the differences in the base from which the voting percentages are calculated (see U.S. Bureau of the Census (1975), p. 1067).

[b] No popular vote was counted for southern States in 1864 and 1868.

slump was of shorter duration. Also, in the United States (in contrast to Britain) the recovery was only partial. In America, from 1840 and up to the end of the nineteenth century, over 70 per cent of those eligible to vote actually came to the polls. The proportion dropped to 65 per cent after the turn of the century and plunged to below 50 per cent in the early 1920s. The figure rose to above 60 per cent in the 1950s and 1960s but once more feel below 60 per cent in the 1970s. In Britain, on the other hand, the pre-slump level of voting participation was re-attained and turnout never fell below 70 per cent again.

Two converging explanations have been offered for these slumps, (though not for the differential recoveries). Newly enfranchised groups – it is suggested – temporarily have relatively low political involvement; they require some time to catch up with the voting turnout of previously enfranchised groups. Hence, as increasingly larger groups were enfranchised (especially women), there was a considerable (though temporary) drop in the proportion of actual voters to eligible voters.

Furthermore, the groups enfranchised during the course of the nineteenth century belonged to relatively higher socio-economic strata that already had a high level of political involvement; those enfranchised toward the end of the nineteenth century belonged to the lower strata, which usually have low political involvement. In the United States, the newly enfranchised at the turn of this century included large numbers of new immigrants whose political alienation was based not only on their low socio-economic status but also on their cultural estrangement. It is not surprising, then, that lower percentages of these people exercised their right to vote. This, however, would not explain why Britain regained its pre-slump level of voting turnout while the United States did not; and why turnout in the United States, today, lags not only behind that of Britain, but behind that of other Western countries as well.[19]

Key (1964, p. 576) points out that there are some problems in comparing voting turnouts in different countries. The electorate data for most Western countries do not include persons who are disqualified from voting for various reasons (such as criminal offences). The American figures, on the other hand, include such persons – which artificially lowers the turnout. However, Key concedes that even after allowing for shortcomings in comparability, the fact remains that voting participation in America is lower than in other major democracies. This is partly due to America's more complicated registration requirements and greater geographical mobility; more people in the United States moved recently, and thus do not meet the residency requirements. Nevertheless, Key maintains, it is also due to a lower level of political involvement than in other democracies. It is not clear, however, why this should be the case.

A simpler trend of electoral participation is displayed by Australia's Commonwealth elections. From 1901 to 1922, voting turnout followed a more or less steady pattern; a little more than half of the electorate participated. This followed the trend established in New South Wales's State elections towards the end of the nineteenth century; the turnout at most of these elections was close to 50 per cent, although exciting elections like those of 1882 and 1891 could bring out more than 60 per cent (Hawker, 1971, ch. 2). The trend was continued in Commonwealth elections until 1922, when voting was made compulsory; thereafter the turnout was always over 90 per cent. In contrast to Britain and the United States, Australia thus presents a case in which changes in turnout were affected more exclusively by legislative reform rather than by socio-economic developments.[20]

Despite such differences, the three countries – together with other Western democracies – show a common trend: since the beginning of the nineteenth century, a steady increase in voter participation as a percentage of the total population has been registered. This may be due partly to the gradual extension of the franchise[21] and partly to the growing political involvement of the population. But, in Lane's (1959, p. 18) words: 'Whatever the reason, it is significant that generally speaking, decade by decade . . . A constantly increasing proportion of the population has registered its preference in national elections.' This, of course, is in line with the optimistic theory of public participation in the political process. Strangely, however, this growth in participation has not been matched by a growth in the public's sense of political influence (commonly referred to as efficacy).

Political efficacy

While it is rather easy to measure voter participation, it is much more difficult to measure the public's sense of political efficacy. There are no official statistics – and only a few research surveys. Moreover, such data become meaningful only when there have been repeated surveys using identical questions on identical samples of the population, from which longitudinal trends can be established. Such longitudinal data are scarce; they are mainly American and do not antedate the 1950s.

At any rate, it appears that the American public's sense of political efficacy has not risen in recent years. On the contrary, Converse (1972) shows that between 1952 and 1968 there was a slight decrease.[22] It is interesting that this occurred at a time when voter participation of one significant population group (blacks) was still rising, and when other avenues of political participation (such as direct action) were also getting more use. As Converse (1972, p. 334) put it:

Indicators of political attentiveness and activism appear to have edged forward over the past two decades . . . And these trends stand in rather marked contrast to the evolution of feelings of political efficacy in the population. it has shown a marked regression during the middle 1960s.

One explanation for the divergence between the trends of political participation and those of political efficacy is that increased participation may cause expectations for fuller participation to grow even faster. If expectations outpace achievements, blocked expectations may lead to a sense of political impotence. This explanation may best be couched in terms of Shils's (1975, p. 14) perceptive analysis of the contemporary political scene:

To a greater extent than ever before in history, the mass of the population . . . feel themselves to be 'part' of their society . . . They have ceased to be primarily objects of authoritative decisions by others; they have become, to a much greater extent, acting and feeling subjects with wills of their own which they assert with self confidence . . . Men have become citizens in larger proportions than ever before . . . Nonetheless this greater incorporation carried with it also an inherent tension. Those who participate in the central institutions and value systems, who feel sufficiently closer to the center – also feel their position as outsiders, their remoteness from the center in a way in which their forebears probably did not feel it.

Another explanation for the discrepancy between political (especially electoral) participation and political efficacy, may be given in terms of the pessimistic theories of public political participation. These claim not only that political manipulation of the public has biased the democratic process, and therefore rendered increasing voting participation futile, but that, for this very reason, such manipulation has also caused *feelings* of political futility (Mills, 1959, p. 324).

The following chapters analyse one type of political manipulation in Britain, America, Australia and Israel, and examine the extent to which such manipulation has in fact biased the democratic process an rendered it futile, as pessimists such as Mills believe. The four countries are analysed in the order in which elections were introduced, beginning with Britain.

2   Political manipulation of material inducements in Britain

In certain periods of Britain's history the exchange of votes for material inducements came to be rather well-established practice. Since the end of the nineteenth century, however, the practice has all but disappeared. The distinguishing feature of this exchange while it took place was that the material benefits passed out to voters accrued mainly from the candidates' (or their sponsors') own resources. It was mainly a private exchange between rich men who wanted political careers and poor men who did not care.

Early developments

In Britain, as in the other countries studied, the employment of material inducements in the electoral process developed with the development of democracy itself. As the representative institutions gained in importance and became more powerful, as the franchise was extended and as voters became increasingly independent of their traditional patrons – the practice of eliciting their votes by material inducements became more prominent.

According to Gwyn (1962, ch. 1), one major key for understanding the growth of corrupt electoral practices lies in the relation between supply and demand. As long as service in parliament remained an onerous burden to be avoided, the cost of elections remained low and men would serve only when they could not avoid the duty. Such was the condition until about the middle of the fifteenth century, when the importance of the House of Commons gradually grew and men first began to vie with one another for seats in it. The struggle over seats was intensified in the following century when Henry VIII, finding most of the clergy and many of the peers aligned against him, made the House of Commons rather than the House of Lords his principal partner in the legislature. When the

35

limited number of seats in the Commons became very desirable, many persons were willing to pay a great amount of money to gain them, although there was a certain time lag in the evolution of that trend.

Throughout the Tudor era the demands for seats in parliament rose, but illegal expenditure on bribery and treating was still rather small. This was so, because at that time, the respect and fear of the common men for the powerful and influential magnates were much stronger than in the years that followed, and they were inclined to cast their votes as directed by these magnates. Hence bribery was superfluous.

The practice of treating voters to food and drink began during the sixteenth century, but in the few boroughs where such treating initially occurred, the bill was paid by the community itself. This suggests that the practice was initially part of a public celebration, rather than an inducement for voting for one candidate or another. By the latter part of the sixteenth century treating became a well-established practice and it was now customary for candidates for parliament to foot the bill. But even then such treating was not necessarily aimed at influencing voters, for an occasional successful candidate would entertain not only his supporters but also those who had voted against him.

It was during the years between the death of Elizabeth and the restoration of Charles II that, for the first time, bribery of voters became common practice. By the beginning of the eighteenth century, it was apparently common for the people of a borough to sell their votes to the highest bidder, wherever they were not committed to vote as directed by their patrons. It was during this time that other items of dubious expenditure developed as well: the payment of voters' travelling expenses (which could be consider-able in large counties); the hiring of superfluous committeemen; the distribution of money after an election. Similar practices continued throughout the century; in some of the elections that took place during that century, considerable sums of money were spent in this manner.

As the century progressed, the rising costs of elections had the effect of preventing constituencies from being contested. For example, in only forty-one English boroughs (out of 204) was there a poll held in 1761. In the remaining boroughs, either the weaker candidates conceded to the stronger or a compromise was reached whereby each party returned one of the constituency's two members.

The beginning of the nineteenth century: the flourishing of material inducements

At the opening of the nineteenth century, we learn from Gwyn (1962, ch. 2) close to one-fourth of the members of parliament were returned from rural county constituencies where much of the electorate (including tenants and craftsmen) was still controlled by one or more of the landowning families. Also, in many of the smaller boroughs, the adjacent landowners' influence was often decisive in the choice of candidates; this control rested on a mixture of traditional patterns of reverence with economic pressure. Towards the middle of the century, new centres of economic power arose where employers controlled substantial portions of the electorate, as a function of their control over the voters' means of subsistence.

In such 'locked in' electorates, where votes were practically predetermined, not much direct bribery and treating of voters was going on. It was easiest for the candidate to get in touch with the master who could deliver the votes *en bloc*, and strike a bargain with him. Hence bribery arose mainly where leading families competed with each other and a floating vote thus existed.

In other electorates, especially boroughs, where electors were more independent, both bribery and treating were common. There were constituencies in which a majority of the voters were bribed. In such constituencies there developed the career of a 'borough-monger' who organized a large group of electors and negotiated a price for their votes *en bloc*. Payment for votes took on a variety of forms: free meals and drinks, entertainment, hiring of large numbers of non-working committeemen and direct cash handouts. As members of parliament often had a say in the awarding of local patronage jobs, the manipulation of public office thus came to be important in the winning of elections.

It was not until the general election of 1831, with the impending reform, that a majority of electors went to the polls not for those who would bribe them but for those who pledged themselves to follow a particular public policy. But as soon as the agitation ceased and politics resumed its normal course, elections tended once more to be corrupt. Some of the boroughs that during the reform had rejected corruption later succumbed to it. Indeed, electoral corruption was, if anything, more common after the Reform Act than before.

The Reform Act of 1832 greatly reduced the number of 'pocket boroughs', as the control of the landed oligarchy declined and new urban voters gained the franchise. It was hoped that this would eliminate venal elections, but it did not have this effect. The new electors, apparently, were no less susceptible than the old. Indeed the abolition of many pocket boroughs gave an impetus to bribery since the new electors could not be by-passed in favour of patrons and had to be won over individually. Thus the 'democratization' of electoral corruption also led to its extension.

Violence or intimidation at elections was also common at this period. In most of the large urban constituencies, electors were often terrorized on polling day by gangs of hired bullies and deterred from voting. Sometimes the candidates encouraged this intimidation.

Although observers agree that electoral corruption increased after 1832, the incidence of such corruption is difficult to ascertain. In nearly every constituency there was the possibility of some bribery and treating, a possibility realised whenever the balance of power was nearly equal. In the counties, the principal means of corruption was treating; in the boroughs it was frequently supplemented by outright money bribes. During the first decade following the first Reform Act – it has been estimated – as many as two-thirds of the electors accepted bribes[1] (see Gwyn, 1962, ch. 3; Scott, 1973, ch. 6).

Mostly the candidates themselves would not be directly involved in these practices. In order to circumvent the law, they attempted to keep separate the legal and illegal aspects of electioneering. This was done through what would now be called the local party. Such groups had existed embryonically in many boroughs throughout the eighteenth century, but it was not until the nineteenth century that they evolved a complexity of structure. Election to parliament was impossible without their assistance, but this assistance often proved to be a liability to the candidate, as the local politicians were not averse to accepting bribes either.

After the first Reform Act, candidates were even more at the mercy of local supporters: as the number of small pocket boroughs was considerably reduced, the number of boroughs where control was lodged in a committee of local inhabitants was proportionally increased. In 1835, the Municipal Reform Act was passed, abolishing in the large towns the closed corporations which previously had been the prevalent form of local government and providing for popular elections in 179 municipalities.

To finance these contests parliamentary candidates were frequently called upon for liberal donations, under the assumption that these would be advantageous for their own elections. In the ninety boroughs with identical parliamentary and municipal boundaries, the practice seems to have been to employ the same machinery in national and local elections. In order to return a majority of members to the town council, it was necessary to have permanent organizations in the town's wards. For parliamentary contests these organizations were co-ordinated by a central association composed of the most important citizens who were usually also the holders of municipal office.

This central association was usually little more than a formal body; the real direction of the contest being in the hands of a much smaller group of party leaders (usually referred to as the finance committee) who met secretly to plan electoral strategy and to allocate the funds provided by the candidates. In smaller boroughs the machinery was far less complicated but the decisions concerning the spending of the candidate's money remained with the same type of persons (Gwyn, 1962, ch. 3).

But although the manipulation of voters by material inducements was frequently carried out with the aid of local party organizations no political machines proper[2] developed. According to Scott (1973, chs 6 and 7) the obstacles blocking the creation of such machines were formidable. First, the persistence of a good many patron-dominated constituencies throughout this period afforded their representatives a measure of independence from party discipline. Second, and more importantly, the resources available from governments for engineering elections were rather meagre. Beyond a small amount of cash that might help win a few close races, and a number of safe seats in seaports and garrison towns, the government had only marginal control over recruitment to parliament. Even such limited government resources gradually diminished and lost their effectiveness and hence could not be decisive in a majority of constituencies.[3]

To this must be added the fractionalized nature of political parties, which were also limited in their resources. The fact that candidates could not rely on party resources to finance their elections meant, of course, that they were less amenable to party discipline. This, in turn, further detracted from the parties' power. Thus the parties did not command the combination of power and material resources that could have served to fashion a disciplined and durable political machine of the type that developed in America.

Electoral corruption was thus established to a large extent on an individual basis; on an exchange between the individual candidate and the voter. The growth and persistence of electoral corruption of this brand into the nineteenth century was related to several factors. One important factor according to Heidenheimer (1970) was the further growth in strength and political significance of the House of Commons as a representative institution. While this growth was going on, party politics remained decentralized. Hence election contests that had greatly gained in importance, yet remained the private concern of the adversaries involved, who thus retained great freedom in shaping their own campaign practices. Even after the electoral reform of 1832, the state remained in a low profile as far as elections were concerned. This exclusion of the state from taking the initiative in elections prevented many instances of corruption from being brought to light and punished.

The second half of the nineteenth century: the decline of material inducements

Nevertheless, as the century progressed, important developments took place. One of these was a change in the incidence of treating versus bribery. King (1970) reports that at the beginning of the century bribery was more widespread than treating, but toward the latter part of the century, treating was displacing bribery as the more common form of manipulative technique. This is attested to by Table 2.1.

TABLE 2.1   *Election petitions[a] from English boroughs[b] – 1832_1885*

Years	No. of petitions	Bribery	Treating
1832–67	125	86	39
1868–85	99	49	50

Source: King (1970), p. 389.

[a] Such petitions were presented by losing candidates to claim their seats or to force new elections. It should be taken into account that not all cases of corruption resulted in such petitions (for instance, when both sides had been guilty, no petitions were made) but such petitions are the only data that allow for an approximation to a quantitative analysis of electoral corruption.

[b] These include all English borough constituencies outside London.

Also, to evade bribery laws, outright bribery was increasingly substituted by the employment of voters (or their friends and relatives) in large numbers in election campaigns. Ostensibly they were employed as messengers, chairmen, flagbearers and the like, but in reality the main purpose was to influence their votes. In addition, programs of entertainment interspersed with indoctrination – carried out between elections – replaced to some extent previous methods of manipulation.

Another method of manipulation was that of 'nursing' a borough by gifts to the constituency. Such gifts usually consisted of building a church or a school, subscriptions to charity and the like. This practice which had first evolved at the close of the Tudor era was even more prominent during the nineteenth century. The Acts limiting direct bribery did not include this practice. Unless the money could be proven to be connected with the next election, it was considered as merely promoting the general popularity of the candidate. In fact, however, a candidate who refused to patronize social functions and was niggardly about his subscription to deserving causes in his constituency stood less chance of election than one who was generous. Such contributions, then, were a counterpart to the more direct exchange of benefits for votes on an individual basis.

Material inducements in nineteenth-century Britain may thus be arranged on a continuum from the more blatant and outright to the more devious and subtle ones. On the end of the continuum there was outright bribery of voters, followed by treating in return for votes. On the even more subtle side there was the ostensible employment of voters by candidates or the overcharging of candidates for various services by voters, and the nursing of the constituency. As the nineteenth century progressed there was a clear shift of emphasis from the more blatant types of manipulation to the more subtle ones: from bribery to treating and from that to the even more sophisticated forms of rewarding voters.

This shift was related to a general decline of electoral corruption first evident towards the middle of the century and after. However, up to the 1880s, electoral corruption, though it had diminished, was still prevalent. It had been estimated that between 1865 and 1884 at least sixty-four English boroughs, returning 113 members or nearly one-fifth of the House of Commons, were undoubtedly corrupt. The general election of 1880 was still not free from undue influence and corruption. In that year, tenants still tended to be docile and to vote as their landlords directed. This was partly from general deference, and partly because landlords possessed the right to evict their tenants, usually without paying compensation. Also, employers who had a monopoly of jobs in their towns had no difficulty in determining the outcomes of elections.[4]

Such powers were less effective in towns where there were different employers. Hence, bribery and treating were still widespread as well. Particularly vulnerable were medium-sized boroughs with 1,000 to 8,000 voters (smaller ones were apt to fall into the hands of single families and in larger ones there was a restraint in the great cost of bribery). However, the 1880 general election marked a transition: it was the last to be disgraced by widespread corrupt practices (Lloyd, 1968, ch. 5).

At the turn of the century, electoral manipulation through material inducements to individuals had all but disappeared. A Royal Commission in 1906 found 500 venal votes in Worcester – but this was the last revelation of systematic electoral bribery (Fredman, 1968). Even after that some small-scale treating and

41

bribery still occurred[5] and could still go undetected – but not malpractices on a large scale. Hence, it is significant (as Gwyn reports) that an investigation carried out during these years was unable to discover extensive electoral corruption.

The virtual disappearance of electoral corruption is documented in greater detail in Table 2.2, which lists electoral petitions during the years 1832–1900. Although it cannot be assumed that all illegal

TABLE 2.2   *Number of petitions succeeding on the ground of bribery, etc., 1832–1900*

Parliament	Number of petitions presented	Number successful
1832	23	6
1835	16	2
1837	47	4
1841	26	10
1847	24	14
1852	49	25
1857	19	5
1859	30	12
1865	61	13
1868	51	22
1874	22	10
1880	28	16
1885	8	3
1886	3	0
1892	12	5
1895	7	1

Source: O'Leary (1962), Appendix 1.

electoral practices resulted in an election petition (see Table 2.1, note a), O'Leary holds that the petition trial is throughout that period the main barometer of electoral morality. Hence, this reduction in the incidence of election petitions may be taken to indicate a reduction in the general prevalence of corrupt and illegal practices.

The nursing of constituencies was apparently perpetuated much longer. In the Conservative Party in 1944 the speaker's conference on electoral reform singled out for censure the continuation of large contributions from candidates towards nursing their constituencies (Gwyn, 1962, ch. 9). But manipulation of material inducements to individuals had all but disappeared; as O'Leary (1962, p. 1) put it: soon the control of votes by 'influence' and their disposal for a consideration had become an ugly memory, and 'the characteristic purity of British elections was held up as a model for other countries'.

In recent years

Observers usually agree that no significant dimensions of electoral corruption are to be found in Britain in recent years. According to McCallum and Readman (1964, ch. 2), the franchise has been exercised without fear of misconduct on the part of the officials responsible and without any serious direct corruption or intimidation of one citizen by another. This is not to say that nursing of constituencies has entirely disappeared or that no general promises of benefits (to the public as a whole or to parts of it) are being made. Such phenomena (or similar ones) are part of all political life and it is difficult to think of any system from which they could be absent. But there is no obvious bribery in the sense of some citizens paying others for voting in a certain manner.[6]

In Leonard's (1968, pp. 192–3) words:

> In practice, people involved in electioneering in Britain have proved extremely law abiding and after each general election there are never more than a handful of prosecutions for election offences. The last time an election was invalidated because of an election offence was at Oxford in 1924.

In Britain, concurs Birch (1973), electoral expenses which were first regulated in 1883 as part of an attempt to stamp out electoral corruption, continue to be under control, and this control has been progressively tightened since then. This, perhaps, is one of the reasons for what he refers to as the honesty, the lack of passion and the lack of money in present-day British politics.

Legislation and the waning legitimation of material inducements[7]

How was the manipulation of material inducements eliminated from the British political scene? Ever since the emergence of such corruption successive attempts were made to check it through legislation. At first, bribery and treating were illegal, but only by common law. As Gwyn (1962, ch. 3) reports, the first statute that attempted to define corrupt electoral practices was passed in 1669. By this Act, members of parliament were to lose their seats if, before their election, they (or persons acting for them) had given or promised voters money or other rewards. But this legislature had poor results and parliament therefore passed another Bribery Act in 1729, intended to prevent electors themselves from being tempted. Among other things, any elector discovered to have accepted a bribe was to be fined £500 and to forfeit his franchise. The effectiveness of this act was as slight as that of the preceding one.

Since the beginning of the eighteenth century and until the middle of the nineteenth century, a number of additional legislative Acts were introduced, but these never went very far. The penalties imposed were far too strict to be regularly enforced and the machinery of enforcing them was too cumbersome to be effective. Only in the second half of the nineteenth century was successively more effective legislation introduced. This legislation provided for the reduction of election expenditure, introduced the secret ballot, entailed more realistic penalties for corrupt practices and made electoral proceedings easier to control.

The first real effort to cope with electoral corruption was made in 1854 when a comprehensive Act was passed which provided a working definition of the chief corrupt practices, practicable penalties for venal candidates and voters, and additional machinery to deal with controverted elections. The old £500 fine, long a dead letter, was abolished. But electors accepting treats or bribes were prevented from voting and candidates offering them were prevented from being elected during the existing parliament. However, even this law brought little improvement and the penalties imposed were not an effective deterrent.

The next step to curb electoral corruption occurred in 1868, when an attempt was made to improve the method of trying election petitions. The right to try such petitions, which previously had been held by the House of Commons, was put into the hands of the High Court judges, and petitions were to be heard in the constituencies involved. Thus, the system of jurisdiction over controverted elections which had produced much expense, inefficiency and partisanship was replaced by a more efficient and objective system which was much more likely to lead to convictions of the guilty. The Act also stiffened the punishment for bribery without making such punishment unrealistic. Anyone guilty of the practice was not allowed to be in parliament for seven years. If he knowingly engaged an agent who had been guilty of the practice his election was voided.

In 1872, the Australian secret ballot was introduced, designed to curb bribery by making the briber uncertain of a return on his money. But the law did not fulfil its promise and, even after its introduction, more subtle forms of bribery and treating continued.

The Corrupt and Illegal Practices Act of 1883 incorporated and considerably improved all foregoing legislation on the subject. Transgressors of the law were submitted to much more severe (though realistic) penalties than before (including imprisonment for up to one year). The most important aspect of this legislation was that which concerned electoral agents. Candidates for parliament had been employing agents for a long time but until the middle of the nineteenth century they were employed principally to make payments about which candidates preferred to be ignorant. In 1883 the appointment of an agent was made compulsory; it was also provided that the candidate must not incur any election expenses except through his agent and that the agent must submit all accounts to the returning officer. The agent's accounts were then to be published so that they could be open to public scrutiny.

At the same time, a severe limit was set to the amount the agent might spend on behalf of his candidate, and election expenses were thus considerably reduced. As the campaign expenses were restricted to the bare minimum, this made it rather difficult to have funds left over for the purchase of large numbers of votes. The law also facilitated control over corrupt electoral practices by making it necessary to prove only the relatively simple accusation that money had been spent, not the obscure accusation that it had been spent corruptly.

This Act had a greater success than previous ones, as evidenced by the fact that corrupt practices vastly diminished and were virtually eliminated towards the end of the century, and by the fact that election expenses were in fact greatly reduced. However, although the Act was successful, it is doubtful whether one can attribute entirely to it, or even to the cumulative effct of all legislation, the rapid decline in corruption which marked the two last decades of the century. The Act of 1883 made bribery more difficult and its punishment more severe, but it was not impossible to circumvent this law as others had been circumvented before. Perhaps part of the success of the Act was that it was more thoroughly enforced than previous laws, as the courts now built up a tradition of severity towards electoral manipulation and there was now a tendency towards harsher treatment of offenders. Consequently, many who would have considered giving or taking bribes must have reconsidered the matter.

The increasingly effective anti-corruption legislation and the stricter enforcement of this legislation was in turn related to a change of attitude toward electoral manipulation among the elites and eventually among the public as well. Eighteenth-century politicians had held the belief that there was no effective way of preventing electoral corruption and had come to regard it as a necessary evil. It is quite possible that this belief, in turn, had acted as a self-fulfilling prophecy and was in itself one of the bases for the ineffectiveness of eighteenth-century anti-corruption legislation.

Looking back upon the early parts of the nineteenth century one gains the impression that at this time politicians were not seriously concerned with eliminating corrupt electoral practices either. According to the moral code then obtaining among the political elite, these electoral practices were not unequivocally considered corrupt. Some observers go so far as to claim that either such practices had no moral significance or they were actually considered desirable. Thus treating and other colourful political practices of the period were practised with an openness that shows that they were not regarded as improper by those whose opinions mattered. For most of the century – writes Gwyn (1962, ch. 3) – a man was not considered immoral for buying his way into the House of Commons. In fact, a man known to have bribed or actually having been convicted of bribery was no less respected by the majority of the House. For this reason, perhaps, anti-corruption legislation could not be effective at that time either. Also, many politicians who would have dispensed with corruption were reluctant to support stern measures for fear that through no fault of their own they would be unseated because of the illegal activities of their supporters.

One important reason for such positive or indecisive attitudes towards venality, holds Gwyn, was the failure of organized religion to throw its weight solidly against it. In the eighteenth century the chuch had held immense political power and many churchmen had been actively involved in politics. Although not many of these clergymen had distributed actual bribes, the majority had been too actively employed in politics to oppose it. In a somewhat less sordid form, the church retained this character during much of the nineteenth century. Political sermons continued to be delivered at election time, and some of the clergymen even participated in corrupt practices.[8]

If most members of the elites continued (throughout a large part of the century) to find that neither their interests nor their consciences forbade them to distribute bribes, the persons receiving these perquisites were much of the same mind. Political leaders felt obliged to look after their supporters but did not feel it incumbent upon them to educate those supporters in the value of democracy.

It is not surprising, then, that for a large part of the century most voters considered their franchise mainly as a financial asset in the narrowest sense of the term and only a minority conceived of their votes as a means of actively participating in the political life of the country. In the pre-reform era, the moral awareness of the electorate concerning the sale of their votes was not highly developed. During the general election of 1831, the electorate was very reform conscious but the effect of the reform movement was not lasting. Soon after the reform many voters once more came to claim their bribes as a right founded upon prescription.

One election committee after another discovered that voters who had accepted bribes felt no shame about their actions. It was not that they were immoral but simply that they could not see anything wrong with selling their votes. Although some progress eventually occurred in the moral awareness of the British electorate concerning the sale of their votes, it was slow and gradual.

Looking at the nineteenth century as a whole, King (1970) contends that there were two political sub-cultures: pre-industrial and industrial, with distinctive attitude differences toward the political process. The older sub-culture encouraged the continuation of what he terms pre-democratic forms of political persuasion. It put little emphasis on platform – or program-oriented campaigns; the purpose of voting was to acquire material rewards. The more modern culture condemned such an outlook, but it became dominant only towards the end of the century.

The turning point came in the latter part of the century: it was then that the political elite turned unequivocally against electoral manipulation. At this point the desire to wipe out electoral corruption was common to the leaders of both parties; in addition, the Royal Commissions investigating corrupt practices now took a grimmer view of the situation and raised the demand for a more drastic solution to a problem that was considered more crucial than formerly.

At that time, too, there were various organizations that strove to turn public opinion against electoral corruption. Trade unions, chapels, friendly societies, all instilled into their members the virtues of democratic participation. In line with this general climate of opinion among politicians and leaders of various organizations, newspapers now strongly opposed electoral corruption and frequently exposed it. The amount of publicity given to the subject far exceeded that of previous eras. Especially the popular radical newspapers (which were now more widely read because of the rise in the literacy rate) emphasized the use of the vote as a means of gaining social reforms, not as the method of acquiring beverages or money.

As the elites changed their attitudes toward electoral corruption, so too, did the public, which gradually became socialized to the new style of political culture. According to Gwyn, the old, venal electors were outnumbered by a public to which corrupt practices were alien and moral revulsion against corrupt practices became widespread. None of the statutes would have been effective had there not also occurred a revolution in the outlook of the mass of the people – admittedly very much influenced by legislative reform – which gradually transformed their perceived role from a relatively passive to a relatively active one. However, as O'Leary (1962, p. 233) points out, when all is said, it was the members of the House of Commons who set the moral tone for the changes in public opinion. 'Parliament managed within one generation to sweep away traditions that were centuries old'.

Manipulation of material inducements and class interests

Thus the British political elite – which at first had sponsored the system of electoral manipulation – later on took an active part in its condemnation and in its elimination. How can this change of attitude be explained? This question can best be dealt with by analysing the class affiliation of the British elite, the class interests thus served by electoral corruption and those served by its elimination.

Up to the turn of the present century, membership in Britain's political elite was virtually monopolized by the propertied classes. Throughout the Tudor era this monopoly was solidified by the pattern of deferential voting whereby the great landowers determined the voting of their dependants. In the following centuries deferential voting gradually lost importance but even in the nineteenth century it had not disappeared.

However, as deferential voting gradually diminished, the cost of a political (especially a parliamentary) career became one of the chief bases of upper-class monopoly of political power. This cost had several sources. Until the beginning of this century, membership in parliament carried no salary. According to Gwyn, the increasing attractiveness of membership in parliament during the Tudor era brought to the decline of a medieval system of public payment; the last members of parliament to receive payment for their boroughs served at the end of the seventeenth century. Henceforth members were not paid and those who were not wealthy were at a considerable disadvantage by having to carry the burden of an additional occupation. Some of the more able members of the government's party might be awarded a salaried position in the government, but in these cases the members were left without funds when their party fell from power.

Election expenses which mostly accrued from private resources afforded another political advantage to the upper classes. There were first the legitimate expenses of electioneering. Initially they were not significant but they grew considerably with the successive growth of the electorate, especially throughout the nineteenth century. In addition, as bribery, treating and the nursing of constituencies developed, election expenses soared to ever greater heights. Consequently, only the wealthy could undertake the financial burdens of standing for parliament.

Those who were not wealthy themselves had to have a wealthy

patron to sponsor their parliamentary careers. Frequently, landed aristocrats were willing to spend large amounts of money to back their own candidates in order to perpetuate their influence and prestige in their localities. Ostensibly, this pattern facilitated the access of lower-class persons to political power. However, it entailed the obligation for parliamentarians who did not belong to the propertied classes themselves to represent the policies advocated by their propertied sponsors. When they were not inclined to do so they frequently resigned.

Throughout the eighteenth century candidates willing to follow the government's lead could usually depend on it for some financial aid in elections if they were unable to raise their own finance. But the funds a government could give its candidates were seldom more than a fraction of their electoral expenses. In any event, the use of public and royal funds for electioneering was discontinued towards the beginning of the nineteenth century; thereby access to political leadership was even further restricted.

Another source of financial assistance to candidates was from wealthy friends and relatives. This, however, meant that candidates had to be well connected. Subscriptions were sometimes raised from supporters through political rather than friendship motives. Also, during the nineteenth century both the Conservatives and the Liberals set up election funds which were meted out to aid candidates. But most subscriptions and party contributions covered only a part of a candidate's expenses and they were by no means present in all constituencies. Most Conservative and Liberal candidates could not expect party assistance and only in a very few instances could candidates stand at no expense to themselves.

As a consequence, both the Liberal and the Conservative parties drew their candidates, their parliamentarians and their cabinet members from the same economic classes: mainly the landed aristocracy and – to a much lesser extent – the capitalists. Some wealthy professionals were also included; but middle-class persons without ample means found parliamentary careers an excessive burden; small tradesmen and members of the working class were entirely excluded. For instance in 1840, over 80 per cent of the members of the House of Commons were landholders and 5 per cent were manufacturers or mine-owners (Guttsman 1976, ch. 7). The same principle in cabinet is illustrated by Table 2.3.

As corrupt electoral practices contributed substantially to election expenses, they had a very real share in bringing about this situation. They also helped to reinforce the political passivity of the lower classes. While material inducements were handed out by members of the upper classes, the acceptance of such inducements was most common among members of the lower classes – the poorer

sections of the population. As Gwyn noted, many voters who came
before election committees could neither read nor write. But there
were also many persons investigated for taking bribes who had
some education. In 1880, the voters unable to read in England and
Wales comprised about 1 per cent of the electorate, a figure well
below the most conservative estimate of the percentage of corrupt
voters even at that time. While not all venal voters were illiterate,
many of them were poor. To poor agricultural workers earning two
shillings a day the offer of even half a crown might be an irresistible
temptation.[9]

TABLE 2.3 *The social structure of cabinet membership, 1830–68*

Large territorial lords and their sons	56
Country gentlemen (lesser landowners)	12
Mercantile and administrative upper class (mainly rentiers)	21
'New men' (mostly lawyers)	14
Total	103

Source: Guttsman (1963), p. 38.

There were some poor men who rejected bribes and many well-
to-do tradesmen and professionals were not averse from receiving
them. Indeed there is only a thin line between the acceptance of
bribes and the overcharging of candidates which was practised by
tradesmen in every constituency. Professional men also looked to
elections as an opportunity for augmenting their incomes. For
solicitors there was money to be made as election agents and
newspaper owners charged candidates double the normal rate for
election advertisements. But the main recipients of material
inducements were none the less the labouring classes and the poor,
and the political manipulation of such inducements thus served to
perpetuate their exclusion from political power.

It is not surprising then, that for a long time the upper-class-
dominated political elites did nothing to discourage the lower
classes' willingness to be bribed, on which much of their own
political power was founded. Nevertheless these elites were also the
ones who eventually initiated the elimination of the exchange of
bribes for votes. A major reason for this, no doubt, lies in the
individual nature of the exchange and in the exorbitant expenses
caused by it. As the practice was carried out mainly by individual
candidates for parliament, there were little or no vested interests of
political machines to back them up.

Also, throughout the nineteenth century the expenses caused by

the practice continued to soar. Together with the legitimate electioneering expenses they ran into thousands of pounds for each
constituency. The election of 1880 was probably the most costly
ever held: over two million pounds were spent. As the individual
candidates and their sponsors bore the main burden of this expenditure they were increasingly harassed by it. Even the wealthy now
found the system an increasing financial strain and hence many of
them were not sorry to see it go.

The question still remains, however, why the upper-class-
monopolized political elite could not have found a way of tapping
state resources to cover the increasing expenses of political corruption as elites in other countries had done so successfully (see
following chapters). It must be taken into account, therefore, that
the years between 1868 and 1883 were a period of constructive
rethinking of various other areas of socio-political life as well and
that this era was also productive of more reformist legislation in
other fields than any comparable period in British history.[10] The
rethinking of electoral malpractices and the legislative reforms
designed to eliminate them were thus only one aspect of a wider
trend toward socio-political reforms (O'Leary, 1962).

In any case, the fact is that by taking the initiative in eliminating
material inducements, and thus helping restrict election expenses,
the upper-class political elite helped relax the restrictions on working-class access to power. As property restrictions on voting were
also eliminated during the same years (see chapter 1) it is not
surprising that this was also the time in which labour effectively
organized for political action, shortly afterwards, to achieve a share
in political power.

Beforehand, and even around the middle of the nineteenth
century, there had been no substantial working-class electoral
organization. Chartism, the most important lower-class political
movement, never produced an organization to promote parliamentary candidates. Only towards the end of the century did the first
Labour candidates win admission to parliament; even then, and for
some years to come, their numbers were rather small and their
influence therefore negligible.[11] The Labour Party itself was not
founded until 1900 and was first admitted into the government
coalition during the First World War; the first Labour government
was formed in the 1920s.

Although salaries for parliamentarians were introduced in 1911,
Labour Party representatives were not necessarily working-class
people themselves. Indeed, in 1951 and 1970 only 37 and 26 per cent
respectively of Labour members of parliament were actually
manual workers (Butler and Pinto-Duschinsky, 1971, p. 302).
Nevertheless class representation in the political elite shifted

considerably around the end of the nineteenth century and the beginning of the twentieth, and the monopoly is no longer in the hands of the propertied classes. For instance, while in 1840 the dominant classes accounted for over 85 per cent of the House of Commons (over 80 per cent landholders and some 5 per cent capitalists) and workers were not represented at all, the situation had changed substantially by 1910. The upper classes now accounted for about 63 per cent of parliament (some 25 per cent landholders and some 38 per cent capitalists) and workers now had a 22 per cent share of the house (Putnam, 1976, ch. 7). While the working class had not been represented in cabinet throughout the years 1868–86, it accounted for 21 per cent of all cabinet members throughout the years 1935–55 (Guttsman, 1963, p. 242).

Also, in all Labour cabinets from 1924 until 1950, over half of the members have been of working-class background (Guttsman, 1963, p. 242). Most importantly, however, the Labour Party is backed by trade unions and a large proportion of Labour politicians are sponsored by them; and, as Laski (1945) has pointed out, the Labour Party's essential direction and its program is implied in the economic interests of its Labour sponsors and supporters.

Material inducements and the democratic process

The virtual elimination of material inducements – in which the elites' initiative had such a substantial share – was thus instrumental in widening the social basis of political power. In addition, it was also significant for other aspects of Britain's democratic process. For while material inducements had emerged with the initial emergence of democratic institutions, their decline was closely interlinked with the further development of these institutions. The growth in the power and political significance of the House of Commons had been related to the development of electoral corruption. But the extension of the franchise towards the end of the nineteenth century and the beginning of the twentieth to the point of universal suffrage coincided with the decline of such corruption. The quantitative extension of the franchise, the qualitative extension in the political significance of this franchise and the widening class basis of political power thus all went hand in hand.

Britain is usually considered as a country with a long-standing democratic tradition, in fact one of the oldest, if not the oldest, democracy in the world. Yet, as the foregoing analysis has shown, for the better part of the nineteenth century the extension of material benefits to voters had a major share in determining the outcomes of elections and thus greatly biased the democratic process especially in favour of the wealthy. Even in Britain, therefore, an (in this sense) uncorrupted democratic system is of more recent vintage than is popularly thought to be the case. What does count is that the transition to such a system did occur; which is more than can be said about the United States – our concern in the next chapter.

3 Political manipulation of material inducements in the United States

When material inducements flourished in nineteenth-century Britain, they were handed out largely by individual candidates and their agents. In America, on the other hand, such benefits have reached the voters mainly through tightly woven party organizations known as political machines. Perhaps for this reason, the practice has been more resilient in this country and although it has recently declined, has not been eradicated.

The party political machine

The American political machine is an organization that has used various methods to gain political support: intimidation, violence and fraud on the one hand, and charisma and ideology, on the other. But the major basis of its power and cohesion has been the use of material inducements. One characteristic feature of the machine is that it has dealt with *particularistic* inducements to families and individuals. This personalization has been the machine's main attraction; it has stood in marked contrast to the impersonal treatment that could be expected from the authorities (see Merton, 1957a). Benefits handed out by the machine have traditionally included cash, gifts, loans, jobs, welfare payments outside the bounds of legality, and help or 'pull' in dealing with authorities. These established debts which the machine could call in on election day (Scott, 1973, ch. 6).

Another characteristic feature of the machine is its organizational structure. According to Key (1964, ch. 12), the classic party machine is a hierarchy. A 'boss' stands at the head of an organization whose workers are held together by the benefits they receive and the benefits they pass out. A large proportion of the machine's officials have simultaneously held public office (appointive or elective). Such employment in the public administration (patronage)[1] came to be an important factor in building and sustaining the machine – especially in establishing lines of command and creating cohesion.

Sometimes the organization is a dictatorship. More often it has consisted of clusters of personal loyalties around certain individuals who, in turn, would be bound to persons higher up in the hierarchy, often by materialist ties. This has given more or less effective control of the machine to a few individuals.

A prominent figure is the precinct captain because he is the link between the machine and the voters. He organizes the support of his family and friends, and of those who can be recruited with various election-day perquisites. He usually has the power to designate two or three precinct election officials, and thereby acquires their votes and those of their families and friends. Funds are allocated to him for election day expenses; with each addition to his payroll, a few votes are added to his little bloc.

The precinct captain works throughout the year as well, accumulating electoral support through services and benefits to the voters of his precinct. Especially in the poorer neighbourhoods, he is a social agency of sorts; in time of stress the people turn to him (and, through him, to the party organization) for assistance without the red tape that characterizes government social agencies.

The precinct captain also helps citizens in their contacts with authorities. He helps aliens through naturalization procedures; he helps people to get jobs, especially on the public payroll; as Key (1964, p. 340) put it, he would even 'see the judge and attempt to mix mercy with justice'. Governmental agencies are so complex that the average citizen is often bewildered. The precinct captain knows the ropes, and thus can be of service even when no favouritism is involved. By such devices, the machine precinct captains deliver large numbers of votes in support of the party.

This combination between a tight organizational structure and the material benefits at its disposal has enabled the machine to wield enormous power in American politics. It has determined the party's nominations and exerted a mighty influence on elections – especially, but not exclusively, on the State and local levels. If the party was not rent by dissention, the machine could usually control the primaries – and 'if one controls the primary, he has gone a long way toward controlling all' (Key, 1964, p. 339). In its most developed form the machine became the *de facto* government – since many major decisions were made by party functionaries who managed their puppets in public office. Although the American political machine has been characterized by some typical long-term features, it was by no means an unchanging structure; growth, heyday, and eventual decline are traced below.

The nineteenth century

The American political machine came into being with democracy itself. In the 1820s and 1830s, as soon as large numbers of Americans had the vote, there came into existence an organization to bring voters to the polls and to manipulate the electoral process itself. At that time there was inadequate control over parties and elections; this situation was utilized by the evolving machines, and the electoral system came to be riddled with abuses (Epstein, 1967, ch. 5).

The machine issued identifiable printed ballots to voters at the polls. Candidates for office were required to pay the party to get their names on these ballots – thus confining the race to rich men, or to those willing to borrow (expecting to recoup the debt when in office). Such receipts were extensive, and provided a generous pool for the bribing of voters.

Such bribing of voters by agents of the political machine was a widespread practice. The simplest form of bribery occurred when district captains paid voters at the polling place. Since the ballots were coloured or otherwise recognizable, and the voters were followed to the ballot box by agents, it was easy to ensure delivery in return for bribes.

Also, generous provisions were made for party workers on election day. In some districts, as many as 20 per cent of the voters were paid in one way or another. Payments were made partly from party funds, partly from assessments on the candidates, and partly from public funds. Party leaders gave themselves full-time jobs on the public payroll. A country clerk told a legislative committee that he was paid a substantial sum each year, from which he paid another clerk a small salary to do most of the work while he himself attended to the machine's business (Fredman, 1968, ch. 2).

The most disorderly elections occurred in the big cities and metropolitan centres, where there were concentrations of poor people and recent immigrants unused to the franchise; the strongest and most effective political machines came to be located here. The first and most long-lived machine was Tammany Hall; it began as a benevolent masonic society, but then went into politics to promote Thomas Jefferson for president. It set the pattern for other urban machines – such as Philadelphia's Republican Gas Ring, which for decades did an equally effective job in controlling elections (Steinberg, 1972, Introduction).

By the 1870s, many people were aware and highly critical of the abuses with which the American elections were beset. In response, the States began adopting the Australian secret ballot from 1880 onwards; by 1910, it was being used in all States except Georgia and South Carolina. It was thought that this would make bribery unprofitable, since a party worker could not check whether a bribed vote had been delivered. The possibility of the Tasmanian Dodge (see chapter 4) remained – but various systems of numbering were devised which precluded this dodge without destroying the secrecy of the ballot.

It soon became clear, however, that despite all this, bribery had not been eliminated; indeed, its extent became quite alarming. For instance, McCook (1892) concluded that 16 per cent of the voters of Connecticut were for sale. At that time, it further became evident that the Australian ballot had not seriously weakened the party machines. Although it had made direct bribery and intimidation much more difficult, indirect bribery by party machines remained.

The beginning of the twentieth century

Despite the secret ballot, therefore, party machines reached unprecedented dimensions around the turn of the century. Describing the situation around 1905, Speed (1970, p. 422)[2] wrote:

> Such a large proportion of voters in every closely contested election in the United States is corrupt that enough votes can be bought at elections to decide which side will win. Moreover, these purchases are made . . . the purchasable element can decide between the great parties whenever there is money enough to secure their votes.

As an example, the author presented the case of New York city. He concluded that more than 70 per cent of the voters were honest, but these were divided between the parties, so that the minority of purchasable voters could tip the balance. The author reached these conclusions on the basis of interviews with politicians; he found nobody willing to confess that they had bought votes or corrupted voters – but the politicians were usually willing to tell what their opponents had done.

Speed calculated that around 24,800 persons were 'employed' by the parties' precinct captains; most of them did not actually do anything to earn their pay, except vote for the party that paid them. Speed (p. 424), further reported:

> I found that the venal vote, besides the workers, was 155,000. To these add the workers and we have a grand total of 179,800.

Some few of these workers really do work so I take off about one third, and leave the net total at 170,000.

Since 652,116 votes were cast in New York City, Speed concluded that between a quarter and a third of the voters were venal. The winning candidate for mayor (McClellan) had only 63,636 more votes than his opponent (Low); two years earlier, the winning candidate (Low) had only 31,638 more votes than his opponent (Shepard). Consequently, wrote Speed (p. 423),

> when we consider the phalanx of venal voters – 170,000 strong –
> it is evident that the men who have the money, in alliance with
> those who know how to spend it, can control the city at any time
> and every time, except on the rare occasion when the really good
> people of all parties get together to protest against excesses.

Given the rudimentary research methods of that time, it is doubtful whether the reported number of venal voters was accurate – but, as a rough approximation, the estimate is nevertheless illuminating.[3]

The majority of voters who could be (and expected to be) bought, lived in tenement houses in crowded districts. 'They are distressingly poor, and the offer of two, three, four or five dollars on election day is a temptation too sore for them to withstand' (p. 423). The most miserably poor were the men who, some thirty days before an election, were colonized in lodging houses; they were glad to get free lodging. The men who worked along the riverfronts were said to be almost universally purchasable, and the rowdies who belonged to gangs sold their votes as a matter of course.

Many of these people were newly naturalized citizens. Also, nine out of ten blacks were willing to sell their votes. In a presidential election, blacks did not tend to vote against the Republicans – but they would take bribes not to vote at all. In non-presidential elections, New York's blacks generally had no preference; they banded into associations, and their leaders tried to sell them *en bloc*. In general, Speed concludes, the people who sold their votes were the unclassed – that is, people who lacked position and a definite stake in the community.

Regardless of whether the figure of 170,000 venal votes is accurate, it is clear that sizeable parts of the New York population were willing to sell their votes – and it is quite likely that such paid votes often tipped the scale. The effectiveness of these machine payoffs was underscored by the failure of reform movements. Reform governments soon discovered that the cost of eliminating corruption was a marked loss in popular support (Scott, 1973, ch. 9). This is one reason why attempted reforms did so poorly and political machines reasserted themselves in all major urban centers.

While some observers maintain that party machines had their heyday at the turn of the century, others claim that bossism was never more powerful than during the 1920s and 1930s (see Steinberg, 1972, Introduction). Some believe that the machines were undermined by the depression, which reduced their resources, and by the New Deal, which increased the government's involvement in the welfare of the people. Thus, argues Greenstein (1966), the private 'welfare' programs of party organizations were undercut by social security, minimum wage legislation, and relief programs.

Not so, reasons Steinberg: bossism did not fade away with the advent of the New Deal. Certainly, the widespread machine practice of distributing food baskets and shoddy clothes to the needy as a means of buying their votes was antiquated by the billions of dollars in federal welfare funds. But most bosses grew even stronger – because they became the distributors of this money, they determined who would get it – besides being able to perpetuate other machine practices as well. In Steinberg's words (pp. 8–9): 'The significance of the bosses of the twenties and thirties was that they collectively made the profession of democratic government and civil rights a hollow phrase in their time.'

For instance, Frank Hague of New Jersey ran a powerful machine based partly on intimidation and violence. Objective poll-watchers were beaten or locked up in police stations. Opponents were frequently beaten as well, or deported from Jersey City. Hague also engaged in blatant fraud to ensure his victory at the polls. Steinberg (1972, pp. 34, 40) commented:

> With the inevitable Hague vote counters on hand he made certain his victory would be one-sided. For instance, in his home second ward only his act of generosity permitted his opponent to get 120 of the 4,620 votes cast . . . A Jersey City philosopher once observed: 'It ain't how the ballots go into the box that counts. It's how they come out.'

But intimidation and ballot-stuffing were not Hague's only methods of winning elections. He knew that unless he could also control voters, the outrage of an antagonistic majority would eventually defeat him. So he sought to control the 600,000 residents of Hudson County by constant pressure from his political machine. He had thousands of election workers. Every home was under the care of a precinct worker. These precinct workers, who were the lowest echelon in the party-machine pyramid, organized clubs and excursions, passed out food, clothing and coal, found jobs for the people of their neighbourhoods, and served as a buffer between them and the police. For these activities, the machine expected and got votes in return.

Hague's reward to his machine was to saddle Jersey City and Hudson County with the largest city and county payrolls in the United States. Many of his lieutenants were given titles and salaries without any duties. He also raised money for the church to gain its support; he quieted the opposition of priests, ministers and rabbis by making them paid chaplains for hospitals, the prison, the police and the fire department.

The effect of Hague's machine was not limited to the local level. Hague helped Roosevelt get into the White House by controlling New Jersey's delegation to the national convention, and by piling up a heavy Democratic vote in Hudson County. This was one reason why Hague's political power remained strong during the 1930s; not until the 1940s did it wane.

Hague's machine was not unique in those days. Steinberg describes several other machines which followed the same pattern – thus demonstrating the power of the machine and the widespread employment of material inducements throughout the 1920s and 1930s. One of the most powerful machine systems was in Chicago, where bribery and other material inducements continued to be the accepted practice. The Republican machine collapsed in the depression because of the greatly reduced city treasury, fewer city jobs to dispense, and a huge drop in private contributions. However, as Gosnell (1937) indicated, this merely marked a changeover from a Republican machine to a Democratic one; the basic machine model persisted to the 1970s (see below). Other American machines resembled Chicago's in most important respects, except that not many of them were so successful for so long.

The middle of the twentieth century

Although the New Deal could not eradicate political machines, several other developments of that time had an adverse effect on these organizations. Posts and other benefits from the public administration diminished. After the First World War, immigration was limited, and previous immigrants had become somewhat acculturated – so there were fewer immigrants for the machines to work on. When the depression ended, the standard of living rose, as did the level of education. Yet poverty – especially among blacks – was not eliminated, and pockets of manageable voters remained.

Partly in response to these developments, party machines have undergone substantial alterations since the 1920s and 1930s. Tightly managed, Statewide organizations became the exception; they were largely replaced by loose, factionalized cliques of professionals within each party. Several machines were weakened, so that their capacity to control nominations declined markedly. Those organizations which retained a semblance of unity devoted greater attention to public action. In a few States, new-style organizations developed; these were based more on a common policy viewpoint than on material benefits.

The weakening of party machines in the 1940s was patently evident. The executive director of the Republican National Committee reported that 357 counties had no Republican chairman or vice-chairman in 1948, and that 28,000 (almost one-fourth) of the precincts had no Republican leadership. In the same year in Oregon, the Democrats had operating organizations in only 13 of 36 counties. Nor were all (or even the largest) cities thoroughly organized. For instance, it was reported in 1949 that no Minneapolis ward had a party organization adequately covering every precinct throughout the year; except in the weeks just before an important election, roughly 100 of the 634 precincts had no captains, and not more than half of the captains were active party workers who could be depended on at all times (Morlan, 1949, as quoted by Key, 1964, p. 341).

The situation was similar in the 1950s. The Survey Research Center found that only 10 per cent of a cross-section of citizens said that they had been contacted personally by political party workers during the 1956 presidential campaign. Even if only non-southern cities of over 100,000 population are considered, the percentage is still less than 20. This is a far cry from the situation that would have prevailed if party organizations had been well developed.

But national statistics conceal quite a bit of local variation. A survey of Detroit voters found that only 6 per cent had been approached by party workers; reports from other cities (such as Seattle and Minneapolis) show a similar neglect. On the other hand, 60 per cent of the voters interviewed in New Haven, Connecticut, in a 1959 survey said they had been contacted by party workers; most of these workers belonged to Mayor Lee's old-time party organization, which was mobilizing votes and welding together the city government (Greenstein, 1966).

Philadelphia's old-style machine also showed continuing vitality in the 1950s. The committeemen still tried to control votes by acting as go-betweens for their constituents with the police and other government agencies and by extending small benefits and loans to the needy. According to Reichley (1966, p. 264), 'A committeeman whose constituents have received ungenerous treatment in the magistrate's court may easily consign him to oblivion on election day.'

There were still divisions in the city where a committeeman had absolute control over 100–200 voters. There were about 200 controlled white divisions and 300 controlled black divisions. The other thousand-odd divisions were either independent or had ineffective committeemen.

If each controlled division had 100 voters firmly loyal to their committeeman, these 500 divisions together held a core of 50,000 votes for the organization. Since even a committeeman who was ineffective or who was located in an independent division was expected to control at least ten votes among his family and friends, the remaining precincts added a minimum of 10,000 votes, for a subtotal of 60,000. Committeemen who could account for 200 or more votes easily boosted the organization's rock-bottom minimum to 90,000 or 100,000. In a primary election (which rarely attracted more than 200,000 voters in either party when there was an important fight), such a base would obviously be decisive. In a general election, on the other hand, it need not necessarily be so – particularly if the opposition party had controlled divisions of its own; but when the sure vote was added to the party's habitual voters, the result was very difficult to overcome (Reichley, 1966).

Further evidence of the persistence of old-style party activities came from an ingenious questionnaire administered by Richard T. Frost in 1957. Party workers from eight New Jersey counties reported that they performed a wide range of traditional services.

TABLE 3.1   *Services performed by New Jersey politicians*

Service	Percentage performing it 'often'
Helping deserving people to get public jobs	72
Showing people how to get their social security benefits, welfare, unemployment, compensation, etc.	54
Helping citizens who are in difficulty with the law to get straightened out	62

Source: Greenstein (1966), p. 260.

The machine in its classical form is an urban phenomenon and mainly a phenomenon of the great cities. But not all urban centres have retained machines. They remained in some portions of several cities, while other cities seem to have been free of them. Why they persisted in some settings but not in others is not fully clear. Greenstein (1966) suggests that the old pattern continued in eastern industrial cities (New Haven, Philadelphia, and many parts of New Jersey) which had sizeable low-income groups in need of traditional party services. However, there were also some cities of this type – such as Minneapolis and Detroit – in which weak, disorganized parties were reported.

In many of the machine cities the legal impediments to party activity were minimal: Connecticut, for example, was the last State to adopt direct primaries. (Significantly, non-partisan local election systems were generally less common in industrial cities.) On the other hand, non-machine cities quite often had non-partisan institutions.

There have been some rural or small-town machines, but their resources have been much more limited. One setting that has traditionally been virtually free of machine-dispensed material inducements to individuals is the American suburb. Suburbanites usually have relatively high socio-economic status, and are keen to preserve their respectability – so the petty resources offered by the machines had little or no appeal for them. Suburban bosses (or party leaders, as they were more commonly referred to) had to be especially subtle; the standard techniques for manipulating voters have not been countenanced. Consequently they focused on making sure their suburbs as a whole received the largest possible share of benefits and appointments, on maintaining contact with the party's State organization, and on broader policy issues.

Recent developments

In the 1960s, machines continued to decline. It has been claimed that at that time they no longer tipped the scales in elections. An analysis prepared by the Republican National Committee showed that in the principal cities, where the party's organization was weaker than that of the Democratic Party, the Republican's share of the vote did not fall off more than it did in suburban areas (where the Republicans had an organizational advantage over the Democrats). Furthermore, Democratic support in presidential elections was not appreciably greater in those cities in which the party was more highly organized (Rourke, 1970).

Nevertheless, a few highly disciplined and effective organizations continued to survive and maintain their power. One such machine was that of Mayor Daley in Chicago. Often referred to as the last of the great bosses in American politics, Mayor Daley could still deliver Chicago's (and, to a large extent, Illinois's) votes to Democratic candidates for governor and president. Indeed, presidential candidates could not hope to gain Illinois's electoral votes without his support.

Daley's ability to deliver the votes stemmed from his double position as Mayor of Chicago and chairman of the Democratic Committee of Cook County – which made him boss of the Democratic machine (or 'the organization', as he called it). The city employed masses of municipal workers who were expected to vote for the party on election day. Businessmen who supported the party financially received preferential treatment from municipal authorities; supporters of the Republican Party were flatly discriminated against. The machine penetrated into all neighbourhoods by means of the traditional machine methods, and delivered large numbers of votes to Daley and his chosen candidates.

Although Daley was accused of wide-scale corruption, it was also admitted that he was a very effective mayor. During his unprecedented twenty-two years in office, Chicago developed and fared better than did many other large cities in the United States. Daley's machine proved its effectiveness in 1960, when it was a crucial factor in the close presidential contest. Daley made sure that the Democrats carried the State by 8,000 votes, thanks largely to the overwhelming majority his machine mobilized in Chicago. Illinois's electoral votes, in turn, were crucial for John Kennedy's election; it was reported that Kennedy had to wait for the results in Illinois before being assured of victory (Fredman, 1968, ch. 5).

Political machines remained a vital force in several other urban centers as well, and lavish election-day expenditures closely approximated bribery; election workers were still expected to 'vote right' and to induce their relatives and friends to do the same. But the extent of this practice differed from place to place (Key, 1964, chs 12 and 18). In Arkansas, for example, it was alleged that many votes were bought in state hospitals and similar institutions during the 1964 election campaign (Epstein, 1967, ch. 5).

Campaign ethics became a live issue in America in 1967 when attempts were made to unseat Congressman Adam Clayton Powell. It was thought that the large costs and hidden financing of campaigns opened the door to bribery of voters. Although there are legal limits on campaign expenditures by candidates and national committees, there is no control over private committees that pick up the bills without the candidate's 'knowledge'. Furthermore, most primary elections (which are often the decisive elections) are unaffected by these laws (Fredman, 1968, ch. 5).

Therefore, legislative measures seem to have had little to do with the further decline of political machines in the late 1960s. At that time even the power of Daley's machine began to wane, partly because of the mayor's deteriorating relations with the black community in Chicago. In 1968, when riots broke out on the west side of the city, the mayor ordered the police to shoot to kill looters – virtually all of whom were black. In 1969 several Black Panthers were killed in a raid on their home by police from the State's attorney's office which was controlled by Daley. Thereafter a considerable proportion of the blacks (who had long been a decisive element in Chicago's voting population) deserted the mayor, thus detracting substantially from his strength.

Despite the deterioration of political machines, the practice of exchanging benefits (to individuals) for votes was not yet defunct at the beginning of the 1970s. Describing the elections to city councils, Schlesinger (1975) reports that the candidates still had to pay off their supporters. Everyone who had voted for a candidate who won by a narrow margin, seemed to think that he was one of the marginal voters who had brought victory; hence, all of the supporters felt that they had valid and substantial claims on the winners. Winning by a narrow margin, 'rather than reducing the number of payoffs which the office holder had to make, actually appeared to heighten the expectations of payoffs' (p. 842). And in the 1976 presidential election campaign, money was still being passed to voters, even though machines evidently continued to decline.

Mayor Daley attached his prestige and that of his organization to the Carter bandwagon because he believed that a strong national Democratic ticket would help him regain control of the State government – which for eight years had been in hostile hands.[4] But, despite his machine's exertions, he could not deliver Illinois's electoral votes to Carter. Ford carried the State, and Republicans beat the mayor's candidates for governor, attorney-general and State's attorney of Cook County (*Economist*, 6 November 1976).

Daley could still turn out the vote: of Chicago's 1.6 million registered voters, 79 per cent went to the polls – only 5 points below the average since 1960. But because of the city's loss of residents to its solidly Republican suburbs, the Daley organization could no longer guarantee Democratic victories in either the county or the State. In 1976, Chicago contributed only 25.7 per cent of the statewide vote – down from 35 per cent in 1960, when Daley's Cook County machine had provided enough votes for Kennedy to win the state and the presidency (*Time*, 22 November 1976).

Other Democratic machines still retained a limited amount of power. Carter received narrow majorities in States and districts that returned Democratic senators and congressmen by generous margins; these narrow victories were due mainly to the last-minute efforts of local machines. If they had begun earlier, they might have brought better results (*Economist*, 6 November 1976).

In Baltimore, too, an old-style machine survived until the 1976 election campaign. According to the *Economist* (30 October 1976), Maryland has had a reputation for political corruption second almost to none (as illustrated by former governors Spiro Agnew and Marvin Mandel). Machine workers have traditionally turned out the vote with the help of lavish amounts of 'walking-around' money for distribution. But Carter's people, from either prudence or poverty, gave out nothing. This alarmed local Democrats, who warned Carter not to take the State for granted.

On the other hand, it was reported that $5,000 was given out as walking-around money for the use of four black ministers helping Carter in San Francisco during the California primary; these sums had not been properly accounted for, and the suggestion was that the money had gone for the ministers' own personal use. In response, Carter asked for a complete inquiry. He admitted that the episode had damaged him politically – but added that candidates were almost powerless to prevent this sort of thing altogether (*Economist*, 4 August 1976).

Money apparently played a decisive role in the gubernatorial campaign in West Virginia. One candidate in the Democratic primary, Ken Hechler, rejected the traditional buying of votes (for money and whisky) which had been rife for many years. He naively imagined that he could break this pattern by refusing all contributions and doing without a campaign organization. He was defeated for the nomination by John D. Rockefeller IV, who admitted to spending close to $2 million in the primary – as against $33,000 spent by Hechler (*Economist*, 30 October 1976). Rockefeller won the governorship as well. As the *Economist* (6 November 1976) put it: 'A young Democrat winner is Mr John D. Rockefeller IV, who ran for governor four years ago and lost. This time he took no chances. The State was almost paved in Rockefeller money (from his own fortune)'.

In some regions, therefore, machine politics or material inducements from other sources still played a role in the 1976 elections – though not as great as in previous campaigns. With the death of Mayor Daley shortly after these elections, many claim, the era of American bossism and machine politics has come to an end. Whether this is indeed so, and whether material inducements to individuals have generally disappeared from the American electoral scene, will become evident only in the next elections.

Manipulation of material inducements and class interests

Why were material inducements, handed out mainly by political machines, so difficult to eradicate from the American political scene? Can their greater resilience (as compared to Britain for instance) be explained by the fact that they served the economically dominant classes' interests?

In the United States, as in Britain, the political elite has been practically monopolized by the socio-economically advantaged strata. In that country, too, a political career has long been a rather expensive venture; while the private expenditures necessary for political careers have declined in Britain, they are still very substantial in America. This is so because to this day the problem of raising money in support of political campaigning is not entirely one of party finance, but in large measure one of financing individual candidates. In substantial degrees, American politics is atomized and each candidate must in some way or another cover his own campaign expenses. The problem of the individual candidate is most pronounced in campaigns for nomination; there funds must be available not to support the party, but the candidate in particular. The ability of a candidate to finance a primary campaign frequently becomes an absolute requisite for a serious fight for a contested nomination, and thus for the launching of a political career.

This, of course, gives an advantage to well-endowed candidates who can use their own funds in primaries and to supplement party funds in elections proper. Thus, in 1972, with the new reporting requirements of the Federal Election Campaign Act of 1971, a total of 247 candidates for federal and State offices reported that they had contributed to their own campaigns.

Moreover, campaigns for office cost more than candidates – even wealthy candidates – are able or willing to spend. Hence, few candidates can even begin a political career for local, State or federal office without first securing financial support from wealthy patrons; there are few congressmen, representatives, or senators, who do not have wealthy financial sponsors. Evidently, candidates of favoured social background, besides having their own funds to invest in political campaigns, are also more likely than others to be well connected. The well-endowed and well-connected also find it easier to obtain credit whenever needed for their campaigns (Key, 1964, ch. 17; Alexander, 1976).

Thus American political reality continues to favour candidates with ample means who are also integrated into the social networks of the well-to-do strata. It is not surprising then, that, while in Britain the social background of the political elites changed substantially throughout the last hundred years, no parallel change occurred in America. Top governmental position holders, senators and representatives are seldom recruited from the lower classes; only few are sons of wage earners or salaried workers – most have their origin in the well-educated, high-income, prestigiously employed, successful and affluent social circles. The occupational characteristics of governmental position holders and of congressmen themselves also show that they are of higher social standing than their constituents.[5]

In spite of all this, what strikes one in comparing American political leaders to their British counterparts, is that from the beginning the former have been much less than the latter, the representatives of the dominant classes proper (either landowners or capitalists). For most of the nineteenth century, the British political elites were practically monopolized by landowners and at the beginning of the present century almost two-thirds of the membership of the House of Commons was still recruited from the landowing and capitalist classes (see chapter 2). In the United States in contrast, the political elites have been recruited to a much larger extent from the professions. Admittedly political leaders were successful and affluent professionals, but landholders and capitalists as such, accounted for a smaller proportion of the political elite. This can be seen from Tables 3.2 and 3.3.

TABLE 3.2   *United States presidents, vice-presidents and cabinet members' initial occupations (percentages)*

	1789–1824	1825–76	1877–1934
Professionals	77	89	81
Proprietors and managers	13	8	13
Large landowners	8	2	0
Other farmers	2	0	2
Clerical and manual workers	0	1	3
	100	100	99

Source: Putnam (1976), p. 187.

TABLE 3.3   *United States senators' initial occupations (percentages)*

	1820	1860	1900	1940
Law	42	38	42	41
Other professions	5	11	13	17
Business	9	27	34	27
Agriculture (including landowners)	44	24	11	10
Labour	—	—	—	4
Housewife	—	—	—	1
	100	100	100	100

Source: Putnam (1976), p. 187.

A similar situation still prevails: As Dye and Zeigler (1975, ch. 4) note, top leaders in government are still recruited predominantly from the legal profession (56.1 per cent), from government itself (16.7 per cent), and from education (10.6 per cent). The situation is not greatly different with regard to the family background of political leaders. Mills (1959, pp. 400–1) reports that of the top political leaders[6] between 1789 and 1953, 44 per cent were sons of professionals, 25 per cent were sons of businessmen and 27 per cent were sons of farmers (although many of these were prosperous farmers, by no means can all of them be classified as large landlords).

So, although in both countries, the political elites were monopolized by the socio-economically advantaged – they were not equally monopolized by the economically dominant classes – those actually in charge of the means of production. Clearly, in nineteenth-century Britain, the dominant classes had a greater monopoly over political power than was the case in America at the time. From a Marxist (class model) viewpoint, it could have been expected, therefore, that the British dominant classes would have been keener than their American counterparts to preserve every aspect of the system – including the manipulation of electors through material inducements – since they were more clearly advantaged by it and had more to lose by its disintegration. Yet it was in America rather than in Britain that the system was perpetuated.

This was so, of course, because in nineteenth-century Britain most of the cost for such inducements had to be borne by candidates themselves, and came to be a heavy burden on them. In America, candidates had heavy campaign expenses as well, but the resources for material inducements as such came predominantly from the political machines that drew on party funds and public payrolls. The development of these machines thus helps explain the perpetuation of material inducements for a much longer time in the United States as compared to Britain.

Hence it is particularly relevant to note that while American political leaders in general were recruited predominantly from the more advantaged strata, this was not so for political machines whose bosses and personnel were recruited predominantly from the less advantaged. Many machine activists were Irish Catholics and from other non-WASP lower background sub-groups. Indeed Merton (1957a, p. 71) in his succinct analysis suggests that the political machines have been so tenacious despite 'the manifold respects in which [they] in varying degrees, run counter to the mores' because they have furnished an important channel of social mobility for individuals whose ethnic background and low class position blocked their advancement in more 'respectable' channels.

Could it be that although machine politicians were not themselves from wealthy strata they served the interests of corporate wealth? To be sure, there has been a rather evident connection between machines and wealth (corporate or otherwise), but this does not mean that the connection has been shaped primarily according to the interests of the wealthy and has been retained chiefly to bolster up those interests. The machines have evidently served the wealthy in several ways. For while the petty material inducements which the machines had to offer went mainly to the poor and needy, the 'pull' that the machines exercised with the authorities could serve as benefits for the wealthy as well. The machines thus served their capitalist clients by arranging for the adjustment of taxes in their favour, for monopolies of local transport, water and gas supply, or for the awarding of construction or production contracts. They also served their wealthy clients by 'honest graft' that is by making available to them inside information on probable development and construction sites – from which enormous pecuniary advantages were to be gained (see also Chapter 8).

But this was by no means a unilateral transaction for the benefit of the wealthy. Just as members of the capitalist classes benefited from the machines – so did the machines benefit from those members: the favours awarded by the machines were used to extract financial and political support from them, which in turn served to enhance the machines' power. Moreover, the financial contributions which capitalists had to make in order to gain favours from the machines promoted their individual but not their class interests. For while some members of the capitalist classes were advantaged by such favours, other capitalists were (by definition) disadvantaged by them. Therefore it was to the benefit of some capitalists to promote and support political machines – but it was by no means to the collective benefit of the capitalist class as a whole to do so.

On the other hand, the people who ran and manned the machines did not have to make any private contributions and at the same time gained power and pecuniary benefits from them. They thus had little to lose and much to gain by the system and they developed strong vested interests in its persistence. It must be concluded, then, that the political machines manipulated the capitalist (as well as the poor) more than they were manipulated by them; and that they (and the material inducements they disposed of) survived as long as they did not because they served the interests of the capitalist classes, but rather because they managed to manipulate those interests to their own advantage.

Material inducements and the democratic process

This, of course, is not saying much for American democracy. Indeed, many observers feel that throughout a major part of its history, America's democratic process has been rendered highly questionable by precisely this manipulation of pecuniary interests. It is widely agreed that throughout the nineteenth century, the

American electoral system retained little democratic value; many observers hold that from the turn of the century through the 1930s, material inducements could still tip elections and thus invalidate the democratic process in large parts of the United States – especially in urban areas. In the 1940s and 1950s, a perceptible decline in political machines and electoral corruption became evident, and observers felt that political machines were no longer the decisive factor in American politics.

However, this does not mean that machine politics became extinct at that time, or even that they could no longer bias the democratic process to some extent. Machines in Philadelphia and Chicago for example, could still have an overriding impact on elections in their areas, which, in turn, could significantly affect the outcome of nationwide elections (as the returns in Chicago and Illinois influenced the 1960 presidential election).

In the 1960s and early 1970s, political machines and the electoral malpractices they perpetrated declined further. But even in the 1976 elections, old-style machines and pecuniary inducements still played a role, although it is difficult to assess the extent of their influence. While they may not have tipped the scales in the presidential election, they almost certainly did so in at least one State's election for governor.

Since de Tocqueville's days, America has had a reputation of being one of the most truly democratic countries in the world. It pioneered in extending the franchise, it outranked other Western countries in the number of offices filled by election, and it had a fairly regular rotation of parties in office. Yet the substantial black portion of the population – especially in the south – was barred from participating in the democratic process until very recently (see chapter 1). And, throughout a major part of its history, America's democratic process had been riddled by manipulation that has rendered it highly suspect even for the rest of the population. Such manipulation has declined in recent years, but only future election campaigns will reveal whether it has disappeared for all practical purposes.

4 Political manipulation of material inducements in Australia[1]

As in both Britain and the United States, there has been a progressively diminishing use of direct material inducements to individuals in the Australian electoral process. But the extent of this diminution is closer to the British trend than to the American: the employment of such benefits has all but disappeared.

Material inducements to constituencies

Although this analysis is concerned primarily with material inducements on the micro (i.e., individual) level, some mention ought to be made of inducements sought and offered to Australian constituencies. This is so because of the extensive weight they carried in nineteenth-century Australia, and because at times they shaded over into individual inducements.

In the second half of the nineteenth century, according to Quaife (1969), a major factor in Australian politics was the conflict between localities for roads, railways and bridges. Electorates tended to elect candidates who felt obligated to attend to the wants of their districts – and roads, railways and bridges were the most common and the most pressing of these wants.

It has been claimed[2] that there were certain geographic constraints on determining the location of such projects – especially those caused by existing population centres – so that options were not as wide as has usually been thought. The major options, according to this view, centred upon the timing of construction and around improvement of existing facilities, and it was mainly here that political influence could be extended.

More common, however, is the view expressed by Knight (1961), who attested that in New South Wales, for instance, expensive railways, roads and bridges were constructed without regard to any

72

consideration other than satisfying the demands of the parliamentary representatives for their own districts. Consequently, there was hard competition among the parliamentary representatives for as much local expenditure as they could procure for these respective districts.

Morrison (1966) reports that in Queensland, too, members of parliament were often interested only in what they could get for their constituencies. A road or bridge in their own districts seemed to be more important to them than was solving the colony's overall transport problems.

Serle (1971, pp. 31–2) has a similar story to tell about Victoria. He writes that the railway was the great prize in rural politics, and a member of parliament was judged more often by his lobbying powers than by his views. In Tasmania, Clark (1947, ch. 10) reports, Bills for public works were usually presented to parliament backed only by departmental reports and the influence of the local member – a method which was increasingly criticized in parliament on the ground that the information presented was not impartial.

The fact that a politician endeavours to promote the material benefit of the community he represents is by no means unusual. What is noteworthy about nineteenth-century Australia is not the phenomenon as such, but the great weight that – according to most views – political pressure carried in determining the location and timing of public works, and the even greater weight which this issue carried in Australian politics. In fact, state Miller and Jinks (1971, ch. 2), such benefits were often the deciding factor in local politics.

There were several reasons for this. In the first place, there was 'the tyranny of distance' which made an adequate transport system a matter of primary importance. For, as Serle points out, the future of a district depended on its transport system; a good one raised property values and reduced farmers' marketing costs. Since the communications system was still in a rudimentary state in many isolated country electorates, it was felt that a transport system was well worth investing in, in terms of electoral support. Moreover, because of the great distances and the slow methods of communication, it was most unusual for a single great colony-wide issue or set of issues to decide the result of a general election in all of the districts. Consequently, local development projects tended to dominate the campaigns (Hawker, 1971, pp. 20–36).

In this era of 'one settler – one road', the allocation of public works to a certain district not only benefited the community as a whole, but sometimes was of even greater benefit to an individual settler or a group of strategically situated settlers. As Miller and Jinks (1971, p. 33), put it: 'The distribution of these throughout each colony offered plenty of opportunity for horse trading and logrolling.'

Where did the funds for the enormous stretches of roads and railways come from? According to Miller and Jinks (1971, ch. 2), these public works were paid for partly by the sale of public lands, but principally by loans from Britain. Australia got her share of the tremendous outflow of British capital in the second half of the nineteenth century. Since this capital flowed to the colonies through their respective governments, the government candidates – not surprisingly – enjoyed a certain advantage over their opponents (see also Quaife, 1969). Governments at that time were changing rapidly, so these advantages were rather short lived. Even so, it is noteworthy that British and Australian government resources did serve as a means for electoral manipulation, and communities (and even certain individual settlers) took advantage of it.

Eventually, some reforms were introduced. In New South Wales, for instance, the Parliamentary Standing Committee on Public Works was established at the close of the 1880s. Its task was to ensure an independent investigation of the allocation of public works, and to free the government from the political pressures of members of parliament for public works in their constituencies. However, Hawker (ch. 9) demonstrates that the Committee was not the independent, neutral body it was expected to be, since the government held a majority on it. Nevertheless, it was considered to be one step forward in making the allocation of public works a neutral process. At the beginning of the twentieth century, Miller and Jinks (p. 38) report, the operation of such public utilities as railways and water supply was placed in the charge of bodies more capable of resisting political pressures than were ministers – although political considerations were not totally eliminated.

Clark (1947, ch. 10) writes that Tasmania passed the Public Works Committee Act in 1914, providing for a statutory body of five – three from the assembly and two from the council – to investigate and report to parliament upon any major proposed public work. It had the effect of putting parliament in possession of more objective information, thus minimizing the weight of political influence.

Similar reforms were introduced in other States, so that today the situation has undergone a rather substantial change. Nevertheless, it has been pointed out[3] that a party in power may still do something special for certain areas with electoral rather than national considerations in mind; and that representatives frequently exert pressure on other politicians for regional or local benefits. MacKerras (1975, p. 219) notes that localism in elections has not disappeared completely; even today, a candidate may sometimes help his chances of being elected by promising to build a college or some other such benefit for his constituency. However, what is still left of this phenomenon is not beyond what may be found in other democratic systems. Our purpose, however, is to focus on what is peculiar to certain democratic systems as distinct from others; hence we turn to material inducements for electoral support below the community level – mainly on the level of families and individuals.

Material inducements to individuals: a historical perspective

While material inducements to constituencies are not considered to be entirely legitimate, they are still regarded indulgently as part of what one must accept – politics being what it is. Not so for material benefits for smaller social units, especially individuals. These have usually been quite clearly labelled as electoral corruption.

There has never been corruption of this kind in Australia to match the extent of that in eighteenth or nineteenth-century Britain. Neither have there been electoral scandals to compare with those in American history; bossism, machine politics and the spoils system never developed in Australia to the extent that they did in the United States. Yet historical evidence (though incomplete) points to the occurrence of certain malpractices in nineteenth-century Australia that as a rule no longer occur today.

It must be born in mind that the secret ballot was introduced fairly early in Australia; in fact, it originated there, and the terms 'Australian ballot' or 'Victorian ballot' and 'secret ballot' are synonymous. Before the introduction of the secret ballot, electoral malpractices – including bribery and treating – had apparently reached sizeable dimensions. Scott (1920) asserts that the vices of the *viva voce* method flourished in Australia, though not more so than in Britain. On the other hand, there was no lengthy period during which these malpractices could entrench themselves, as the first elections did not occur until the beginning of the 1840s, while the ballot was introduced in most States in the 1850s.[4]

The secret ballot hindered the use of material inducements, and thus may have helped keep the practice from reaching the blatant dimensions of pre-reform Britain. However, it did not eliminate the practice. For one thing, the ballot could be circumvented; in fact, the 'Tasmanian Dodge' (see below) was invented explicitly for this purpose. Also, the use of benefits is based largely on tying beneficiaries to the party by a bond of gratitude (as did the American bosses, for instance). Moreover, the material benefit frequently accrues only if the candidate or party comes to power (or is maintained in power), which makes his or its election a matter of self-interest to the beneficiaries. This 'honour' system of building a bond of obligations, and the even safer system of building a bond of interests, are other reasons why the secret ballot could not eliminate material inducements.

New South Wales

This is illustrated by developments in New South Wales. Loveday and Martin (1966) explain that for more than thirty years after the introduction of responsible government in this State (1856), no political parties emerged in the legislatures; the government functioned through majorities organized around parliamentary factions. These factions lacked the stable structure of modern democratic parties, and had no coherent and distinct bodies of doctrine (although their members did have political opinions); nor, as Nairn (1967) points out, did they present any platforms of practical objectives. The factions were political bodies in which alignments were fluid and governments were maintained in power by shifting combinations of groups. Hence, he adds, men, not measures, were the main basis of politics.

Since there were no firmly demarcated parties, and since the factions rarely comprised a majority in the assembly, each faction leader had to compete not only for the support of new members and independents, but for the others' followers as well, so that they could form and maintain a ministry.

To help faction leaders to elect candidates who were likely to support them in parliament, Loveday (1959) reports, rudimentary political organizations were established in the electorates. These usually consisted of one or more agents in personal contact with the faction leader, a few close political associates of the leader who were willing to take seats if elected, and more or less ephemeral committees composed of local worthies. Through these organizations, the faction leaders employed various kinds of manipulations in elections, and generally did their best to build up local networks of influence. Since they operated chiefly through local people, the organizations often outlasted the election campaigns.

Loveday and Martin (1966) report that the first tentative steps toward electoral manipulation of this kind were made in the 1856 election by the leaders of what became the liberal faction in the first parliament. Within the next ten years, such intervention became an established practice of all faction leaders. Some, such as Parkes, Cowper and Robertson, became extremely skilled in finding candidates likely to follow them in parliament and amassing electoral support for them.

What place did material inducements for individuals hold in these manoeuvers? According to Loveday and Martin, a faction leader could frequently win the support of a candidate or member of parliament by meeting his requests for administrative action in his electorate – often on behalf of interests he personally represented – or by finding posts in the civil service for him or his political friends. Other persons who were helpful to parliamentary leaders in election campaigns (such as local agents) were rewarded in a similar manner (see also Nairn, 1967, esp. pp. 5–6; Martin, 1958; Loveday, 1959). As Bland (1944, p. xi) put it: 'loyalties were measured by the yardstick of personal advantage that accrued to individual members and groups as a condition of their support of particular leaders.'

Occasionally, politicians accused each other of using bribery to gain political support. For instance, Martin (1958) reports that one of Parkes's defeated candidates (Walter H. Cooper) claimed that his followers had been wooed away by bribes of all kinds. At the same time, Parkes's agents themselves wooed everyone who had influence over groups of voters; when money was needed, it came from Parkes's wealthier political associates or from subscription lists. His methods were copied by opposing leaders, which testifies to their effectiveness.

In the same vein, Dickey (1969) presents a collection of letters and his own comments on the situation in New South Wales during the second half of the nineteenth century. According to him, political followers who had local influence wanted their support to bear fruit in the form of a flow of roads, bridges and building jobs which would enhance their own status in their communities. They also considered it justifiable to extort favours from political leaders for themselves and for their friends, and did not hesitate to apply pressure for that purpose.[5]

The letters presented by Dickey also attest to accusations of electoral malpractices:

> I shall at all times look back with feelings of pride to the position I took during the late political struggle and shall at all times attribute the defeat to dishonest, corrupt, malignant, and ignorant practices, the only object being 'Election at any Cost'
> . . . When I calmly reflect upon the influence with which I had to contend, I cannot imagine how we polled so many votes. Bags of flour sent to poor families, men who had not been able to pay rent for weeks past can now pay off the landlord and a little to spare. Is it not discreditable that our Attorney General should obtain his seat by such means, God forbid – that I should ever be a party to such vile practices.
> . . . I do not think . . . under the extraordinary circumstances since come to light, that we would have secured a seat (in the

electorate of the Hume). On Saturday week last, a Mr. Coe and I drove to Mulwalla (8 miles west from Corowa) and on reaching the Post Office hotel at that place, the proprietor – a Mr. Burley, an old Victorian, the licensee, recognised me as an old friend and as he did not know the purpose of my visit, he, in reply to my request anent how he found business in New South Wales, said – 'I am doing pretty well between the Hotel and contracting. I was at Albury yesterday securing a good thing in the form of a payable contract to build an approach to the Yarrawonga and Mulwalla bridge, and Mr. Hayes became my bondsman conditionally that I would work for him and Lyne to get them returned', and as Mr. Burley's hotel is almost opposite the Court House where the polling took place we had an excellent opportunity of seeing how faithfully he, Burley, and many other hirelings acted during the day in fulfilment of the bribery arrangement. From 8 to 4 there was one incessant stream of half-muddled creatures led like sheep to the slaughter between two or more agents over to the booth, and on entering which, a printed paper (copy annexed) was placed in their hand until I captured one about 3 p.m. when they ceased to issue them . . .

Burley's hotel was placarded off as Lyne and Hayes' committee rooms and drink was freely administered minus payment by the drinkers. Cabs were also flying about having 'Vote for Lyne and Hayes' placards affixed on the sides, and as they arrived agents jostled them through the hotel to get primed with drink and then led over to the booth. The document signed by Hayes on behalf of 'Burley' for the corrupt work is with the land of revenue officer at Albury. Mr. Coe and another will verify the above statement. I am of the opinion that equally desperate means were adopted all over the electorate . . .[6]

We shall have a great contest in East Maitland. Money and the damd grog his already at work but I shall beat Dodds.[7]

Not surprisingly, the critics of the day felt that the system involved a dubious bidding for votes, and that corruption, nepotism and electoral malpractices were common (Hawker, 1971, p. 21). However, the question is: how widespread were such practices in fact? Hawker (ch. 2) claims that although the electoral system in New South Wales was slow in working, and although some of the reforms made in other Australian colonies were adopted in New South Wales only reluctantly, there was little to show that the State was beset by large-scale corruption. He finds evidence for this in the works of the Parliamentary Elections and Qualifications Committee. This Committee, according to Hawker (p. 58),

investigated some seventy petitions between 1858–1900, most of
which came from candidates who claimed that they had been
defeated by foul means. The committee sustained less than a
third of the objections. Its reports exposed some careless
returning officers and proved or suggested the existence of some
cases of personation and bribery, but that was all. The
committee, perhaps, was not the very best judge, for its members
were members of Parliament who might have an interest in the
result in a particular constituency. But even if electoral
corruption was widespread and well hidden, it seems not to have
worked to the systematic political benefit of anyone.

From 1887 onwards, Loveday and Martin (1966) report, the
patterns of the previous thirty years were gradually replaced by a
new order of party organization and discipline. By 1887 there were
two political groups, the Freetrade Group and the Protectionist
Group, which in effect were parties. By 1899, a basic change had
taken place: although overtones of the old factional system survived, it was no longer the mainspring of the colony's political
institutions. In 1891, the Labor Party was established; it developed
a total program and far greater internal discipline than had previous
political groups. The Labor Party also helped introduce major
changes in the parliamentary system, since its economic interests
coincided with general demands for reform (Nairn, 1967).

One of the reforms pertained directly to electoral inducements:
since 1890, the electoral law has forbidden treating and other forms
of undue influence on electors. But, as Parker (1960, p. 69) reports,
'The final blow at the good old Eatanswill type of election was the
Liquor Amendment Act of 1905, which requires public houses to be
closed during the hours of polling.'[8]

Queensland

In Queensland as in New South Wales during the second half of the
nineteenth century, no formal parties had yet been established,
although there were some informal organizations. This made it
harder for political leaders to win and hold the support of a majority
in the house (Morrison, 1953 and 1960–1). Apparently, the effect of
this situation on electoral manipulation was similar to that in New
South Wales.

Consequently, material inducements were at least as widespread
in Queensland as in New South Wales, and perhaps even more
prevalent than in other States. Morrison (1950) reports that after
Queensland's first election in 1860,[9] both losers and winners
published advertisements in which they claimed that various

malpractices had been employed successfully or unsuccessfully to keep them out of office. It was even claimed that treating had decided the election in one constituency. By 1863, Morrison notes, treating was even more widespread. In the 1870s, Morrison (1951) further notes, claims were made in the town of Ipswich that workers in industry were hired and fired according to the criterion of political support, and that the workshops were packed for political purposes.

A similar picture emerges from Bernays's (n.d., p. 48) analysis. Bernays writes about George Thorn, who made his debut in parliament in 1867 and later became premier: 'He was adept at electioneering and in days when the laws were less severe than they are now, he perpetrated . . . many a smart trick which would unseat a man in 1919'. Of Patrick Perkins, Bernays tells (p.83) that he secured a seat in the lower house in 1874 as a result of his electioneering capabilities. One railway contractor, an intimate associate of Perkins, loaded half a dozen trucks with Perkins' Ale and a vast number of labourers – and toured the electorate,

> recording an uncountable number of votes at each little polling booth for the owner of the beer . . . In the opinion of the navvies it was good beer and the owner worthy of an unlimited number of votes. Perkins won the election hands down . . .

Later, however, Perkins was charged with bribery and corruption, and the election was voided.

According to Bernays, the electoral system – especially the 'voters' rights'[10] prevalent before 1874 – was thought to be a direct incentive for bribery. He notes that although the voters' rights were abolished by the Election Act of 1874, this act did not succeed in eliminating corrupt practices. In 1885, for example, twenty Mackay planters sent a letter to the governor protesting the 'political immorality' in Queensland; it referred to fraud, and to the judgeship and other high offices given as rewards for political services to disreputable persons whose characters would not bear scrutiny (Bernays, n.d., p. 514).

The Election Act of 1885 had special provisions for preventing corrupt election practices. These provisions were based on the British law of 1883; the offences covered were 'treating', 'undue influence', 'bribery' and 'personation'. Persons guilty of such corrupt practices were prohibited from voting (Bernays, pp. 292–3).

A further improvement was the Election Tribunals Act of 1886, which introduced a new method for trying election petitions. Previously, these had been handled by a Parliamentary Elections and Qualifications Committee. However, since the party in power held a majority on the Committee, there was more than a little suspicion that unconscious bias had governed many of its decisions. The new law provided for the trial of election petitions by a Supreme Court judge, with six assessors chosen from a panel nominated each year by the speaker. Even here there was some room for bias, since the ruling party invariably had more assessors than did the opposition. But the bias was much smaller, and the moral effect of having the sessions presided over by a Supreme Court judge made the public regard the decision as substantially just (Bernays, p. 284).

In this manner, successive legislation gradually put increasingly stringent controls on electoral corruption. Also towards the end of the nineteenth century, the Liberal Party and other party organizations began to take shape (Morrison, 1953). This development, too, may have contributed to the eventual decline in electoral corruption in Queensland.

Victoria

While some observers claim that nineteenth-century Queensland had more than its share of electoral corruption, others demonstrate that Victoria did not fall short on this count, either. Victoria also lacked firm party organizations (Mills, 1942), and thus faced the same problems in forming and keeping a parliamentary majority. Hence, writes Serle (1971, p. 2),

> The notion prevailed of Parliament as a collection of individuals, whose prime duty was to act as agents for local constituents.
> Governments almost always had to purchase the support of some 'independent' members and give favoured treatment to nominal supporters as well as staunch adherents.

Similarly, leading politicians trying to create a faction around themselves would promise future bounty to would-be supporters.

Not surprisingly, similar practices prevailed at elections. By 1851 (before the introduction of the secret ballot), bribery and treating at elections had apparently become a well-established custom (Jenks, 1891, p. 162). Some Victorian politicians of the time alleged that such malpractices were rife, others belittled the phenomenon, although they did not deny it (Fredman, 1968, ch. 1). A contemporary newspaper claimed that politicians who opposed the ballot did so in order to preserve the system of bribery, favours, and coercion from which they benefited.[11]

The secret 'Victorian ballot' pioneered in Victoria, was used at the first election (1856) after the advent of responsible government. There is little doubt, writes Fredman, that the new system put at

least a temporary halt to bribery, lavish treating and various disorders at elections. Other observers, however, express different
views. Mills (1942) writes that bribery and treating did not disappear at once with the introduction of the ballot, although the
ballot did modify the electoral proceedings. Scott (1920) states that
the new system worked perfectly and produced the expected
results, but was particularly effective in reducing threats and
violence.

Quaife (1967) supplements this by saying that more subtle forms
of malpractices could still be found in the 1856 election. Agents
canvassed the electors and solicited pledges to vote for their candidates. Many of these agents were willing to use any means to obtain
such pledges, and came close to breaking regulations designed to
prevent treating and bribery. One candidate, Robert Bennet, paid
agents to get people to the polls, and lavished upon them a surfeit of
ham and wine; as a result, his election was declared void. However,
this was an exception. On the whole, says Quaife, there was little
evidence of outright bribery, although treating was more widely
practised. In one case, voters pledged to one candidate were treated
by another – who subsequently won the election.

Serle (1963, ch. 9) reports that in the 1859 elections in some
constituencies (such as in Kilmore), the principles of the secret
ballot were largely forgotten. Around 1870, some of the former
disorders had evidently recurred, especially after the invention of
the Tasmanian Dodge (see below). Thereafter, methods had to be
devised to ensure that the ballot a voter deposited was in fact the
ballot he had received; for example, numbers were put on the
ballots and on perforated counterfoils (Fredman, 1968, ch. 1).

Tasmania

In Tasmania, according to Clark (1947, ch. 3), the first exercise of
the franchise in 1851 involved actions which no longer characterize
Australian elections. The newspapers published advertisements by
the committees of the various candidates, naming the public houses
at which they would meet – a practice which opened the door wide
to 'unblushing bribery, which was by no means uncommon' (p. 19).

In 1958, a year after its introduction in New South Wales, the
secret ballot was adopted in Tasmania. Thereafter, contested
returns and charges of corruption diminished but did not disappear.
One of these occurred in 1880, reports Clark (ch. 8), when the
Elections and Qualifications Committee voided the election of a
candidate because of extensive bribery by his agents. The Committee further decided that the district should be disfranchised for a
time because of corrupt practices during this and previous elections.

Other election contests after the introduction of the secret ballot were not free from large expenditures of money 'in ways which have long disappeared' (Clark, p. 45). One of these ways, which achieved world-wide notoriety, was the Tasmanian Dodge – also called the Simpson system, after its originator.

The idea of the Tasmanian Dodge was rather ingenious. The party agent lined up his followers, and sent the first one in to vote a blank and bring out an unmarked ballot – for which the voter was then paid an agreed sum. The agent filled in the ballot himself and gave it to his second voter, who deposited it in the ballot-box and brought out another ballot – in return for a similar remuneration. In this manner, the agent rewarded any voter who would deposit a ballot marked by the agent and return to him an unmarked one. This system made it possible to bribe the voters despite the secret ballot, and the party agents could ensure that they were obtaining a full return for their money.

How widespread in Tasmania were such malpractices based on material inducements? Something on this may be learned from the election petitions analysed by Townsley (n.d.). Under a statute passed in 1858, bribery, treating and other forms of corruption were declared illegal and punishable by a large fine. The electoral law provided for appeals to the Supreme Court for any malpractice (in earlier days, petitions were received by the house). According to Townsley, such petitions were by no means rare in the second half of the century, but only a few were upheld.[12]

Material inducements to individuals: recent developments

From 1890 onward electoral malpractices gradually diminished and in the twentieth century they practically disappeared. During the depression in 1931 there were allegations that the Labor treasurer had distributed relief work among the unemployed in his own electorate on the basis of political allegiance.[13] Although these allegations were not proved conclusively, they were sufficient to defeat the government.[14] But this was the last time a government was defeated on such grounds.

Nowadays, observers generally agree, electoral malpractices based on material inducements to individuals have been largely abandoned. In New South Wales, for instance, Parker (1960, p. 61) states, the strategic balance between contending parties and interests probably accounts for the general fairness of the State electoral system.

Where there are high stakes in the manipulation of State power or the use of public money, there have naturally been intrigue

and attempts at corruption, but with few exceptions since the
turn of the century . . . these have had more success in the
internal affairs of political parties and the administration of
urban local authorities than in State government itself . . . with
political forces so diverse and so evenly matched, the party
struggle is keenly and on the whole cleanly contested.

As for Queensland, we have Bernays's (n.d., p. 55), statement
that the 'free and easy methods of the past are happily no longer
possible in the twentieth century'. In Victoria, electoral corruption
faded in the early twentieth century as anti-corruption Acts (passed
in the nineteenth century) came to be rigorously enforced.[15] In
Tasmania, Townsley (1960) asserts, politics is played somewhat
roughly, but not without respect for acepted rules of conduct. Reid
(1960) writes that apart from the distribution of assembly districts,
the South Australian electoral system is unexceptionable. There is
no reason to suppose that the elimination of corrupt practices has
been any less in the remaining States.

According to Davis (1960, p. 586), there is an occasional tendency to stretch the rules a bit:

But on the whole there is in all States a predominant desire for
legitimacy, and on the whole it is – for all the occasional suspicion
or proof of venality – exceptional for the constitution of any party
in any State to be so corrupted that it gives a distorted reflection
of the life within it.

National elections were introduced in Australia at the beginning
of the twentieth century, when reforms in the States' electoral
system were well under way. They have never been subject to the
malpractices of material inducements on the subcommunal level to
any sizeable extent. As Crisp (1965, p. 14) put it: 'Australian
national elections, which have from the beginning been conducted
by secret ballot supervised by career public servants, have usually
been entirely free even of serious suggestions of such malpractices.'[16]

Observers occasionally refer to the 'political machines' of the
parties (especially the Labor Party). However, this term covers a
variety of meanings that unfortunately are not always clearly
specified. The impression one gains is that the term 'machine' is
associated by these observers with internal party control, rather
than with the handing out of material benefits to the public. In any
event, it is usually agreed that such machines are fading away – if
they have not already done so.

For instance, Jupp (1964, ch. 9) reports that a number of
Australian empires have been run in a pale imitation of the city

machines in the United States. They controlled municipal and even parliamentary positions for many years – such as the Labor Party's control of the Sydney City Council and the Richmond and Carlton Councils in Melbourne. However, Jupp does not claim that these machines handed out material benefits to members of the public. Furthermore, both the Melbourne and Sydney mayoral nominations were eventually brought under State executive power. A similar analysis is presented by Parker (1960) concerning the Labor Party of New South Wales. He, too, shows that erstwhile corrupt practices were concerned with internal (especially pre-selection) procedures, and that lately a variety of safeguards have diminished or eliminated these practices.

Today, no instances of electoral corruption involving material inducements to individuals are known, and it is reasonable to assume that if such practices did occur in significant dimensions, they would have become known and would have been reported by the media (which make it their business to find out things of this nature). Nowadays there are few electoral disputes; and if it does happen that an occasional member of parliament is unseated, it is usually because of an infraction of rules other than the ones concerned with material inducements.[17]

It has also been pointed out[18] that while members of parliament occasionally build up their personal following by looking after the needs of their constituents (and this may occasionally include material benefits to individual families) this does not take the form of bribery before elections or 'machine politics' based on payment for political support. The assistance (when it occurs) is more in the nature of representing the interests of constituents before the authorities; mainly expediting procedures that would have occurred (albeit more slowly) in any event. For the most part, members of parliament who choose this path fulfil the function of an ombudsman, obtaining for their constituents what they are entitled to, to begin with. Only in a minority of cases (as far as this can be ascertained) do MPs obtain for their supporters illegal favours or favours which are on the borderline of legality. In any case, such favours – whether lawful or not – are usually trifling. So this practice never even remotely approaches the American dimensions.[19]

Even if politicians wanted to hand out material benefits on a large scale, they would be unable to do so – since they usually do not have the necessary private means, and their parties do not have sufficient funds either. Election expenses are relatively low in Australia;[20] and they scarcely cover the cost of advertising – to say nothing of material benefits to individual voters. It is thus generally agreed that, out of conviction or out of necessity, Australian politicians do not resort to material inducements in any significant dimensions –

and that there is no longer substantial bribery, treating or anything of that nature in the Australian electoral process.

Manipulation of material inducements and class interests

Can this pattern of material inducements and their decline be explained by the Australian dominant classes' political and economic interests? As in Britain and the United States, there was a rather clear relationship in Australia between the political system and the class structure: the economically advantaged classes had a near-monopoly over Australian politics, a situation that was maintained almost to the end of the nineteenth century. This near-monopoly resulted from the way in which the political process was conducted.

As Loveday, Martin and Parker (1977, ch. 1) point out, property qualifications for members of lower houses were abolished by 1859 in all colonies except Tasmania, but payment of members was not introduced until the 1870s in Victoria, and in the late 1880s in most of the other States. The frequency of elections and the cost of going into parliament meant that many members spent only short terms there. Even so, this situation, as well as inequalities in the electoral system which remained up to and beyond 1890 (see chapter 1), all no doubt contributed to the failure of lower-class social groups and interests to win representation in parliament.

Until payment of members was introduced, men had to be able to afford to go into parliament and that meant having independent means, or being at least moderately well-to-do by colonial standards. Since few members were full-time politicians and given that legislatures normally sat in the evenings, it was possible to combine some city callings, particularly in the professions, trade and commerce, with a parliamentary career. However, countrymen with modest means were at a disadvantage, and even wealthy squatters, landowners, farmers and businessmen found parliamentary life difficult because of the regular attention demanded by their distant enterprises.

A few men from the working classes reached the parliaments but before 1890 their numbers were negligible. Generally speaking members were drawn from three broad groups in society: the pastoral and landholding section, the professions and commerce. None of these three groups was homogeneous, each spanning a wide range of social positions and economic interests; nevertheless the membership of the lower houses could be described – in the most general sense – as middle-class and above.

It must be taken into account that the middle class in Australia at this time was particularly new, open, and not yet clearly set in its attitudes and life style. Many persons had rapidly attained their positions without gaining many of the attitudes that might be regarded as the marks of a middle class in a more settled society. By their own personal experience and the immediacy of their contacts with the electorates, the members of parliament thus provided a broader representation than might appear when members' occupational and economic positions alone are taken into account. It remains a fact, however, that the lower-class sections of the community had no independent avenues to political representation.

Also, organizations of economic interests which took part in politics before 1890 were representative of the better-off sections of the community: such organizations included for instance chambers of commerce, chambers of manufacturers, free selectors' and farmers' associations. The main political work of the first two types of organizations was to express their views on current legislation and administration directly to government and to members of parliament, many of whom were merchants and manufacturers and sympathetic to, or indeed members of, the chambers. Farmers' and selectors' organizations were different: they were organized for electoral work intended to return members to parliament. Their main purpose was to promote combined action on their behalf by their representatives in parliament; they were often attacked for pushing sectional demands in parliament and for turning members into delegates. Despite these differences the various organizations had this in common: they all worked for the promotion of their own economic interests.

Working-class people, on the other hand, did not have political organizations to match and confront those of other sections of the community and it was not until late in the century that the working-class organizations undertook sustained political action. The trade unions of this period were avowedly non-political; their members were not connected with any one party or political organization. It was realized that there were many social and political reforms for which working-class organizations could agitate; this led to the formation of workingmen's political associations in several of the States. But these political organizations had no continuous existence and rapidly fizzled out.

It was easy enough for such organizations to draw up programs but it was another matter to get the candidates and the votes, or to secure the backing of unions and Labor councils. These were frequently afraid that workers would alienate sympathetic governments and friendly members of parliament if they took independent electoral action. So in Victoria, for instance, as late as 1885 and again in 1889, the Trades Hall Council decided not to back working-class candidates even though a handful stood and sought its support.

In Sydney, the Trades and Labor Council tried to win Labor representation in parliament, but the experiment, which did result in the election of one member, was not a success from their viewpoint and was not repeated before 1890. In Brisbane the Trades and Labor Council nominated four Labor candidates in the elections of 1888 but all were defeated, chiefly because of apathy among Brisbane workers, and three of them were then victimized by their employers for standing.

Given the hold which the better-off sections of the community had over the political system, the employment of material inducements (which only the wealthy could afford) as political manipulation might have been used to the advantage of these groups, to solidify that hold and to keep Labor out. In nineteenth-century Australia, the political authorities were clearly in charge of allocating some vital economic resources – such as transport systems that could greatly enhance property values and the like. Australia's advantaged strata could not but have been aware of the economic leverage to be gained from continued control of the political process. Yet material inducements which could have fortified that control were eliminated, thus helping to pave the way for working-class participation in political power.

And, in fact, the period in which manipulation of material inducements to individuals declined was also the time at which working-class organizations began to take an active part in politics, at which Labor parties were established and at which a clear alignment of Labor against non-Labor emerged. At the turn of the century, in little more than two decades, Labor and Liberal parties had been formed in all States and clearly stood in opposition to each other (Loveday, Martin and Parker, 1977, ch. 9).

It is true that the advent of the Labor Party did not revolutionize the actual representation of working-class people in politics. The Party first contested an election in 1891 in New South Wales, and, as a result, 13 per cent of New South Wales's parliamentarians throughout the years 1891–8 were manual workers. While this looks like a promising start, workers' representation in parliament was not significantly augmented later on: in the 1958–61 federal parliament for instance, there were only nine manual workers. Almost the same holds for State and Commonwealth cabinet ministers. Of the 147 individuals who had held ministerial posts betwen 1945 and 1958 and on whom information was available, only 18 had been manual workers, and only 20 were sons of manual workers.

This may be attributd to the fact that, even in the Australian Labor Party itself, worker representation was not as great as could have been expected, and even declined as time went on. However, a large proportion of Labor Party representatives were union officials, either salaried or honorary: in the whole period since federation union representation has rarely fallen below half of the parliamentary party (Encel, 1970, ch. 12). The advent of the Australian Labor Party thus obviously resulted in a better representation of working-class interests than would have been the case had no Labor Parties gained political representation, and the political near-monopoly which the advantaged enjoyed in the nineteenth century was consequently – if not abolished – at least substantially modified.

Looking at internal developments as such, one therefore wonders why the economically advantaged were quick to give up material inducements which could have stablized their power monopoly. Looking at the problem from a comparative perspective, however, one notes that although political power in nineteenth-century Australia was monopolized by the socio-economically advantaged, it was not monopolized by the landowing and capitalist classes proper to the same extent as was the case in Britain. Given the relative openness of the class system, and the lack of long-term crystallization of classes, the Australian pattern of class representation in politics resembled the American more than the British one. Yet Australia followed Britain rather than America on the path of relatively early elimination of electoral corruption.

Apparently, this is so because in Australia, as in Britain, a substantial part of such corruption was financed by private resources of wealthy politicians, and the practice might have become too expensive to make its continued employment economically profitable or even feasible. Since no American-style party machines developed, public resources were not increasingly mobilized to substitute or supplement private ones for the purpose of electoral manipulation. It is this omission, then, rather than dominant class interests which explains the decline of electoral corruption in Australia.

Material inducements and the democratic process

However the decline of material inducements may be explained, it is clear that even in the heyday the dimensions of such inducements were rather modest in Australia in comparison to what was taking place at that time in Britain and the United States. Inducements to constituencies (in the form of roads, rails and bridges) may have heavily influenced the outcome of elections, but this was far less true of benefits given directly to individuals. Benefits for individuals probably affected some elections in some constituencies, but it seems most unlikely that they biased a majority of the elections in a majority of the constituencies, and hence that they offset the democratic process to a considerable extent.

The States' parliaments (it has been claimed) were on the whole rather ineffective at the time; although social problems existed, parliaments were frequently unable to grapple with them. Hence, it might be argued that it was of little importance who was elected and by what methods. Yet – as we saw – political authorities were in charge of substantial material resources. Thus it did make a great deal of difference whether or not the voters had a genuine impact on the (political) allocation process.

Consequently, the gradual extention of the franchise, the development of political parties (which, according to some theorists enhanced the influence of increasingly wider social groups on the political process) and the virtual elimination of material inducements were not without significance in Australia. Moreover, parliaments gained in importance and passed more significant legislation towards the end of the nineteenth century – just as the elimination of material inducements was taking place. Thus, as the participation of the public in the political process grew, it also became increasingly meaningful. Today, certainly, the electoral process is not distorted by material inducements to any appreciable degree. In this, the Australian system differs considerably from that of Israel, to be dealt with in the following chapter.

5 Political manipulation of material inducements in Israel

Of the four countries analysed, Israel seems to be the one in which the giving of material inducements in return for electoral support is still the most firmly entrenched. Israel does not surpass the activities in nineteenth-century Britain or those in the heyday of the party machine in the United States, but, with the aid of its own party machines, it seems to have maintained this practice to the greatest extent – more so, even, than the United States. While there may have been a recent decline in its prevalence, clearly the practice has not been eliminated.

The pre-state (Yishuv)[1] era: the flourishing of material inducements

The practice had its beginning with the beginning of modern Jewish colonization of Palestine at the turn of the century, and it evolved with the evolvement of the political system itself. The budding Jewish community (or the Yishuv, as it is commonly referred to) had not yet attained statehood; the country was under Turkish (Ottoman) rule – and then, after 1918, under British Mandatory rule. This did not prevent the Jewish settlers from setting up their own voluntary organizations. These included a variety of political movements and parties, among which the labour movement and its parties were the most prominent, the Histadrut (the federation of Labour unions) and a Jewish authority for self-government[2] which was eventually recognized as such by the British Mandatory Government.

Each political movement had its own ideology to which its faithful were intensely committed, and which it attempted to propagate among the community at large. Ideological commitment was especially intense in the dominant labour movement and its major party, Ahdut Ha-Avoda;[3] but it was also intense in the community at large (see Chapter 6).

91

Nevertheless, the political movements and parties (Ahdut Ha-Avoda included) did not rely on ideological persuasion alone to acquire and retain political support. They deemed it necessary to bolster ideological propaganda with a wide array of tangible inducements.

Even though the elections to the Yishuv's national institutions were by secret ballot from the beginning, this did not prevent activists from employing such inducements, as they sought to bind citizens firmly to their parties by a paternalistic system calling forth gratitude and self-interest. They tried to reach potential followers while still abroad or immediately upon arrival. They frequently sponsored their immigration, and supplied them with essential services without which life in the under-developed country would have been even less bearable. In return, they pressured the immigrants to join their parties – expecting electoral support to ensue as a matter of course.

Most political groups established impressive networks of banks, housing construction companies, loan societies, economic concerns, labour exchanges, health services, homes for the aged and other social, educational and cultural services for both new and veteran settlers. Also, land was allocated to new immigrants through political organizations – so that land settlement served as another device for mobilizing support (Eisenstadt, 1967, ch. 9).

While all of the major parties employed these devices, the Histadrut and Ahdut Ha-Avoda were most prominent in turning them into a fine art. Although the Histadrut was set up in 1920 as a federation of Labour unions, it did not (and never intended to) confine itself to traditional union activities. One of its chief functions was to provide employment for workers by pressuring the weak private sector into hiring Jewish labour (rather than cheaper Arab labour) and by establishing its own numerous and increasingly powerful economic concerns. It also set itself up as a political organization in which the workers' parties were represented according to their strength in internal Histadrut elections.

The strongest and most energetic among these parties was Ahdut Ha-Avoda, whose aim was to gain hegemony in the Histadrut. Shapiro (1977, ch. 5) reports that it did so not only by ideological campaigns but also by developing a full-scale political machine focused on material inducements as the basis of its success. This machine was of central importance for the entire political system: it set the patterns for all subsequent political interaction; it also served as a blueprint on which the other political parties modeled their own machines, even though they could never hope to equal its efficacy.

Ahdut Ha-Avoda's political machine was manned by a highly loyal, closely knit and well co-ordinated group of people. This group was also in co-ordination with the party's central leadership, whereby a division of labour took place between the two groups: the central leadership shaped the party's policies and manned its foremost positions; it was thus constantly in the public limelight. The group of machine functionaries, on the other hand, was content to wield power behind the scenes and to utilize that power to mobilize support for the party's leadership, without the public ever being fully aware of its existence.

Ahdut Ha-Avoda's machine functionaries in the Histadrut were rewarded for their loyalty to the party not only by power as such but also by a variety of material benefits for themselves. Their major activity however, concerned the handing out of such benefits as political inducements to rank-and-file members of the Histadrut. These benefits included posts in the Histadrut hierarchy itself, in its numerous concerns, or in related institutions, and grants or loans on easy terms from the Histadrut's financial or welfare institutions or from any other institution where the party had made inroads.

The party-machine activists tried to form personal relationships with Histadrut members so that these members would turn to them in time of need. Hence, members would frequently approach those activists for help in solving their employment or housing problems. The machine functionaries would then activate their connections in the Histadrut, the party and the municipality until a suitable position was located or financial aid for the purchase of an apartment was forthcoming. In return, these members were expected to support the party and be active on its behalf at elections.

People who were helped by the party machine were not free to change their allegiance at will. It has even been claimed that those rebels who tried to do so (and they were not too numerous) were dismissed from their jobs or even evicted from their apartments.[4] Although the practice contradicted the Histadrut's regulations, this fact did not seriously hamper its development or reduce its efficacy – as was proved by the Histadrut elections, in which Ahdut Ha-Avoda first gained a plurality and then an absolute majority. With the aid of its political machine Ahdut Ha-Avoda thus succeeded in setting itself up as the dominant party in the Histadrut and through it in the Labour Movement.

In 1930, Ahdut Ha-Avoda united with another Labour Party to form Mapai,[5] which gained hegemony not only in the Histadrut but in the Yishuv's national institutions as well, and hence in the Yishuv as a whole. Thereafter, Shapiro (1977, ch. 5) reports, the same practice which had proved to be so effective in the Histadrut was stepped up in the national institutions as well.

Medding (1972, ch. 8) describes the Mapai party machine in the 1940s. Its dominant group, known as the 'Gush',[6] was located in

Tel-Aviv. Its functionaries continued to generate support by helping people to solve their financial problems. A functionary would accrue political debts from top leaders and develop widespread institutional connections throughout the party and the Histadrut. He would call in these political debts on behalf of rank-and-file members, to aid local sub-leaders who required some favours for their supporters, or to reward the sub-leaders themselves for their party service. In this manner, he would build up his power base over the years – and use it to the party's advantage at election time.

After independence: the persistence of material inducements

The attainment of statehood did not basically alter the party composition of the Jewish community: Mapai remained the dominant party until 1968, when it merged with two other Labour Parties to form the Israel Labour Party (ILP). In 1969 it joined forces with yet another Labour Party to form the Alignment. In this format it retained its dominant position as the key partner in all government coalitions and the major force in the Histadrut and in the Jewish Agency until 1977 when it lost its hegemony. Thus Israeli Society had been under uninterrupted Labour hegemony for almost half a century, and the Alignment, alias ILP, alias Mapai, alias Ahdut Ha-Avoda, has been the dominant party throughout this whole period.

As a result of this continuity political practices prevalent in the Yishuv – including those of handing out material benefits to service political goals – were carried over into the state era. Indeed the massive influx of new immigrants which occurred with the establishment of the state opened new vistas for these practices. A large number of these immigrants originated from traditional (mainly Middle Eastern) countries, and both the culture of democratic elections and the ideology of the Israeli parties were entirely alien to them. At the same time, most of them had neither the financial means nor the professional skills necessary for making their way in a relatively more modern occupational structure so they were greatly dependent on the representatives of the absorbing society for their livelihood. The situation was aggravated by the difficulties involved in accommodating a large number of immigrants quickly.[7] It was practically impossible to provide adequate housing and employment for everyone at the same time, and priorities were entirely at the discretion of the functionaries in charge of immigrant absorption.

The parties did not hesitate to take full advantage of the situation. As Eisenstadt (1967, ch. 9) maintains, the parties tried to incorporate the new immigrants into their own frameworks not so much by ideological persuasion (which in any case would have been futile), but by a network of financial assistance which eased the immigrants' passage into the new society. Hardly any major party refrained from using material benefits to gain the immigrants' political support but the Labour parties headed by Mapai had an obvious advantage in this respect.

The federative arrangements of resource allocation handed down from the Yishuv era were maintained and extended. The parties confronted the new, somewhat bewildered immigrants with a network of economic aid extended through banks, housing companies, economic concerns, labour exchanges and the like just as they had done in the Yishuv era. They also continued to send their representatives abroad to prepare potential immigrants for immigration (and thus create political indebtedness).

In the Yishuv, the parties had divided the new immigrants among themselves by the party political key; each party had been in charge of a number of immigrants in direct proportion to its strength in the most recent election. This custom was perpetuated after statehood, ensuring that each party gained new manpower in rough proportion to its existing strength, thus stabilizing the dominance of the Labour camp.

The handing out of material inducements to new immigrants flourished in rural areas and in the development towns where a large proportion of these immigrants were concentrated and employment and housing were under the control of veteran Israeli functionaries. A large proportion of the population in these development towns was dependent on such functionaries for its very livelihood.

This dependence developed from a socio-economic fact into a socio-psychological fact as well. The new inhabitants of these small towns acquired the habit of moving from office to office and presenting their demands for employment, housing and welfare. Since those in charge of the resources needed the immigrants' political support, they could not afford to be unresponsive to their demands. Consequently, they tended to supply services which at times exceeded what the immigrants were entitled to by regulations. Among other things, they provided state-sponsored public work projects regardless of whether these were necessary or even useful. By this device, large-scale unemployment among immigrants was prevented, and political support for the well-established parties was promoted.

Eventually, a symbiotic relationship developed between immigrants and party activists, from which each side gained essential advantages. Cohen *et al.* (1962, p. 101) report, on the basis of their research in a development town in the late 1950s:

There is a tendency, especially among newcomers to turn any social framework in the town into a device for gaining concrete benefits . . . The parties and their leaders utilized this tendency before the election in order to secure the inhabitants' votes and presented the parties as instrumental in providing such benefits. Phenomena such as promises of work, housing, etc., in exchange for votes were mentioned many times by the respondents.

In his study of the 1965 and 1969 election campaigns in another small town, Deshen (1970 and 1972) tells of an intricate combination of symbolic devices and concrete benefits employed (especially by coalition parties and their affiliated political bodies) to increase electoral support. The benefits consisted of religious articles donated to the congregations, and more tangible benefits such as jobs, housing loans, or other financial aid. Similar conclusions are reached by Aronoff (1972, p. 161). Referring to a senior official in Mapai – which had now become the ILP – he writes:

From his dominant position he ran the 1969 election very much like a classic political boss, offering manifold resources to those who would comply to his dictates and threatening sanctions to those who would not. The object was victory for the party in the election.

Sometimes the device of exchanging benefits for votes was intermingled with another manipulative device: that of co-optation, especially of ethnic and immigrant leaders in development towns. In its rudimentary phase, this combined mechanism utilized local leaders as middlemen in the bargaining process, turning it into a three-way exchange: the leaders would mobilize their followers in support of the party in return for various benefits for these followers, and thereby enhance their own leadership positions. Further elaboration of this device incorporated the local leaders into the party's own hierarchy and granted local power positions to them; in return, they would elicit the support of their followers for the party (Zamir, 1964, pp. 10, 51; Medding, 1972, pp. 69–71).

The political use of material benefits after independence was most conspicuous with new immigrants in rural and semi-rural development areas. However, the majority of the Israeli population resides in urban areas; hence, it would be surprising if the parties had not attempted to employ similar devices in these areas – and to the veteran population as well. There is some evidence that they have in fact done so. Medding (1972, p. 38) tells how the dominant party in Tel-Aviv extended material inducements to both immigrants and veterans. With the establishment of the Israeli government in 1948 and the expansion of the functions of the Histadrut and the Jewish Agency[8] to deal with the new immigrants, a vast number of new positions was created and had to be filled. Hence,

> Subleaders were promoted, rank-and-file became subleaders and in the general proliferation of tasks and branches many advances were to be made, and many rewards handed out to the faithful, or to promising new immigrants anxious to avail themselves of political channels of mobility in Israeli society.

Thus, whoever had the capacity to allocate these positions, advances and benefits could derive significant political advantages in terms of party membership and support. Mapai's Gush in Tel-Aviv performed these tasks more than satisfactorily, and provided the party with many new members to build the foundation of its national success.

In Haifa, too, we learn from Medding, similar methods were used. The Haifa Labour Council (which is part of the Histadrut) was generally headed by a top party leader. This leader usually developed a personal following by taking care of local Histadrut members – for instance, by finding employment for them. The Labour Council was divided into fourteen areas which were subdivided into fifty-seven neighbourhoods. These were serviced by secretaries who, for the most part, were trusted members of Mapai. The secretary acted as a major figure in the neighbourhood committee, and represented it in Histadrut institutions. He was frequently approached by the residents of the neighbourhood with regard to housing, educational facilities, and other problems. He helped place relatives in the Histadrut institutions for the aged, arranged loans or credit, helped workers get promoted, and the like.

Evidently, the Labour Council and its subdivisions were involved in a much wider range of activities than are usually undertaken by such bodies 'thus enabling the party controlling these activities, particularly those connected with the allocation of instrumental benefits and material rewards, to derive direct and immediate political advantages from them' (Medding, 1972, p. 145).

Another way in which Mapai tried to gain the electoral support of various groups was by what Medding (p. 19) referred to as 'organizational penetration'. This mechanism is described by the author as follows:

> Assured support for Mapai among organized interest groups was sought by capturing control of their executive bodies and then co-ordinating their policies with those of the party. On occasion, Mapai even organized the interest group's institutions in order to benefit from its support.

Medding then goes on to describe how Mapai employed this device with a variety of groups such as industrial workers, artisans, professionals, immigrants, ethnic groups, women, etc. (pp. 19–85).

What is noteworthy about this mechanism is that it was closely interrelated with that of handing out material inducements for political support. This is most evident in Mapai's grassroots penetration at the workplace. The basic cell of the Histadrut organization in almost every workplace in Israel is the workers' committee, usually elected by secret ballot among the employees. This committee (especially its secretary) has important instrumental benefits at its disposal; the committee's agreement is required for the dismissal of permanent workers, and it takes an active part in deciding promotions and consequently salary increases. Also, most committees secure loans and other forms of financial assistance for workers.

The allocation of these benefits is not subject to specific Histadrut regulations, and is entirely at the discretion of the committee. 'Such loans can thus be used as political rewards, sanctions or incentives' (Medding, p. 49). Members of the committee also perform significant general service and social work functions for employees. This potential, too, has usually been converted into votes in Histadrut and Knesset (parliament) elections.

Mapai's aim has been to achieve a majority on each workers' committee, and thereby secure the position of secretary. Once it had attained this majority, its members on the committee had no need to withhold services from non-party members; the party could call in debts and obligations which workers had accrued, or workers hopeful of getting assistance from the committee would join the party and work for it, or make the committee's party members aware of their support. 'The establishment of such a network of reciprocal obligation and mutual benefit represents the conversion of trade union functions and social assistance into political advantages for the officials' political party' (Medding, p. 49).

The conversion of individual assistance into political advantage has not been limited to the Jewish population. The traditional pattern of dealing with the Arab minority in Israel has been to reward the 'good' Arabs (the ones willing to support the state, the regime and the political establishment) with a variety of benefits, and to punish the 'bad' Arabs (the ones who oppose both the state and the regime, lending their support to Rakah[9]) by withholding such benefits.[10]

At the same time, it must be noted that the practices of direct bribery and treating of voters about to cast their ballots has not been as well-established in Israel as it had been in nineteenth-century Britain, for instance. Direct bribery has not been absent in Israel;

from time to time, there have been rumours that voters have been paid directly[11] for casting the 'right' kind of vote.[12] These rumours pertain especially (though not exclusively) to voters in the Arab sector and to Jewish voters in poverty-ridden neighbourhoods.[13] But it is clear that, in the main, a more sophisticated device of exchanging material inducements for political support has evolved, and it is this device which has become so widely employed.

However, what strikes one most forcefully with regard to this device is not merely the frequency with which it has been employed. Rather, it is the fact that it has become part of a highly institutionalized system – as in the United States in the heyday of bossism (but unlike Australia, even when such practices did exist there). This system has not been formally recognized as legitimate, but it has largely been accepted on the informal level and has been entrenched in the very structures that carry out the political process in Israel and in the role definitions of those who man those structures.

Recent developments

Has this system changed appreciably in recent years? As the waves of new immigrants in the early years of the state became absorbed, they should have become less dependent on the various agencies for their livelihood, and thus should have become less susceptible to the device of exchanging votes for benefits.[14] But the public's dependence on political functionaries is inherent in deeply ingrained features of the Israeli socio-political system, rooted in a period which long preceded the mass immigration of the early state era. Hence, there is no reason to expect that it would have declined drastically with the decline in immigration.

Moreover, some of the immigrants and their progeny came to be so effectively socialized into the system that they were most reluctant to relinquish it, even when, objectively, they could have done without it. Consequently, the practice of seeking and accepting a wide array of benefits from various political agencies has not been eradicated. In fact, in some sectors and localities, this practice has become part of the local culture – the accepted way of doing things.

Thus Uzi Benziman writes[15] that a distinct sub-culture (or a 'parallel culture', as he terms it) has developed in a large number of settlements, development towns and neighbourhoods – comprising no less than one-sixth of the Jewish population of Israel. The inhabitants tend to base their livelihood at least in part on the public bounty. Many of them have employment of one sort or another, but the remuneration has to be supplemented from public funds. Others are frequently out of work, or subsist on public funds altogether. The political functionaries have got into the habit of channelling large sums of money into these localities. In return, the local inhabitants employ a line of minimum interference in politics; local political bosses are free to do whatever they wish in their domains, without fear of being demoted or rebelled against by their constituents.

As a typical example, Benziman tells of Hatzor, where the local council bases its power on a wide array of benefits handed out to the local population. These benefits perpetuate and even enhance the population's dependence on the political authorities. On its part, the public is willing to close an eye (or even both) to whatever is happening on the local political scene. Since various party constellations take part in the coalitions of the local council, it seems that several parties have benefited from this tacit arrangement.

The people who live in localities such as Hatzor are mostly of Afro-Asian (or Middle Eastern) origin who reached the country at the end of the 1940s or the beginning of the 1950s. By now, with the co-operation of the political authorities, they have succeeded in educating a second generation to the same way of life – a generation which is now in the process of educating its own progeny (the third generation) to the same pattern.

Recent intra-party elections apparently have not been free from the pressure of material inducements, either. In February 1977 the ILP Conference (in which over 3,000 delegates participated) was called upon to elect the Party's candidate for prime minister.[16] The delegates were mostly Party functionaries, and therefore dependent on senior Party officials for their promotion and sometimes even for their livelihood. Hence, their allegiance to one or other of the candidates was greatly influenced by considerations of their own private self-interest.[17]

Neither are there any signs that material inducements employed in other contexts and with different populations for the purpose of securing political support – such as those analysed by Medding (1972) – have been relinquished since that book went to press. We must conclude, then, that although the use of material inducements for small groups, families and individuals may have declined in recent years, it has not done so drastically, and the pattern is still institutionalized in some sectors of Israeli society.

Manipulation of material inducements and class interests

In Israel material inducements were handed out primarily by Labour leaders in the interests of the labour movement, which held hegemony in the major political structures. Moreover, from the Yishuv days and onward the ability of the Labour leadership to hand out such inducements was enhanced by the fact that this same leadership had also shaped the economy which consequently was – in large part – under public (that is Labour) ownership and control: the Histadrut had established a variety of enterprises and these developed into some of the country's major economic concerns. This meant that enormous financial resources were at the disposal of the Labour functionaries who controlled these concerns.

Also, because of the initial harsh economic conditions, large-scale economic resources had to be imported into the country from abroad. These resources, supplied mainly from the World Zionist Organization, were channelled through the Histadrut and the national institutions – which from the early 1930s were under Labour control as well. This further enhanced the resources which Labour functionaries could control and deploy for political manipulation. This also implied that large sections of the population were greatly dependent on such resources. The dependent sections included those employed by Histadrut enterprises, those employed by the national institutions and eventually those employed by the private sector of the economy as well. All of these were considered as potential Labour supporters and the material benefits many of them obtained were instrumental in transforming them into actual Labour supporters as well.

The employment of material inducements in return for political support was thus primarily an exchange between the ruling Labour elite and rank-and-file workers or employees. However, members of other classes, especially owners of private enterprises were not entirely neglected as they, too, became greatly dependent on the Labour-led political establishment.

Initially the founding fathers of the Labour Movement intended to establish an economy that was entirely publicly owned, and thus to prevent the development of a capitalist class altogether. The leaders' financial dependence on the World Zionist Organization – which did not share their socialist views – made it necessary for them to compromise by putting up with private enterprises (and their owners) as well. However, because of the barreness of the land, the lack of natural resources, the under-developed state of the economy and other forbidding circumstances, the private sector of the economy which evolved especially from the 1920s and onward remained rather weak. Subsequent economic crises weakened the vulnerable private sector even further. Thereafter, private enterprises could hardly hope to be profitable or even self-sustaining; they came to rely increasingly on financial aid from Labour-controlled public resources (Shapiro, 1977, ch. 6).

A successively closer relationship thus developed between the political (especially Labour) functionaries who were in charge of resources and businessmen and industrialists who were in need of

101

these resources for the very survival of their enterprises. In this symbiotic relationship from which each side derived essential advantages, the functionaries were unequivocally the dominant partner who called the tune, while the budding capitalists were clearly the dependant.

With the attainment of statehood the dominance of the public sector of the economy was perpetuated and enhanced, as was the inflow of financial resources from outside the country. To the pre-state Histadrut enterprises, state-controlled concerns were now added, as a consequence of which the public sector's share of the total Israeli economy is unequalled today in any other Western society (Barkai, 1964). The inflow of resources from the World Zionist Organization was supplemented and greatly overshadowed by postwar compensation from Germany and by financial aid from the United States. Consequently the ruling Labour elite was in charge of a greater chunk of the economy and greater financial resources than ever before.

While the necessity of encouraging economic development (specifically the import of private capital from abroad) has brought the regime to reluctant concessions to private enterprise, it has seen to it that the private sector of the economy remain directly or indirectly under government control. The continued ascendency of the public sector over the private sector of the economy and the continued vulnerability of Israel's capitalist class has been facilitated by the ruling elite's commitment to the socialist ideology (see chapter 10) and the close co-operation between the government and the Histadrut.

All this meant that after statehood, large parts of the Israeli population have made their livelihood with the direct or indirect aid of the government and the Histadrut. Some 40 per cent of Israel's workforce has been directly employed by the public sector of the economy – that is by one of these two agencies – and most private concerns have been able to sustain themselves only with the aid of various loans, subsidies, tax exemptions, foreign currency concessions and other such benefits from the government. Since the allocation of the benefits has been governed by rather loose regulations, various high-ranking public officials and other elite members have been in a position to grant these benefits largely at their own discretion. Accordingly, they have been in an especially advantageous position to utilize these benefits for political manipulation and large parts of the Israeli public – both employees and self-employed, both workers and capitalists – have been greatly susceptible to this device.

Clearly, both employees and entrepreneurs would have been better off had there been unequivocal, objective guidelines for the allocation of resources and had they been less dependent on the political establishment and thus less vulnerable to manipulation through such resources. Had this been the case, they still would have obtained the same benefits, but with greater dignity and without having to make any political concessions in return. The ruling elite, on the other hand, would have been substantially weakened. It is too early to tell as yet whether and how the situation is likely to change with the advent to power of the right-wing party – the Likud[18] – following the last election. Until recently, in any case, material inducements have clearly benefited the ruling Labour elite rather than the capitalist class and it is by the former, rather than by the latter, that they have been sustained for so long.

Material inducements and the democratic process

To say that the Labour elite has been the main beneficiary of manipulation through material inducements also implies that the dominant Labour Party has benefited disproportionately from this practice. The Alignment (alias ILP, alias Mapai, alias Ahdut Ha-Avoda) has been able to utilize a disproportionate amount of benefits – accruing from its lengthy control over Histadrut and national resources – to promote political support for itself. This is not to say that other parties have not benefited from such resources as well. The religious coalition party and right-wing parties have done their best to compete with Labour in this respect. But having been the major power in the Israeli government since independence, and in the Histadrut and the national institutions long before that, the ILP could command much larger resources than any of the other parties. It also had the most energetic activists and functionaries, who seemed to be most skilful in employing these resources for the party's benefit. The Labour Party thus outranked all other parties both in resources and in resourcefulness.

It seems reasonable to conclude that this double advantage goes a long way towards explaining the Alignment's (and its predecessors') political dominance for close to half a century. The fact that the Labour Party's forerunner, Ahdut Ha-Avoda was the first to set up an effective, large-scale party machine – explains, in large part – how it gained control of the Histadrut and later (under the name of Mapai) of the national institutions as well. Thereafter, the resources it commanded and its resourcefulness in their utilization formed a combination that was hard to beat. The establishment of the state did not alter the basic situation, except that Mapai now gained control of the lion's share of the government's resources as well. When it merged with another party in 1968 to form the Israel Labour Party, and joined forces with yet another party in 1969 to form the Alignment, the new political body derived no less of an electoral benefit from the practices which had served its forerunners so well. Apparently, the same methods still fulfilled an important role in ensuring the Alignment's re-election in 1973.

Elsewhere (Etzioni-Halevy, 1977, ch. 5) it has been shown that in recent years there has been a substantial decline in the popularity of the Israeli government, as measured by opinion polls.[19] Assuming that the samples interviewed represent the voting public,[20] the substantial decline in support for the government from the time of the 1969 election to the time of the 1973 election was not matched by the decline in electoral support for the Alignment which headed this government. While the said survey research indicated a decline of 20 percentage points in support for the government from October 1969 to December 1973, the electoral support for the Alignment declined from 46.2 to 39.6 per cent in the same period, i.e., by 6 percentage points only. In other words, the control which the establishment (headed by the Alignment) has had over electoral support is greater than the control it has been able to exert over public opinion.

This may be interpreted in a number of ways – for instance by some voters' customary allegiance to 'their' party, by reluctance to endorse an alternative that might have seemed less promising, or by the fact that responding to a questionnaire does not entail the same degree of commitment as does the casting of a ballot. I suggest, however, that a complementary explanation could be supplied in terms of material inducements.

It may be reasoned that both electoral support for the Labour Party and oral support for the government are influenced equally by the government's national policy and by symbolic persuasion or propaganda. On the other hand, oral support is likely to be less susceptible to material inducements than is electoral support. Hence, the fact that between 1969 and 1973 the latter declined to a lesser extent than did the former may be attributed, in part, to the contribution of material inducements to the mobilization and pre-servation of electoral support for the ruling party.

Thus, it seems plausible that at least until 1973, the handing out of material inducements has significantly affected the outcome of the electoral struggle in Israel – and hence, significantly biased the democratic process. Material inducements have clearly biased many elections in other countries, such as in nineteenth-century Britain and in the heyday of the party machines in the United States. But nowhere in the other countries analysed have they done this so consistently in favour of one party. Nowhere have they so stubbornly prevented the orderly replacement of the ruling elite – one of the most basic criteria of democracy – and maintained one-party rule (though mitigated by coalitions) for such a long time.

Nevertheless, even in these years, the growing dissatisfaction of the public with the establishment had resulted in a moderate decline in electoral support for the ruling party. The reasons for this dissatisfaction are beyond the scope of the present analysis.[21] What is of significance in the present context is the fact that such a decline did take place notwithstanding the employment of material inducements. Even at that time, then, democracy in Israel, though obviously far from perfect, was still viable to some (albeit limited) extent.

Moreover, in the most recent election, in May 1977, the Alignment secured only 24 per cent of the votes as against 32 per cent netted by the Likud, and thus lost its long-standing hegemony. In the absence of hard-core research data on this last election, it is difficult to say whether this was *despite* the disproportionate application of material inducements by the dominant party, whether it resulted from the fact that other parties had overtaken the Alignment in the employment of such inducements, or from the fact that there was a general decline in the employment of such inducements by all parties. But whatever the explanation, and whatever one's private feelings concerning the electoral victory of the right-wing Likud, one cannot but conclude that even in Israel (where the practice of material inducements in the electoral process has been the most firmly entrenched in recent years) the democratic process has eventually made some headway. It must be kept in mind, however, that in the absence of material inducements the Alignment, or the Israel Labour Party and Mapai before it, might have been replaced a long time ago.

6 Political manipulation of material inducements: an explanation

The gist of the preceding four chapters is that the manipulation of material inducements[1] has been prevalent and has declined to some extent in all of the countries studied. But the form of the manipulation as well as the timing and extent of its decline have differed: in Britain and in Australia where material inducements have been handed out primarily by wealthy elite members, the decline has taken place chiefly towards the end of the previous century. While some remnants of the practice could still be found in Australia at the beginning of this century, it was no longer widespread; in both Britain and Australia it no longer existed on any significant scale towards the middle of the century and onward. It cannot be asserted with certainty that manipulation of votes through material inducements (to families and individuals) never occurs in these countries, but if practices of this nature persist, they do so in a rather mild and innocuous form and are within or around the range of what is legitimate by present democratic standards and laws. If any manipulation of a different nature occurs – which observers agree is doubtful – it is clearly the exception rather than the rule.

In the United States and in Israel, where material inducements have been handed out chiefly by party machines, the decline in this type of manipulation was only partial and came about much later. In the United States, party machines have been active during the nineteenth century, but have apparently reached or at least maintained their peak at the beginning of the twentieth century. Since about the middle of the century a significant decline in these machines has been evident, but the employment of material inducements has not disappeared completely from the political scene and some of it has still been evident in the most recent elections.

In Israel the system of handing out material inducements was developed by party machines from the beginning of this century and especially from the 1920s and onward, and it was maintained and even elaborated in the 1950s and 1960s. Although there has apparently been a certain decline in the efficacy of this practice in the most recent election, this decline has been even smaller than in the United States and the practice has certainly not disappeared.

It seems, then, that in the matter of electoral corruption there has been a certain similarity between Britain and Australia – which is not surprising, as the Australian political system was modelled to some extent on the British one. By the same token – and despite all other major socio-political differences between Israel and the United States – there seems to have been a certain similarlity between them in electoral manipulation and its development over time.

This raises the question of how the similarities and the differences among the countries may be explained. Let it be said at the outset that (as should be evident to sociologists) laws against electoral corruption, no matter how stringent, can explain neither the similarities nor the differences, neither the evolution of nor the decline in material inducements. On the face of it, the legal reforms, especially in Britain and Australia, go a long way towards explaining the elimination of corrupt electoral practices in them. But what a sociologist would want to explain is why these legal reforms came about in the first place. Moreover, initially, several legal reforms were less than effective because they were not properly enforced. It may thus be argued that what counts is not so much the stringency of the newly enacted laws but rather the stringency of their enforcement. This once more raises the question of why such laws should be more stringently enforced in one country, or at one time – rather than another – so that additional explanations must be looked for.

The populist conception: characteristics of the rank-and-file

Some observers have attempted to explain electoral manipulation of material inducements by certain traits of the rank-and-file public that is being manipulated. The public's ideological awareness, immigration and consequent disorganization, poverty and education have all been suggested as explanatory factors. How powerful are these explanations?

Ideological commitment

Scott (1973, p. 104) offers a theory by which manipulation of material inducements (or machine politics) develops when the public is no longer automatically loyal to its traditional patrons and thus is not enmeshed in a system of deferential voting, but on the other hand has not yet developed intense ideological commitments.

> If correct, this analysis implies that it is especially among new electorates for whom traditional vertical ties have weakened, but have not yet been replaced by new ideological class ties, that machine politics is most likely to flourish.

The first part of this thesis does not pose any special problems. Where deferential voting is prevalent, bribery of the electorate is obviously superfluous – although one might argue that bribery (as well as intimidation) are implicitly built into the situation without having to be resorted to explicitly.

The second part of the thesis seems plausible too. But does it fit the four countries investigated? Actually it does not. Take the case of Israel, for instance. In the Yishuv era, politics were on a high ideological pitch, and ideological commitment was intense, yet the employment of material inducements in the political process flourished. Moreover, in the labour movement, ideological commitments were specially intense. As Gorni (1973) shows, Ahdut Ha-Avoda, the major Labour Party, was ridden by intense ideological arguments among its various factions. The intensity of these ideological debates has probably rarely been equalled. Yet this same party was the originator and the chief perpetrator of the system of material inducements.

Ideological commitment was by no means restricted to leaders and was intense among the rank-and-file as well. The end of the nineteenth century and the beginning of the twentieth was a time of large-scale migration of Jews from Eastern Europe overseas. The overwhelming majority of Jewish migrants went to the United States and only a tiny fraction came to Palestine. For instance, in the years 1904–14, 1,195,423 Jews immigrated to the United States from Eastern Europe, while only some 25,000–30,000 made their way to Palestine (Gorni, 1970). The minority who made this choice were obviously the most committed ideologically.

This can be seen among other things from the fact that their socio-economic status differed widely from that of the immigrants to America. While the latter were usually of rather low socio-economic status,[2] evidently trying to raise their standard of living by immigrating to America, the former were generally of a much higher social background and they were willing to *lower* their standard of living by coming to Palestine.

Furthermore, early in the twentieth century, while only 1.3 per cent of the Jewish immigrants to the United States were professionals, 14 to 17 per cent of the immigrants to Palestine were. Many more were students who had interrupted their course of study to immigrate, or high school students who had not been accepted at the Russian universities because of the *numerus clausus* imposed by the Russian government on secondary and higher education for Jews. Thus, a disproportionately large number of them belonged to the 'intellengenzia' which usually is characterized by high ideological awareness (Shapiro, 1977, ch. 7).

Evidently this ideological awareness had a lot to do with their coming to Palestine. After all, what but an urgent Zionist commitment and intense national loyalty could have induced people to face the adverse conditions of an under-developed, barren country where, initially, it was a problem even to subsist. This point is supported by Gorni's (1970) analysis of a 1930s study of 1,000 old-time immigrants who had reached the country at the beginning of the century. He concluded that it was difficult for them to find their place within the spectrum of political parties because their political involvement was so high and their affinities so well crystallized that they were reluctant to compromise with existent political frameworks. And yet, in wooing these people, the leaders of the various political parties (headed by Ahdut Ha-Avoda) felt it incumbent upon them to back up ideological commitment by material rewards, and such rewards were not rejected.

On the other hand, immigrants to Australia were apparently not motivated chiefly by considerations other than those of improving their lot, and their ideological commitment could not in any way have matched that of the Zionist-motivated immigrants to Palestine. This goes apparently for the general Australian political scene as well. Australia has been characterized as a society in which ideology does not play a major part in politics and in which the controversy between the parties revolves around the material interests of their supporters more than it does around ideological issues. Indeed, it has been claimed (Parker, 1968, p. 23) that Australian politics are specifically characterized by 'the low importance ascribed to non-material values – especially those associated with . . . political ideology'. It has further been claimed (Emy, 1974, p. 347) that 'Australia . . . seems to have combined a hedonistic culture with a distinctly low-keyed instrumental view of politics'. Yet recent Australian elections (like British ones) have been least beset by electoral corruption.

Moreover, the 1950s in the United States have been characterized as a period when one-time ideological commitments – especially those of intellectuals – had been eroded and no new commitments had taken their place; a period, in fact, characterized by 'the end of ideology' (Bell, 1960). Yet the 1950s were also a period in which a partial decline in material inducements was evident, and when some of the foremost party machines were on their way down.

Ideological commitment of the public, then, explains very little in the matter of electoral corruption. Indeed, as Parker (1968) has pointed out, intense ideological commitment among public and leaders alike, may intensify the drive and hence the struggle for power. It may therefore increase the attractiveness of manipulative devices designed to secure such power. Moreover, excessive zeal may even lead the zealous to feel that the ideological goal justifies the manipulative means.

Immigration and disorganization

Additional factors which, according to Scott (1973) account for the machine (i.e., material) inducements in the electoral process are disorganization – by which he means the presence among the public of large numbers of immigrants as yet disoriented in the new society – and poverty.

But while these factors may serve to explain some of the developments in some of the countries studied, neither of them can serve to explain the differences among them. Thus, the diminution of immigration to the United States after the First World War may be held to explain the partial decline of the party machine from the 1940s and onward. Also, the large-scale immigration to Israel in the Yishuv era and in the 1950s may serve to explain the flourishing of material inducements at these times, and the decline in immigration later on, may possibly serve to explain whatever decline in electoral corruption took place in Israel in the 1970s.

A different picture emerges, however, when the countries are compared to each other. In the nineteenth century, for instance, the United States and Australia were countries of immigration, Britain was not. Yet bribery and cheating flourished in Britain to a much greater extent than they did in Australia and matched or surpassed this practice in the United States. It is true that large proportions of the nineteenth-century immigrants to both America and Australia came from the United Kingdom. Coming from a similar culture, they did not have to face serious disorientation in the new society. But even so, how can Britain's surpassing Australia in electoral corruption be explained?

A twentieth-century comparison casts similar doubts on the thesis. While immigration to the United States has been drastically reduced since the 1920s, in Australia the opposite was the case: after the Second World War a deliberate immigration policy on part of the Australian government resulted in massive immigration. In fact, from 1947 until 1970, 3,593,130 immigrants arrived in

Australia – quite a large number, in view of the fact that the whole Australian population comprised only about 13 million at the beginning of the 1970s.[3] Even if non-British immigrants alone are taken into account (under the assumption that British immigrants are not disoriented in the new country), Australia is still substantially ahead of the United States, having taken in 2,313,58 such immigrants between 1947 and 1970 (Price and Martin, 1976, p. 14). Thus, if immigration were the deciding factor, then, one would expect material inducements to have persisted in Australia to a much later period and to a much greater extent than they did in the United States. Yet, the opposite has been the case.

Poverty

If immigration as such cannot account for the differences among the four countries, can poverty (among immigrants or other inhabitants) do so? The period in which material inducements were gradually eliminated from the political scene in Britain, i.e., the second half of the nineteenth century, was also the time in which a significant rise in the standard of living occurred. As Bagwell and Mingay (1970) point out, real wages rose markedly in the last forty years of the nineteenth century (the increase between 1860 and 1891 alone was in the order of 50 per cent). Moreover, this long-term rise in real wages was supplemented by improvements in housing, education, health and the like. In Australia, too, despite some setbacks, especially in the 1890s, the elimination of material inducements towards the end of the nineteenth century followed a significant trend of economic growth and a rise in the population's general standard of living. The developments in each of the two countries as such, then, would seem to confirm the poverty thesis.

This is not so when the comparative perspective is employed. In America, for instance, the situation was no less favourable. As in Britain, the later nineteenth century was a period of rapidly growing real incomes: wage rates remained nearly stationary while prices fell considerably between 1865 and 1898. Real wages in manufacturing for instance, rose by about 50 per cent between 1860 and 1890 and by another 30 per cent between 1890 and 1913. As in Britain, the rise in real wages in America was accompanied by improvements in the living environment; there was a marked increase in expenditure going to consumer durables such as stoves, iceboxes, etc. (Bagwell and Mingay, 1970). There is no reason to believe that the rise in real income and standard of living was greater in Britain and Australia than it was in the United States. In fact, the opposite was the case, as can be seen from Table 6.1. And yet Britain and Australia far overtook the United States in the elimination of electoral corruption. On the contemporary scene, it seems, the general level of affluence (or lack thereof) cannot explain the differences between the countries either. This can be surmised from Table 6.2 that lists GNP *per capita* in the countries studied, in 1974.

TABLE 6.1   *Growth of national product per capita during the nineteenth and twentieth centuries (product in constant prices)*

Country	Period on which calculation is based	Coefficient of multiplication in a century
United States	1839–1962	4·9
England	1855–1959	3·7
Australia	1861–1962	2·2

Source: Kuznets (1966), Table 2.5, pp. 64–5.

TABLE 6.2   *GNP* per capita *in 1974 (US dollars)*

United States of America	$7,751
Australia	$7,245
Britain	£3,966
Israel	$3,479

Source: Compiled and computed from International Institute for Strategic Studies (1977).

As can be seen, the countries' rating on *per capita* GNP[4] has very little to do with their rating on the exchange of benefits for votes. The United States is the first in affluence, but by no means the first in the elimination of electoral corruption. Britain is almost the least affluent of the countries, but not the least successful in the elimination of electoral corruption.

If a country's general level of poverty *vs.* affluence cannot account for the prevalence of electoral corruption in it, could it be that such practices are accounted for by *pockets* of poverty among the public? This contention seems plausible in view of the fact that the recipients of benefits in exchange for political support have frequently been the poorer elements in society (though not exclusively so). Thus, as pockets of poverty are eliminated, the public, or parts of it, become less vulnerable to material inducements and the petty resources the politician has to offer, become less attractive. Yet, it was seen in the preceding chapters that some of the more affluent elements in society have also availed themselves of material advantages from political sources. Perhaps for this and other reasons, the pockets of poverty theory can only aid in explaining some intra-country developments, especially in the United States (see below), but is of little value in explaining inter-country differences.

In the United States, for instance, despite the rise in the standard of living towards the end of the nineteenth century and the beginning of the twentieth, many immigrants still lived under conditions of extreme poverty, and there remained a mass of poverty and unemployment among the indigenous population as well. About a quarter of the urban workers were unemployed for a part of each year. There was overcrowding in slum tenements, which produced squalor and disease; many new immigrants were swallowed up in these overcrowded slums. In addition, there was also a great deal of rural distress. It has been estimated that all in all, around 1904, no less than 10 million persons lived in poverty.

However, the situation in Britain was not greatly different. Despite the general improvement in living conditions towards the end of the nineteenth century, there persisted a substantial proportion of poverty-stricken slum dwellers who existed at a bare subsistence level. Investigation by Charles Booth in London in 1886 showed that poverty affected about a third of the population: 22 per cent could obtain the necessities of life only by constant struggle and over 8 per cent could not achieve even this. Surveys of other industrial towns confirmed these revelations. By the late nineteenth-century British towns still contained vast slum areas and often were unhealthy and dirty; they still contained a large class of extreme poor whom the benefits of industrialization had largely passed by (Bagwell and Mingay, 1970).

In the United States and Israel, there have certainly been pockets of poverty in recent years as well. It has been estimated that in 1959 there were some 39 million poor persons in the United States making up 24 per cent of the population. At the beginning of the 1960s, it was estimated that there were 36 million people, or approximately 20 per cent of the population living in poverty.[5] Another estimate, accepted by President Johnson and Congress in 1964, was that there were some 30 million destitute poor in the United States at that time. Throughout the 1960s the number of persons living in poverty has apparently declined substantially; since 1969 the decline has all but stopped and in 1976 the poor reached 24 million, or 12 per cent of the population (and half the 1959 percentage).[6] Similarly in Israel, the Prime Minister's Committee on Children and Youth in Distress reported that in 1968–71 about 200,000 children, or approximately 24 per cent of all children, lived in poverty; and that 11 per cent of the general urban

113

population (which accounts for about 90 per cent of the population) were below the poverty line.[7]

But by the same token there has been poverty in recent years in Britain and in Australia as well. Thus, Townsend, using data from the British Ministry of Labour's National Survey of income and expenditure in 1960, estimated that 7½ million people or some 14 per cent of the population were living below generally accepted subsistence standards (Abel-Smith and Townsend, 1965).[8] Also, various studies conducted in Australia have shown that pockets of poverty have been very much in evidence there. Poverty has not necessarily been concentrated among new immigrants: Australia's selective immigration policy has ascertained that new immigrants were absorbed with relative ease into the occupational structure. Hence the extremes of poverty found at the turn of the century among American immigrants are not to be found in Australia.

But pockets of poverty have been located among the general population. In a survey of living conditions carried out in Melbourne by the Institute of Economic and Social Research in 1966, it was found that some 7.5 per cent of the income units were below the poverty line in that they had insufficient income to meet their basic needs[9] (Henderson, 1969). The inner areas of all other large Australian cities were similarly found to contain sizeable populations that require public service payments (such as unemployment or sickness benefits) to reach even a minimal level of subsistence. In addition, there have been pockets of poverty in country areas, which include certain depressed areas of primary industry. Finally, the National Commission's Enquiry into Poverty conducted in 1975 reported that over 10 per cent of all income units in Australia were very poor, as they were below an austere poverty line, and an additional 8 per cent were slightly less poor in that they were less than 20 per cent above it[10] (Henderson, 1975).

It is exceedingly difficult to compare levels of poverty and sizes of populations living in poverty from one country to another. Supposedly, the poverty line is drawn in such a manner that those underneath it are seriously short of basic needs such as minimal food, shelter and medical care. But this line cannot be drawn precisely. Basic needs vary and people (especially from different countries) do not agree on what is minimal. Hence, standards used to demarcate the subsistence level vary from country to country. In the United States, where the general standard of living is highest, the poverty line is apparently drawn at a higher level than it is in Australia, and this may account in part for the larger percentages defined as poor in American statistics.

Nevertheless, the general impression one gains is that the percentages of the population living in poverty are greater in the United

States and in Britain than they are in Australia. But even so it is clear that in Australia, and certainly in Britain, pockets of poverty have been sufficiently large to have warranted the handing out of material inducements by party machines, had there been party machines eager to take advantage of the situation. In the absence (or almost total absence) of organizations geared to such practices, poverty as such could not bring them into existence.

This is not to say that poverty has contributed nothing to the explanation of electoral corruption. Poverty is apparently a fertile ground on which such corruption thrives. The absence or decline of poverty is certainly apt to have adverse effects on it. But poverty among the rank-and-file public cannot initiate the handing out of material inducements when other, more decisive conditions, are absent.

Education

In close conjunction with poverty, low levels of education have also been considered in explaining the exchange of benefits for votes (Sorauf, 1960). And, in fact, it has been reported that in nineteenth-century Britain, voters open to this type of manipulation were frequently (though not exclusively) at a low level of education. In America, too, the people most vulnerable to machine politics were the less educated (frequently, also, new immigrants, and poor into the bargain).

In Israel, on the other hand, the situation is more complicated. While many of the new immigrants of the 1950s (of whom a great proportion came from Middle Eastern countries) were indeed poorly educated, the situation was far otherwise in the pre-state era (see above). Yet the highly educated immigrants (and old-timers) did not hesitate to accept material benefits from political organizations and to pledge their allegiance to these organizations in return.

Moreover, there seems to be no relationship between the four countries' rating on level of education and their rating on electoral corruption. The British system of education has been characterized as an elitist system and the Australian and Israeli systems fit in with this title as well; in these countries, changes toward greater demo-cratization are but slow and gradual. The American educational system on the other hand has been much more mass oriented and the great majority of American youngsters nowadays attain at least a high school diploma.

It may be argued that the American high school diploma cannot be compared with its British or Australian counterparts.[11] But it is significant that a far greater percentage of American youngsters – as

115

compared to British ones, for instance – benefit from education up to a higher age. This difference is certainly not reflected in differences in the countries' manipulation in electoral processes.

Neither ideological awareness nor immigration, poverty and level of education of the rank-and-file public thus seem to explain differences between the four countries in electoral manipulation involving material benefits. Perhaps this is so, because the public is merely the recipient of such benefits. Even if uninvolved ideologically, even if disoriented in a new society and unaware of democratic procedures; even if in dire need of material benefits and willing to accept them in return for political support – members of the rank-and-file public can hardly do so unless introduced to the practice by those who have the power and the resources to perpetrate it. The rank-and-file can make use of the practice (and it certainly helps if they are willing to do so), but they cannot initiate it. Hence the major explanation of political manipulation of material inducements is to be sought not in the character of the public that is the object of manipulation, but in the character of those who seek to dominate the public through such manipulation, and in the structures of domination they have devised. But if so, who are the 'dominators' and which of their traits account for the practice, its resilience or its decline?

The Marxist conception: dominant class interests

Two sociological models have evolved for the conceptualization of social domination. The class model deriving from the Marxist tradition and the elite model deriving from the Pareto-Mosca-Michels tradition (see Inroduction). Both of these are very general and highly abstract, and therefore cannot generate specific testable hypotheses that could account for inter-country differences in political manipulation. Yet, from the logic of each model, certain expectations would follow. From the Marxist model it would implicitly follow that manipulation through material inducements would be most likely to evolve – and once evolved would be most likely to persist – where the economically dominant classes have the clearest leverage over the political system and where, therefore, the manipulation most clearly serves the interests of these classes. From the elite model it would follow that differential developments in the political manipulation of material inducements have very little to do with the degree to which the economically dominant classes benefit from the practice and that the explanation for such differences is to be found in the structural features of the political establishment itself and in the features of the elites which shape and represent it.

The material presented in the preceding chapters shows that this is in fact so. In eighteenth- and nineteenth-century Britain the economically dominant classes (aristocrats and later capitalists as well) had a virtual monopoly over political power; this monopoly was established among other things through the introduction of material inducements into the political process. The perpetuation of such inducements could thus have served the interests of the landed and capitalist classes in maintaining their monopoly. Yet Britain was the first country to relinquish the practice, thereby helping to pave the way for Labour participation in the political establishment. In Israel, *per contra*, an aristocratic class was obviously non-existent. The capitalist class was politically weak and subdued, while the working class and its representatives had a virtual monopoly over political power for close to half a century. Yet Israel is the country in which material inducements have been most resilient.[12]

The elite conception: the role of administrative power

Having eliminated so many alternative explanations, we are left with the ruling elites themselves, and the political process they shape, as the major explanatory factor. But which of their features are to be held accountable? There is no unanimity among sociologists on this point either.

Elite come-back

It has been claimed for instance that the ever tighter proscription of material inducements has been initiated and sanctioned by elites in democratic countries to ensure for those parts of the elite currently out of office a fair chance of returning to power. In other words, in this view, the elimination of material inducement from the electoral scene is a kind of gentlemen's agreement between various sub-groups of the elite to refrain from keeping each other out of power permanently. This, in turn, is seen as being in line with the various sub-groups' own interests – since any of them might find itself out of office eventually.

From this thesis it would follow, however, that countries in which a periodic rotation of the party in power has been institutionalized, would be less subject to the manipulation of material inducements or would be the first to eliminate the practice. Where those sections of the elites that are currently in office have a greater expectation of being out of office following the next elections, they would be more prone to impose effective, restrictive regulations on the employment of material inducements as political manipulation, in order to ensure the possibility of their own eventual return to power. On the

other hand, where no rotation of the party in office is institutionalized, the sections of the elites currently in power would be more
prone to use material inducements with the view of thereby retaining their power indeterminately.

The foregoing analysis has shown that this is not the case. Of the
two countries in which material inducements have been more resilient, Israel would fit the thesis since it has been ruled by one party in
the state and pre-state eras for a long time. The United States
however would not fit the theory since rotation of parties in office
has long been institutionalized there; no less so, in fact, than in
Britain or in Australia.

Centralization of the bureaucracy

Another theory, proposed by Heidenheimer (1970), has to do with
a structural feature of the establishment: the power of the country's
central administrative structure *vis-à-vis* that of political bodies.
According to this theory, electoral corruption and specifically the
offering of material inducements arose where electoral assemblies,
political parties or other political instruments of mass mobilization
were powerful prior to the development of a centralized, powerful,
bureaucratized civil service. Conversely, it was curbed, where fully
developed national bureaucracies antedate the emergence of
political parties. Whatever merit this theory may have in explaining
historical developments in electoral corruption, especially in the
nineteenth century,[13] it is doubtful whether it can serve to explain
the contemporary scene.

Translated into contemporary terms, this theory would imply
that material inducements flourish where political parties are relatively stronger than the public administration, which is relatively
weak. Such a theory certainly does not fit the Israeli case. In the
pre-state era, parties did indeed develop before a powerful indigenous, state bureaucracy came into existence (see chapters 5 and
10). But at present Israel is renowned for the degree of centraliza-
tion and for the power concentrated in the hands of its bureaucracy.
This powerful administration, however, has not weakened (and
perhaps has even strengthened) political parties and it certainly has
not eliminated (and perhaps has even furthered) material inducements in the electoral process. Hence the thesis on the centralized
power of the bureaucracy can hardly explain why Israel has so much
more electoral corruption than does Britain or Australia.

An alternative explanation: politicization of the bureaucracy

While the power accumulated by a country's central bureaucracy

118

cannot serve as an effective tool for the explanation of material inducements, the explanation for this practice can still be found in that bureaucracy. However, it seems that (at least in the countries studied) it rests on a different feature of this structure, namely, the degree of its politicization. Indeed, if the bureaucracy is both powerful and politicized, who or what is to guarantee the harnessing of this power for the prevention of electoral corruption. Is it not rather more plausible that this power will be mobilized to further material inducements in the electoral process?

Therefore, I suggest, it is not the power of the administration as such, but the degree of its politicization that counts.[14] Such politicization may explain the use of material inducements in return for political support in several ways. In the first place, the penetration of political criteria into the administration makes it possible for the party in power to allocate positions in the public service itself in return for political support. Thus, the phenomenon commonly referred to as 'patronage', constitutes in itself an important type of material inducement for the mobilization of political support. Patronage was apparently most effective as an electoral inducement as long as electorates were small and the votes of public servants themselves could easily tip the scales in elections. As the electorates grew, the efficacy of patronage as direct electoral inducement, apparently declined (see chapters 7 and 8). However, patronage is still highly effective in mobilizing party activists who will engage in soliciting the electoral support of *others* (while their own electoral support for the party is assured as a matter of course).

Second, the introduction of political appointees into public administration makes it possible for the ruling party to utilize its influence in the administration to hand out a wide array of additional rewards by political criteria. In other words, whenever public servants owe their appointments to political adherence rather than (or in addition to) objective qualifications, they are likely to be under strong pressure (as well as being highly motivated) to aid in perpetuating the power of their patron party. They will usually do so by allocating whatever rewards they have at their disposal in return for electoral support for the party.

Such rewards as a rule include jobs in public works and government-controlled economic concerns. They may further include anything from preferential treatment in the allocation of (government-sponsored) housing to preferential treatment with regard to income tax; from the allocation of government contracts to the 'fixing' of parking tickets. The politicization of the public service may thus serve as the basis of a 'spoils system' whose fruits may benefit large numbers of the party's potential supporters at the poll and penalize large numbers of non-supporters.

The various rewards handed out by public servants on the basis of political criteria may be further utilized as a source of pressure for beneficiaries to make substantial donations to their benefactor – the party in office. It is in any case common for members of various interest-groups to make donations to political parties in the hope of bending their policies in their own favour. But when political criteria are not confined to the government echelon alone and penetrate the public service as well, the motivation to do so is patently increased, as are the benefits to be gained when the party reaches power. Moreover, in this case the tendency filters through from the middle-range level of interest groups to the micro-level of even small companies and individuals who gain direct benefits from the politicized administration. In this manner the administration serves as a significant source for the enhancement of party funds. These, in turn, may then be offered to voters as additional inducements to be traded for electoral support.

Laws purporting to eliminate such practices and to control party finance (like laws designed to eliminate electoral corruption) are in themselves inadequate to curb such practices. They can usually be evaded with but a little ingenuity. They seem to be useful only when part of a wider tradition of political restraint.

Patronage appointments thus serve not only as political rewards in their own right but also as a source of further benefits to the party's electoral supporters. This evident connection between patronage and material inducements (or machine politics) has been pointed out by several observers. But these have not always presented the connection in its wider context, besides positing (or implying) a causal relationship between patronage and material inducements which seems to be widely open to criticism.

Thus, Scott (1973) conceives of patronage as an important tool in the hands of the party's political machine, but does not relate the phenomenon to the wider context of the politicization (or conversely the political neutrality) of the public administration. Rather than viewing it as an outgrowth of the patterns of administration, he sees it as an outgrowth of party politics. These, in turn, he considers to be decisively influenced by conditions of poverty and disorganization among the public (see above). Hence the causal chain, according to Scott, leads from the character of the rank-and-file to the character of the political machine, and from that to patronage.

A similar causal chain has been posited by Sorauf (1960, p. 34), when he wrote: 'The old machines and local party organizations relied on patronage, but they were rooted in social and economic conditions that are disappearing. As they disappear so will the parties and patronage they fostered.' In other words, like Scott, Sorauf feels that political machines have had their source in certain social conditions and that they in turn have fostered patronage, which they subsequently relied upon to serve their own ends.

As will subsequently be shown, however, the actual causal chain is the reverse of that proposed by the two observers. Patronage is not the outgrowth of the party machine; on the contrary, the party machine is the outgrowth of patronage. This patronage, in turn, is part of public administration; it can be utilized by the party only if the public administration is generally politicized and hence allows for such a utlization, or even encourages it. Where the administration is politically neutral, there is no basis for the emergence of party machines.

The broader framework: elite culture and structural differentiation

The pattern of the administration itself is the outgrowth of certain traditions or codes of ethics which govern the behaviour of political and administrative elites. These role definitions of the elites, in turn, are intricately related with the structural differentiation which occurs in the overall institutions of government in a given society throughout the process of its modernization (see Huntington, 1968). Specifically it is the differentiation between the party-political and the party-neutral structures of the polity which is decisive. Where such structural differentiation has occurred the elites' notions of propriety also draw a clear line between partisan and non-partisan spheres of action and the bureaucracy is defined as a non-partisan sphere. Where no structural differentiation has occurred, the elites' notions of propriety remain ambiguous with regard to party-politics in governmental structures (including the bureaucracy) and political and non-political criteria of action remain fused.

It is not clear whether the structural differentiation gives rise to the normative differentiation, whether the reverse is the case, or whether the two processes are so closely inter-linked that they develop simultaneously. It is clear, however, and it will be shown in the following chapters, that where such processes of structural and normative differentiation took place, they developed over lengthy periods of time and that they long anteceded recent conditions of poverty, immigration or ideological awareness of the rank-and-file public which supposedly explain the existence (or conversely the absence) of twentieth-century machine politics. There is thus a clear chain of influence which runs from the structures and traditions of the governmental institutions in general, to those of the public administration in particular and thence to material inducements in the electoral process. The broader structural and normative patterns set the framework for the politicization or political

121

neutrality of the bureaucracy; this in turn determines whether the resources of the bureaucracy will or will not be available for political manipulation.

In addition, I suggest, there is also a third type of connection between the politicization of the bureaucracy and the manipulation of material inducements: the fact that they both emanate from the same elite culture and traditions which either foster or restrain both. Using Parsons's distinction between universalism and particularism,[15] we may say that an elite culture in which particularism in general is clearly circumscribed, is one in which elites will tend to restrain particularist criteria in the bureaucracy and in the electoral process alike. In a culture like this, the elites will thus tend to curb both party-politics in the bureaucracy and material inducements in the electoral process even when the resources for such inducements do not derive from the bureaucracy. Conversely, an elite culture in which particularism is pervasive will be conducive to both types of penetration, no matter where the resources for political manipulation derive from. This conception will be applied and substantiated, with regard to each of the four countries, in the following chapters.

7 Administrative power in Britain: the separation of administration from politics

Britain is renowned for a career civil service recruited through open, competitive examinations, and for its distinction between elective-political and appointive-non-political offices. This pattern is the outcome of far-reaching administrative reforms which began at the close of the eighteenth century and reached their peak during the second half of the nineteenth century.

The age of politicization

In the eighteenth century there was no clear distinction between the civil service and political personnel. For many public servants, party-political and administrative duties blended into each other. Even lower-rank public servants frequently had political tasks to perform, such as canvassing for parliamentary elections; some of them were zealous in their support of their party, and did their best to convince potential voters of its excellence. Ministers, for their part, spent much of their time on administrative details which their twentieth-century successors now delegate to civil servants. This was the most striking feature of British administration then, and it continued well into the nineteenth century (Parris, 1969, ch. 1).

In the eighteenth century, even the administrative activity in the public service was thoroughly subordinated to political consider-ations. According to Finer (1952), administrative departments were regarded as the private establishments of ministers, and civil servants' fees did not come under parliamentary scrutiny. These were advantages that politicians were quick to utilize, especially to ensure an amenable House of Commons. This was a necessity for the government administration, for although the monarch was independent and irremovable, his ministers were not – and it was through them that he had to carry out his policies.

Hence, patronage was used to detach members of parliament from their private loyalties and get them to support the administration. Since the smooth running of the government rested upon the making and keeping of the House of Commons, there was increasing pressure throughout the eighteenth century to turn more and more posts to political advantage. But although patronage grew steadily, a spoils system did not develop in Britain. For a time, the government created openings for its supporters by dismissing those appointed by its predecessors – but the practice subsided before it became firmly entrenched (Parris, 1969, ch. 7).

Finer reports that from 1780 to 1830 administrative reform proceeded on a considerable scale; by 1830, the trend of divorcing the administration from partisan considerations had become irreversible. Laws were enacted against the sale of offices. To eliminate the corruption of parliament itself by patronage, a series of Acts limited the number of ministerial offices which could be held by members of parliament. These Acts advanced the evolving separation between partisan-political and non-political office, although this conception was not fully realized at the time (Bridges, 1971).

In the 1830s, the more flagrant subordination of administrative efficiency to political utility diminished. But the party in office still endeavoured to allocate jobs to its supporters, and patronage was still helpful in ensuring party discipline in the House. In early Victorian Britain, writes Gwyn (1962, ch. 4), the government still possessed a certain amount of patronage which the whip, as patronage secretary, distributed to loyal members of parliament. Politicians were expected not only to get jobs for their dependants, but also to help them up the ladder of promotion.

The price of patronage, observers agreed, was a lowering in the morale of the civil service. The practice of giving outsiders high posts in the service lessened the chances of promotion for career employees and caused resentment among their ranks. Since political appointees did not make a secret of their party loyalties, ministers sometimes felt they could not trust the civil servants they had inherited from previous governments. Furthermore, after 1832, the supply of patronage fell far short of the demand; for every friend gained through the award of a post, one or more 'enemies were made by the refusal of their requests. For all these reasons, therefore, many politicians came to consider patronage to be more of a burden than a boon, and many saw it as an outright embarrassment (Parris, 1969, ch. 2).

The age of reforms

These developments set the stage for the reforms which eventually made Britain the model for others throughout the world. The reforms were based on the recommendation of the Northcote–Trevelyan Report (submitted in 1854). Their essence was the principle of a clear-cut distinction between appointed, permanent, non-political public servants, and elected, temporary, political executives, and the submission of the former to the latter. Recruitment was to be solely by merit rather than by political allegiance, and civil servants were to be selected by open, competitive examinations conducted by a central board (Birch, 1973, ch. 10).

The implementation of these prescriptions was a gradual process. For a time, the civil service commission (appointed in 1855) had to be content with a system of limited competition – a compromise between the older pattern of undisturbed political influence and the Northcote–Trevelyan system of neutrality. Heads of departments still had something to bestow: the nominations which were required before candidates could sit for the examination. On the other hand, nomination did not ensure victory; the victor was, supposedly, the most efficient. The snag was that none of the candidates nominated might be suitable for the job. One advantage of the new system was that it made it easy for patrons to fob off clients with a minimum of offence, passing the buck to the civil service commissioners. However, it was not until the 1870s that open, competitive examinations were established as the regular method of entry for most of the large administrative departments.

Even then, it turned out, patronage was still tenacious. Neither the setting up of the civil service commission nor the introduction of competitive examinations could kill it. In the 1870s, Disraeli still used posts to which there was no recognized ladder of promotion as political prizes for his followers. In the next decade, non-partisan promotions became more prominent, but some 20,000 posts still remained in the hands of the patronage secretary. However, a convention was established that patronage appointments were to be permanent – not to be disturbed by subsequent administrations. As a corollary, this permanence carried a standard of loyal service to whatever government was in power (Parris, 1969, ch. 2; Bridges, 1971).

This, in turn, was connected with another development: the salary system for public offices was modernized. Before 1870, a great number of clerks were paid by a fee system; therefore internal developments in each ministry were beyond public scrutiny. After 1870 a salary system was gradually introduced, and payment of officials came under the purview of the treasury and of parliament. Parliament had been taking an increasingly close interest in the administration since 1830, and it devised various measures for keeping the administrative machinery under detailed control.

125

Among other things, it now initiated inquiries into the management of departments and the quality of personnel.

Hence, ministers and department heads had an increasing interest in good appointments – especially when these were senior appointments – and not only for reasons of efficiency. It became more and more necessary for appointments to be defensible before parliament, since improper appointments could be injurious to the minister and his party. Furthermore, for patronage to be useful, public opinion had to sanction (or at least tolerate) its employment. As parliament became increasingly critical of patronage after the middle of the century, so did public opinion. These were two of the major reasons why patronage declined gradually throughout the second half of the nineteenth century, and was practically eliminated at the turn of this century (Finer, 1952; Wettenhall, 1973).

The age of political neutrality

The new system based on the Northcote–Trevelyan Report was completed towards the end of the nineteenth century, and turned the English public service into a profession in the sense that it came to be based as far as possible on merit, expertise, detachment and neutrality.

Especially emphasized was the principle of political neutrality, which implied first and foremost that appointments and promotions were non-political; this principle has been maintained to the present day. The Labour government of 1966 gave temporary appointments in the civil service to a limited number of economists of known left-wing views, but it was assumed that these appointments would not be permanent. Permanent appointments are sometimes offered to persons of known political views, but care is taken not to confine these offers to members of the governing party (Birch, 1973, ch. 16).

The principle that civil servants are servants of the Crown, serving with impartiality whichever ministers happened to be in office, was questioned between the wars by a number of left-wing writers. They argued that the middle-class backgrounds of senior officials would make it difficult for them to sympathize with Labour aims and to co-operate fully with Labour ministers. But the Labour Government of 1945–51 carried through a series of reforms with complete co-operation from the civil service.

The principle of impartiality implies certain restrictions on the political activities of civil servants. The present position is that the administrative and executive classes and their departmental equivalents may not take any part in national politics apart from voting, and may take part in local politics only if permission is given by their departments. It is not difficult for executives to secure such permission, provided there is no possibility of a role conflict (as there might be if the official worked in a local office or if he worked in a department having dealings with local authorities). Still, not many executive civil servants do take part in local politics, and administrative officials are almost entirely excluded (Birch, 1973, p. 175).

Political impartiality does not imply that civil servants are unaware of the political implications of their work. As Christoph (1975) remarks, the scope and character of their administrative activities are bound to sensitize them to the political world in which these activities are embedded. Civil servants are beginning to cast off the myth that what they do stands apart from politics, and they usually have their own views on matters of political policy. Moreover, they play some clear political roles which include policy advising, policy implementation and enhancing the minister's political success. To perform these roles, civil servants must be aware of the political implications of various courses of action.

But, despite all this, they are not free to indulge their own political tastes. Their identification with one party over another is sublimated by the requirements of their calling. Thus they cannot easily be applied to on the basis of party ties, and they do not tend to conduct a policy simply because it fits a certain party line.

The role definition of British public servants thus hinges on the distinction between party politics and politics in the more general sense; the latter includes the definition of certain social goals and the formulation of policies for their attainment. While civil servants are necessarily engaged in politics in the broader sense, they are not usually engaged in party politics. This distinction is possible, in part, because some of the political conceptions which guide the activities of civil servants are consensual. As Bridges (1971, p. 57), characterizing the British civil servant, put it (perhaps with slight exaggeration):

> the departmental experience of which he is the exponent – although it is an essential element in the government of the country – is part of the stock of things which are common to all political parties. It is something which stands apart from the creed of any political party and this makes a civil servant avert himself almost instinctively from party politics.

It has been claimed that the British system of administration excells not only in its concern for political neutrality, but also in its concern for the orderly arranging of hierarchy, division of functions and quality of personnel. As such, it has become, in Wettenhall's

(1973, p. 240) words, a 'leading example of bureaucratic organiz-ation about to be immortalized conceptually in the scholarship of the social sciences by the great German scholar Max Weber.'

The fact that the British administrative system has come close to Weber's ideal-type model of bureaucracy does not necessarily imply that it is ideal in the other sense of the term, or that it is not beset by significant problems. It has been criticized, for instance, on the lack of autonomy of its public officials, as compared to the French system (see Shonfield, 1971). This and similar criticisms, however, are beyond the scope of the present discussion.

Recent developments

In the 1960s further reforms were introduced into the British civil service. The foremost of these resulted from the Fulton Report of 1968, which rejected some of the principles outlined in the Northcote–Trevelyan Report of 1854. Among the changes was the establishment of a Civil Service Department (CSD) with central authority on recruitment, training, staffing and salaries. The Fulton Committee further suggested that ministers be entitled to give temporary posts to a small number of experts serving as their personal advisors. None of the changes, however, substantially affected the structure or functions of the bureaucracy; none of them re-ordered the political roles of civil servants in any but marginal ways, and the political neutrality of the service was not basically changed (Spann, 1973; Christoph, 1975).

Will the British civil service remain divorced from party politics? *The Economist* (23 October 1976) reports that, recently, left-wing leaders of the civil service unions have been pressuring the govern-ment to change the rules so as to enable civil servants at all levels to combine public service with party politics. However, the First Division Association, which represents the top 6,000 civil servants, says that its members do not want to be politically free. At any rate, our concern is not with the future, but with past developments.

The politicized administration and material inducements

Throughout the eighteenth century, the politicization of the administration served as a source of electoral manipulation, since patronage was used as one major inducement for political support. The key to electoral victory at that time lay in the pocket boroughs and the closed boroughs; the politician had to address himself to the individuals who possessed the first, or had political influence in the second. To secure the support of these individuals, the candidates handed out sinecures, pensions, etc.; in return, these persons saw to it that members of parliament who could be relied upon to support the government would be elected.

In addition, jobs in the public service were used as inducements for votes. At that time, the electorate was still very small: at the close of the eighteenth century, it comprised no more than 200,000–250,000 voters. Hence, individuals with the right to vote were given preference in appointments to the public service, and were then expected to cast their votes as their administrative chiefs directed. They thus played an important role in securing the return of government candidates: there were no less than seventy boroughs where the elections depended chiefly on the votes of revenue officers (Bridges, 1971).

In the nineteenth century, politicians still endeavoured to translate patronage into electoral advantage. The fact that members of the party in office were normally consulted whenever a local appointment was about to be made in their constituencies gave them a certain advantage over their opponents, who could only make promises.

Patronage apparently had the greatest electoral influence in the smaller (but not the smallest) boroughs. The counties and large boroughs were too extensive for patronage to have any considerable significance, and the very small pocket boroughs were too safe to waste it upon. Thus, as the smaller boroughs disappeared with the growth of national wealth and population and the passage of the Second and Third Electoral Reform Acts, the usefulness of patronage for electoral manipulation seems to have declined considerably. The only constituencies in which patronage could influence a really large number of voters were those in which government dockyards were situated; at mid-century, they numbered about a dozen, and in less than half of those could the government depend on success (Gwyn, 1962, ch. 4).

The value of patronage in elections was also depleted by the general growth of the electorate, because its usefulness depended on the balance of supply and demand. Even when the electorate was very small, the amount of patronage was never equal to the demands made on it – but it was still large enough to be useful. However, the increase in the electorate's size caused by the Reform Acts destroyed this balance, and with it the usefulness of patronage in electoral manipulation. 'Politicians continued to go through the ritual for another generation. But even they came to see that from the practical standpoint of political advantage it had become meaningless' (Parris, 1969, p. 71).

What strikes one about patronage is the fact that its decline was roughly simultaneous with the decline in electoral corruption involving material inducements. The period in which politics pervaded the British administration and patronage was at its peak was also the period in which electoral corruption had its heyday; the reforms in the civil service were roughly parallel in time to the reforms in the electoral system. This parallel development may be partly explained by the fact that patronage itself served as a source of electoral manipulation, especially in the eighteenth century, and this was evidently eliminated by administrative reform. But while patronage declined with electoral manipulation, its *usefulness* for such manipulation had declined much beforehand. How can this discrepancy be explained?

Moreover, we saw (chapter 2) that the most pronounced forms of electoral corruption in Britain were bribery and treating financed by the private resources of candidates and their sponsors (and, to a minor extent, by party funds) rather than government patronage. The fact that such bribery and treating declined together with politicization of the administration seems to be highly significant, and also calls for an explanation.

It seems that there is one explanation for both puzzling phenomena: the simultaneous developments in political administration and electoral corruption stem not only from the fact that the politicized administration supplied some resources for electoral manipulation. It has an additional source: the elites' codes of ethics in which both processes have been embedded. As long as the elite culture was such that it condoned particularism in the administration, it similarly condoned particularism in the handing out of material benefits; when the one came to be condemned, the other came to be condemned as well. Thus the era in which patronage in the administration became illegitimate is also the period in which political manipulation of material inducements to individuals became intolerable. Hence the almost simultaneous reforms in both areas.

The broader framework

The elite culture of political restraints

What, then, is the culture which inhibits politicization of the British civil service and electoral corruption alike, and how did it develop? Basically, it rests on certain rules of the game; on notions of propriety and fairness that pervade the role definitions of the British elites in both the civil service and the political level which controls that service. These notions of propriety include the principles of self-restraint and objectivity. For political neutrality to work, not only civil servants must practice self-restraint; politicians must do so as well. As Sisson (1971, p. 451) put it: the British administration enjoys an extraordinary degree of freedom from political intrusion 'because politicians accept constitutional limitation of their field of influence in a manner which is by no means to be taken for granted in countries outside Britain.'

Accordingly, the rule that governments should not interfere with the impartiality of the public service, and should not show party bias in making appointments, is invariably accepted. The adherence to these rules of the game by the political and administrative elites implies that a party forced into opposition can rest secure in the knowledge that its chances of shaping public opinion and winning the next election are not likely to be biased by government and administrative action. This knowledge makes it easy for the defeated party to accept its role as the 'loyal opposition', and to abide by the same rules and tradition when it itself comes to power (Birch, 1973, ch. 16).

Structural differentiation

How can this tradition be explained? According to Huntington (1968), developments in Britain's public administration should be seen as part of a wider trend of differentiation in governmental institutions that took place in Britain (and in Europe in general) throughout the process of modernization.

In medieval and Tudor England, the differentiation of government functions was not very advanced. A single institution often exercised many functions, and a single function was often dispersed among several institutions. Parliament, Crown, judicature and other institutions each performed many functions which partly overlapped; this tended to equalize power among the institutions. In the seventeenth and eighteenth centuries British government moved toward a concentration of power and a differentiation of functions. Executive, legislature and judicature evolved from a common origin and adapted themselves to specific purposes, thus making the British government more effective than would otherwise have been the case.

For instance, no clear distinction existed between legislation and judicature in medieval and Tudor government. Up to the beginning of the seventeenth century, parliament was viewed as a court, among other things. The courts, in turn, were much more than judicial tribunals; they were regarded as possessing political roles as well. Tudor and early Stuart courts used the common law to control acts of parliament. These actions did not represent a conscious doctrine of judicial review so much as they represented the fusion of legislative and judicial roles. This fusion disappeared in the seventeenth century, with the development of a new doctrine of parliamentary supremacy; from then on, judges could no longer oppose points of sovereignty. By the eighteenth century, no court could declare invalid an Act of parliament – however unreasonable it might be.

In another sense, the politicization of the judiciary continued into the nineteenth century as well;[1] the appointment of judges was still partly by political criteria. Political activity such as membership in parliament was considered to be a valuable experience for High Court judges. In the appointment of such judges by the Lord Chancellor, there was a consciousness of their political alliances to a degree that would be inconceivable today. Such politicization thus, is definitely in the past. Political appointments gradually declined until the new, neutral pattern was finally consolidated after the Second World War. Today, appointments are entirely unpolitical and free of any but objective considerations.

Can present-day British Supreme Court judges influence politics, even though they are not politically appointed? The answer is a qualified no, in the sense that they are not asked the same questions as are their American counterparts (see next chapter). For instance, they are not called upon to decide on desegregation, busing and the like. Nevertheless, even other types of litigation sometimes have ramifications for politics in the broadest sense of the term. For instance, since there is so much state control of the economy, litigation between citizens and the government sometimes results in court decisions that have an impact on the welfare of large numbers of citizens and on the government itself. But party politics, as a rule, do not affect judgments in these areas. In fact, only one Supreme Court judgment in recent years was thought to have ben influenced by partisan sympathies. So, although the judiciary is not completely divorced from politics in general, its separation from party politics is virtually total.

Another type of differentiation, Huntington points out, was that of the military institutions from other institutions of government. This was reflected in the creation of a professional non-political standing army, which dates from the restoration of 1660. Yet another differentiation was that between the Crown and party politics, which began at the end of the eighteenth century; this process was closely related to the separation of administration from politics. Parris (1969, ch. 1) claims that one of the main factors in this separation was the drive to reduce the influence of the Crown in politics – an influence which many felt had harmful effects on the system. For example, members of parliament were often rewarded for their faithful support of the Crown with offices for themselves or their dependents. Hence, to diminish the influence of the Crown, it was necessary to reduce (or even eliminate completely) the number of offices that were compatible with a seat in parliament. It was further necessary to diminish or abolish the patronage at the disposal of the Crown; the reduction in political appointments was partly based on this motive.

It is in this manner that the depoliticization of the administration, and the ethics of self-restraint on which it depended, were bound up with a wider trend of differentiation which characterized the British scene. This trend was much less pronounced in the American system, whose analysis is our next concern.

8 Administrative power in the United States: the partial decline of political involvement

In certain periods, the American public service has been highly politicized. Although lately it has been based more on merit, it has not attained (and perhaps was not meant to attain) the political neutrality of its British counterpart.

The age of political pervasiveness

When the American public administration was created in 1789–92, the penetration of party politics was not as deep as in Britain at the time. Political neutrality was not institutionalized, but neither was the administration hindered by a legacy of politicization, as was Britain. Another contrast with Britain was that the functioning of the administration did not depend on the support of the legislature (because the president was practically irremovable). Consequently, patronage aimed at securing such support was not as widespread as in Britain (Finer, 1952).

However, the American system failed to follow up its initial advantage, and did not keep pace with British administrative reforms. From 1801 until the beginning of the twentieth century, the American system moved no further towards political neutrality; on the contrary, it tended to move in the opposite direction – eventually taking the form of the now famous patronage system.

This system emerged gradually; no single administration may be held responsible for its development; it gained momentum in the late 1820s and 1830s, when many federal employees were spending more time on partisan matters than on administraive pursuits. When President Jackson took office in 1829, he found many federal offices occupied by political opponents. He removed quite a number of them and replaced them by political supporters. From then until the Civil War, the system of political appointments flourished. The most striking example was Lincoln's Republican Party of 1860, where occupants of some 1,200 of the 1,500 available posts were replaced by party faithfuls (Fish, 1900; Heard, 1960).

Some reforms were attempted around the time of the Civil War and in the two decades following it. Acts of 1853 and 1855 established 'pass' examinations which provided that appointees must pass a departmental test before taking office. However, these examinations were non-competitive and unstandardized; competitive examinations open to all were experimented with in 1872, but were not permanently established until 1883.

The Pendleton Act of 1883 provided for competitive examinations, for 10–12 per cent of federal employees and for a civil service commission with some authority over recruitment. Discrimination for political reasons was forbidden. Appointments continued to be a function of the president or the department head, but his choice was limited to those who ranked in the top four on the list of eligibles prepared by the commission. The Act left it up to the president and congress to extend the merit system to other employees (Ferguson and McHenry, 1950, ch. 22).

About half of the States followed the federal government in adopting civil service systems, but these did not necessarily ensure political neutrality. Even less progress was made on the county and civil levels; so, although the system of political appointments shrank (especially on the federal level), it was not eliminated.

While the patronage system in Britain gradually withered away throughout the second half of the nineteenth century, and was practically non-existent in the twentieth, it was still in existence in America at the beginning of the twentieth century, and indeed, reached prodigious levels at that time. For instance, it had been reported that 60 per cent of the party precinct captains in Chicago held municipal jobs in 1928, and almost 50 per cent did so in 1936 (Gosnell, 1937). This situation was not peculiar to Chicago; Gosnell cites comparable data from Philadelphia. Also, various studies conducted at the time show that in Pittsburgh, 73 per cent of the male Democratic committeemen, and 24 per cent of the male Republican committeemen, held public posts; in upstate New York cities, 19 per cent of all committeemen were on the public payroll; in Albany, 35 per cent of the Democratic committeemen were also public officials, and in Syracuse and Auburn, the percentage was 28 (Key, 1964, p. 337). In New York city, as late as the 1930s, the total annual pay for posts exempt from civil service regulations (that is – for political jobs) exceeded 7 million dollars.

According to Key (ch. 13), the politicization of the bureaucracy

135

has been a constant source of pressure and cross-pressure on presidents, department heads, governors, and others in executive positions – so much so, in fact, that a system had to be institutionalized to allocate patronage. Since the party organizations consisted of loosely linked centres of power, the jobs had to be distributed according to the strength of each centre. Ordinarily the chairman of the national committee of the president's party has controlled the distribution of patronage. Also, by custom, certain types of patronage have been assigned to senators in their States and to representatives in their districts. In those states and districts represented in congress by the minority party, the national committee has most often made appointment recommendations.

For top-level posts, the president himself has usually enjoyed some discretion. For less important posts, the power of appointment has customarily lain in the lower levels of the party organization. State and city patronage has varied according to the nature of the party organization. In a State or city with an atomized party, the patronage of each department or agency has generally been used to strengthen the personal following of the head of that agency. In more unified organizations, the tendency has been to bring all patronage into a single pool, and to develop a systematic procedure for allocating it among the principal party functionaries. All in all, concludes Key, although the system came to be fairly well institutionalized, it has not been free of disputes over who gets what.

The partial decline of political pervasiveness

Over the years, the party patronage system has met increasing opposition from people or groups affected by it, and from public opinion in general. Consequently, the civil service reforms begun in the later part of the nineteenth century were expanded by legislative acts of 1907, 1939 and 1940. Under these new reforms, the recruiting, examination and selection of employees were to be conducted largely by the operating agencies (the departments), subject to uniform employment standards to be determined by the civil service commission.

But, as Epstein (1967, ch. 5) points out, by the time these attempts at political neutralization of the public service got under way, politicians, including party bosses and their machines, were deriving so much benefit from government patronage that the vested interest in maintaining the system was much stronger than in Britain. Civil service reforms had to overcome this vested interest, and victory was by no means complete.

The competitive merit system made gradual headway. In 1883, only 10.5 per cent of all federal executive employees had been included in the classified service; by 1940, some 72 per cent were covered. The positions in the classified system were now filled from lists of persons who had passed formal, written examinations. But although the merit system was greatly expanded, 25 per cent of the civil servants (approximately half a million) were still outside its boundaries in 1950 (Ferguson and McHenry, 1950, ch. 22).

In the 1950s, Sorauf (1960) writes, the merit system was further expanded as political appointments were adversely affected by public opinion. Patronage was losing its respectability; for many people, its ethics no longer seemed to be a reasonable ingredient of politics, and it was increasingly considered to be at odds with the civil virtues instilled by public education. Patronage thus became increasingly devalued as a political currency. Also, as Key (1964, p. 359) remarks, the rise of professionalism and the increasing reliance on technical personnel all took their toll. Thus Sorauf claims (p. 28), 'the movement to instal merit systems in place of the older patronage is well on its way to full victory.'

In the 1950s, however, this victory had not yet been attained. Although the system of political appointments had been considerably limited, it had not disappeared – and in some places it still existed unchallenged. It persisted to the greatest extent as the local level, and to a somewhat lesser extent at the State level. But even federal patronage had not disappeared. Indeed Mills (1959, ch. 10) maintains, that the Eisenhower Administration declassified about 134,000 civil service positions and forced many thousands of other position holders to resign on the grounds that they were 'security risks' – thus opening new vistas for patronage.

Sorauf himself reports that at the beginning of the 1950s, patronage was still extensive in Pennsylvania. The State's civil service system covered only 20 per cent or so of its employees. The great majority of the State's administrative and clerical force, as well as field employees in highways, forestry and the like, were still politically appointed. Even at the end of the 1950s, some 50,000 positions in the Pennsylvania State administration could still be used as patronage appointments (Sorauf, 1956, 1960). Similarly, Moynihan and Wilson (1966) report that in New York State in the years 1955–9 (under Governor Harriman), 62 per cent of all appointments in the State administration were political appointments sponsored by the Democratic Party – and another 12 per cent were cleared by the party.

Summing up the situation for the late 1950s, Sorauf (1960, p. 30) states: 'There remain States where merit systems have made few inroads into patronage and where large numbers of positions remain at least technically available for distribution by the victorious.' It has been estimated that at that time only slightly over half of the States had attained relatively complete merit systems operated by a central personnel agency and applying to most employees; and only in a few States, were all employees covered by a merit system (Heard, 1960).

In the 1960s, too, the situation differed widely among States and localities. Some States had civil services that served loyally and impartially whatever party was in power; other States had an almost complete turnover of employees (outside the federally protected departments) when a new party came into office.

Similar differences existed among cities. In a few cities, the number of patronage employees was very small. At the other extreme, almost the entire municipal service of some cities still consisted of persons who gained their positions through party channels and who devoted a portion of their time to party work (Key, 1964, ch. 13). As late as the 1960s, Chicago's politicians still had some 15,000 city and county jobs at their disposal and another 13,000 to 17,000 State jobs. Nor were Chicago and Illinois unique. Pennsylvania still had 50,000 patronage positions as late as 1962 (Epstein, 1967, ch. 5).

As a general trend, Sorauf (1960) notes, merit systems have made their greatest inroads in the well-paid, specialized positions where the need for expertise and training is greatest. The parties are left with the less-desirable, lower-paid positions. 'With continued economic prosperity and high levels of employment', he adds, 'the economic rewards of these jobs . . . are less appealing than formerly' (p. 30). It would seem to follow that in times of economic recession (such as the United States experienced in the early 1970s), these jobs might prove once more to be attractive.

In addition, a large segment at the top of the American bureaucracy is still filled by political appointments. Most persons who occupy these posts are not politicians in the ordinary sense, but persons of administrative experience or ability who have partisan commitments. Although in general, the proportion of political appointments in relation to non-political appointments has been decreasing, Brzezinsky and Huntington (1964, p. 171) note: 'The immense expansion of the federal bureaucracy has multiplied the number of "political offices" at its top.' They claim: "It is not inconceivable that a new type of American professional, bureaucratic politician may be emerging.'

In recent years, the role of the American public service has not been unequivocally clear as far as party politics is concerned. This is illustrated by the fact that the Nixon administration (perhaps more so than its recent predecessors) was able to put pressure on parts of the civil service in order to use it as an instrument for political advantage; it was apt to reward supporters and punish non-supporters by dismissal or demotion (White, 1975, ch. 5). As Lukas (1976, p. 19) noted:

> Although the Hatch Act prohibits federal civil service employees from taking part in partisan political efforts, all presidents have tried to make bureaucrats march to their political tune. But the Nixon effort was unusual both in its scope and in the fierce determination with which it was enforced.

Among other things, pressure was put on the Internal Revenue Service to bear down on people and organizations not politically congenial to the Nixon administration. For this purpose, a special committee (later named Special Service Staff) was set up in 1969; it was dismantled in 1973 after details of its operations came to light. As it turned out, the Internal Revenue Service was not as politically effective as had been expected – because, according to Nixon's men, it was dominated by Democrats (Lukas, 1976, ch. 2). Successful or not, this attempt to utilize the public service for partisan purposes shows that despite the diminution in political appointments, the ambivalent role of that service has not yet been resolved.

This ambiguity has been in evidence even more recently. The *Economist* (22 November 1976) reports that with President Carter's advent to office it was expected that in Washington alone 2,200 Republican appointees (whose posts were not protected by civil service regulations) would be jobless. On the other hand, the *Economist* (24 September 1977) reports that President Carter had made a firm campaign promise that political considerations would play no part in the appointment of attorney-generals where toughness and integrity are so important to the fight against crime and corruption. Despite these promises, political appointments of attorney-generals were still made.

Federal prosecutors are usually expected to offer their resignations when a new president takes office, so that he may choose successors from his own party. This time, several of these declined to resign, relying on Carter's campaign promise. Nevertheless, some were forced out of office; at least thirty-four new federal prosecutors were appointed, all of them Democrats. These in turn, have considerable discretion to choose the lawyers on their staffs. This, of course, is patronage as usual. On the other hand again, Senator Moynihan has refused to go along with this policy, requesting that three Republican prosecutors be retained in New York. So political appointments are not generally pervasive either and an unclear situation persists.

The politicized administration and material inducements

In America, as in Britain, the period of party-political penetration into the public administration coincided with that of the employment of material inducements in the electoral process. But while political appointments and electoral corruption were eliminated in the latter part of the nineteenth century in Britain, the practices were retained well into the twentieth century in America – and only a partial, roughly simultaneous decline in both was evident around the middle of the century. At present, both systems have this in common: although they have declined considerably, they have not been eliminated.

It is quite evident that bureaucratic politicization and material benefits have developed and partly declined along similar lines, because the bureaucracy has provided most of the resources required for these benefits. The positions available have served as rewards for party activists and supporters. Moreover, once the administration was manned (wholly or partly) by party-committed public servants, these could be of further service to the party by using the allocation of public works jobs as a political inducement.

However, as Moynihan and Wilson (1966) suggest, the 'function' of politicization of the public administration for electoral manipulation has not been primarily to win votes in return for jobs on the public payroll. There have been simply too few jobs and, since the introduction of mass suffrage, too many voters. Its contribution has been primarily to lay the basis for the spoils system.

In this system, a wide array of resources – ranging from favourable contracts for public works and business transactions to the actual misapplication of the law – has been employed by politically committed public servants to recruit party support and to penalize opposition. In recent years, the grossness of such spoils has been reduced, but the system itself has not been eliminated. Even in the 1960s, the system greatly enhanced the scope and effectiveness of the party machines; it was still very much in evidence during the Nixon administration (see Lukas, 1976, ch. 2).

The beneficiaries of the patronage and spoils systems have repaid the favours by contributing part of their salaries or profits to party funds. This has greatly enhanced the party's resources, and hence its ability to hand out additional benefits to voters. This practice flourished in the second quarter of the nineteenth century, reaching a peak in the years following the Civil War. Despite attempts at federal and State reforms in the last third of the century, it has been reported that at least 75 per cent of the money raised by the Republican Congressional Committee in 1878, came from federal office-holders; that 94 per cent of the city employees in Philadelphia

140

paid such assessments in 1913; and that in 1933, a substantial proportion of Republican funds in that city still came from levies on public employees (Heard, 1960, ch. 6).

By 1960, Heard reports, federal office-holders were no longer subject to systematic, blanket solicitation – but 'voluntary' contributions from government employees at all levels were still an important source of income for the parties. To keep within the law, solicitations among federal workers were conducted off the job and by persons outside the federal service. There were fewer restrictions in State and local governments, so the frequency of solicitation and compulsory giving has been greater than at the federal level. In a presidential election year, contributions of somewhere between 5 and 15 million dollars have probably been made by office holders at all levels of the United States government.

Beneficiaries of favours other than employment have not been backward in extending financial aid to their parties either; in fact, their contributions have exceeded those made by political appointees to the civil service. These beneficiaries include large-scale profiteers who have found it to their advantage to make large contributions, thus enhancing their parties' chances of retaining (or returning to) power (Heard, 1960, ch. 3). It is in this manner that the politicization of the administration has served as a basis for the thriving of party machines in which material inducements have played a major role.

The broader framework

The politicization of the American administration, in turn, may be explained by the notions of propriety prevalent among the American political and administrative elites and by the overall structure of the American institutions of government. In the British system, professional ethics of bureaucrats and self-imposed restraints of politicians serve as guidelines that safeguard the civil servants' political neutrality. But in America, no similar professional ethics have developed, and the elites' notions of propriety have not been clearly spelled out. This would explain why successively mounting pressure from public opinion has only led to piecemeal reforms: as the elites' notions of propriety have remained unclear, their actions have remained indecisive.

The elites' ambivalent notions, on their part, are related to the overall structure of the American institutions of government. In contrast to Britain, there is, in America, an incomplete differentiation between the party-political and non-political branches. It will be recalled that Huntington (1968) views such differentiation as a major element of political modernization. In America, he holds,

141

this process of modernization was never completed.

America was born with governmental institutions, norms and practices imported from sixteenth- and seventeenth-century Britain precisely at a time when they were being abandoned in their home country; in America, they took root and were retained to a marked degree. In Huntington's words (p. 98): 'The institutional framework established in 1787 has, in turn, changed remarkably little in 175 years . . . political modernization in America has thus been strongly attenuated and incomplete.' And again (p. 129): 'The United States thus combines the world's most modern society with one of the world's more antique polities.'

As a consequence, writes Huntington (p. 132), the present American governmental system can be properly understood only in the light of traditions which run back to seventeenth- and pre-seventeenth-century England. 'This combination of modern society and Tudor political institutions explains much that is otherwise perplexing about political ideas in America.'

The government of medieval and Tudor England it will be recalled, was a government of fused functions. Crown and other branches of government each fulfilled many roles. But in the seventeenth and eighteenth centuries, British government evolved towards a differentiation of functions; the mixture of party-political and non-partisan structures disappeared (see chapter 7). In America, by contrast, the fusion of functions was perpetuated. This pattern can be seen in the mixing of legislative and judicial functions in the same institutions, and in the incomplete separation of the judiciary and the police from party politics.

The judiciary and politics

Political influence has been uncommonly pervasive in the American judiciary, both in the selection of judges and in the extraordinarily wide policy-making functions of American courts. Federal judges have customarily been appointed, while judges in most States are elected. One might assume at first that the two systems are entirely different; actually, it has been observed that they are almost identical. In both, the judges are chosen largely by the party chieftains (Berle, 1962).

For federal judges (including Supreme Court judges), the practice has always been for the president to make the appointment with the advice and consent of the Senate; thus, individual senators are deeply involved in the appointment process. Also, it has become customary for the president to give his attorney-general the responsibility for advising him about judicial appointments. All these people are clearly motivated by political considerations.

It has become customary for the attorney-general to base his choice on the recommendations of his party's State chairmen, usually in conjunction with the party's district leaders and the party's senator (if any) from that State. Although the American Bar Association is also consulted on appointments, observers agree that the party leaders have the most influence on choices (Berle, 1962). Thus it is not surprising that between 1884 and 1941 over 80 per cent (and frequently over 90 per cent) of the appointees to federal judgeships were from the president's own party.

The political significance of the appointment process is somewhat attenuated by considerations of merit; someone who lacks the qualifications is not likely to be appointed. But among the objectively qualified, the politically faithful are given preference. Federal judges have tenure in office – which makes them potentially independent of their party obligations. But this does not alter the fact that the appointment of judges is largely a political process (Evans, 1962; Chase, 1972, ch. 1).

In the case of elective judgeships, the power has been in the same hands; the slates are drawn up by the party leaders; whose decisions are merely ratified by the voters. Consequently many (though not all) candidates are partisan. Judges have been nominated by special judicial district conventions, ostensibly designed to remove such appointments from direct political influence. In practice, however, a judicial convention consists of a slate of delegates put up by the party's district leaders. The electors have little say in the matter, since most districts are 'safe' for one party or the other. In such districts, the party leaders' approval is equivalent to nomination and election (Berle, 1962; Watson and Downing, 1969).

Throughout the first half of the twentieth century, various plans were developed to replace elections with non-partisan selection methods. A non-partisan court plan[1] was adopted by Missouri in 1940. Judicial reforms in other States were delayed by the Second World War, but picked up considerable momentum in the 1960s when they were introduced in a large number of States (Watson and Downing, 1969, Introduction).

Many have sought to depoliticize the process by setting up a special selection commission for federal judges. However, even on the State level 'there is good reason to believe that the merit plan is not all it is cracked up to be' (Chase, 1972, p. 203). According to Chase, the merit plan has been a clear improvement over the previous system – but even, as pioneered in Missouri, it has not eliminated politics. After this plan was introduced, rival Bar groups mounted campaigns to get their men elected to commissions which nominated candidates for the bench. These lawyers' elections have taken on many of the features of a general party system, supported by conflicting ideologies. Consequently, the merit plan has been less effective than expected because politics has pervaded even the American Bar Association.

Moreover, politics does not end with appointment or election. A judge has a considerable amount of patronage to distribute. In the federal courts, he can appoint trustees in bankruptcy, receivers, referees, and so forth. In the State courts, he can appoint special guardians and other court officers. Usually judges appoint people from their own party to these jobs, and civil service reforms have had little effect upon these practices (Berle, 1962; Schubert, 1974, ch. 1).

Political parties are vitally interested in the judiciary, not only as a source of patronage. Federal judges have maintained a high level of personal involvement with the party system at the local level, and have themselves been the political leaders of their communities (Schubert, 1974, ch. 1). This does not mean that judges are dishonest or consciously partisan in their verdicts. In fact, many observers consider the working of the system to be satisfactory or even excellent.

Nevertheless, this articulation of the judicial and party systems is significant in view of the political implications of many judicial decisions. Huntington (1968, ch. 2) points out that foreign observers since de Tocqueville have identified the immense political influence of the courts as one of the most astonishing and unique characteristics of American government. To this day, American courts are guided by questions of policy to an extent unknown now in England. Political parties have always battled over the judiciary – especially the federal courts – because party leaders recognize that it is a major instrument for controlling the substance of public policy (Schubert, 1974, ch. 1).

The policy-making role of the federal courts in interpreting national statutes has grown during the present century. Politically significant judicial decisions include such well-known examples as those in the areas of antitrust action, labour–management relations and desegration. While such decisions may not be consciously or explicitly partisan, they do reflect the judges' basic norms, values and political ideologies. Such political leanings of candidates for judgeships, in turn, carry great weight in their appointment.

The role of ideology can be traced in records of Supreme Court decisions, which have alternated between periods of conservatism and liberalism. These leanings have not always coincided with the ideology of the party in power, because justices appointed by previous presidents continued in office. But appointments made by any particular president have evidently been designed to increase the affinity between his own political leanings and those of the Supreme Court.

The police and politics

Party politics has also pervaded American police forces. Students of earlier police departments found them to be riddled with corruption and filled with political appointees. Corruption and politicization of the police usually went hand-in-hand: the police were used to help to fill the pockets of corrupt politicians. Although reforms have been introduced, many police departments are still held to be guilty of such misconduct. For instance, Bent (1974) holds, selection for the police force usually consists of written examinations, physical agility tests, background investigations and interviews. The interviews are used to screen out applicants with 'incompatible' (including politically incompatible) views, and create a bias in favour of applicants whose political attitudes match those that predominate in the force.

Authority over the police is usually placed with the city council and the city's executive. Bent claims that this has allowed the responsibility for the police to be mingled with the councilmen's interests in other matters, thereby encouraging corrupt political control and favouritism. In most cities with a mayor–council type of government, the mayor is the political authority with control over the police (including authority over appointments). As an elected official, the mayor must yield to various pressure groups for his political survival; hence, his appointments are often political. In fact, in the mayor–council type of city government it has mattered little whether supervision of the police is undertaken by the members of a council or by the city's executive head. In either instance, police administration has been subordinate to political and personal interests (Bent, 1974, p. 65).

The priority given to political interests by the mayor–council structure resulted in reforms such as the commission plan[2] and the city manager form[3] of local government. But police administration has not fared well under the commission plan. Although it initially gave hope for new improvements, it ultimately proved susceptible to political and corrupt exploitation.

The city manager form of government has been considered to be most ideally suited for the constitution of a politically neutral political force. However, this form of government is not widely practised in large cities where problems associated with urban life are most critical. 'Indeed', writes Bent (1974, p. 66), 'it is in the communities where law enforcement needs are most urgent that police administration is forced to submit to political priorities at the expense of public service.'

Political influence over the police has not declined: it has even been claimed (Eidenberg and Rigert, 1971) that it has been growing in recent years. In 1969, for instance, in several cities, the police force campaigned for or against the election of certain mayors. In one city (Minneapolis, Minnesota), 'the police not only had entered the political process . . . they had in a sense taken it over' (p. 291).

The causal chain

The politicized judiciary and police were part of the broader framework for the politicized administration from which party machines derived the benefits they handed out as political induce- ments to the public. The party machines, in turn, had a vested interest in the persistence of both a politicized administration and electoral corruption. The question, however, is: Was the politiciz- ation of the administration an outgrowth of the party machines which, in turn, had their origins in the poverty and disorientation of new immigrants as some observers (see chapter 6) have claimed?

I have attempted to show that this could not have been the case because the politicization of governmental structures i.e., the incomplete differentiation between party-political and non- partisan aspects of the American establishment – antedated the mass immigration from non-English-speaking countries and the poverty which supposedly explain this pattern. Indeed, this pattern is the outgrowth of an elite tradition which has its roots in the pre-reform British system, some of whose elements are crystallized and stabilized in the American constitution. Thus it can hardly be explained by twentieth-century immigration and poverty. This argument gains additional strength from the contrast between the American system and its counterpart in Australia.

9 Administrative power in Australia: the evolvement of political neutrality

The Australian public administration, like the British, now has a large degree of political neutrality – in contrast to when the States' administrations first came into being.

The age of politicization

The British administration of Australia was carried out by remnants of the corrupt civil and military administration of pre-reform Britain, and this pattern pressed its mark on the evolving Australian administrative structures. Five of the six Australian colonies became independent States in the middle of the nineteenth century in the same decade in which the Northcote–Trevelyan Report was submitted, but before the British system of separation between administration and politics was perfected.

Thus Australia inherited the pre-reform British administrative structures. The new states did not immediately introduce far-reaching changes, even though the system was resented by the population. Administrative structures and practices differed greatly from State to State, but all were permeated by political consider-ations, and in all of them the system encouraged direct political intervention in administrative matters. Only towards the end of the nineteenth century were the truly significant reforms introduced (Caiden, 1967, ch. 1; Wettenhall, 1973).

The politicization in the various States' administrations was most clearly evident in the area of political appointments. Observers agree that such appointments were not unusual, although there is no consensus on the dimensions and ramifications of this practice. Bland (1944, p. xi) states: 'There was merely an embryonic public service recruited by the normal processes of political patronage.' Other observers claim that patronage related to only a relatively small percentage of all appointments. Although politicians were constantly offering people jobs, it is quite possible that these were largely jobs that they would have obtained anyway.

New South Wales

The most extensive data available on this topic are in regard to New South Wales. Knight (1961) suggests that the public service was a haven for the friends, relatives and political supporters of ministers and department heads. Loveday (1959) reports that appointments were used by ministries in their struggle to retain a majority in the Legislative Assembly. A parliamentary leader developed and maintained support for his faction *inter alia* by finding posts in the public service for members of parliament's influential constituents, friends, or political supporters, or for the members of the Legislative Assembly themselves.

Between 1856 and 1870, Loveday writes, appointments to the public service were made by the governor upon the recommendation of a minister (before and after that period, applicants for vacancies were required to pass an examination). During those years, therefore, the minister had the disposal of patronage without the restriction of tests. However, Loveday shows that there were other types of restrictions. Appointments had to go through the governor and the executive council after having been considered by the cabinet. Such joint cabinet decisions must have limited the amount of patronage of a purely personal nature, even if they did not eliminate political appointments which benefited the faction as a whole.

There was, besides, a seniority system in promotions. A minister who wished to use patronage for political purposes had to take into account the seniority claims of current employees, as well as the desires of the departmental heads to maintain efficiency and discipline, and balance these against the political demands made on him. Assuming that somewhat more than half of the offices in a ministry were limited by seniority, technical qualifications or other requirements, it seems that each minister had about forty posts a year that he could use as a political tool.

According to Hawker (1971, ch. 5), the constitution prohibited members of the Assembly (except ministers) from accepting any office of profit or pension from the Crown; however, this did not apply to ex-members, or promises to sitting members. Offices of profit were hard to define in any case, especially where lawyers were concerned; the fees received by barristers from governments were sometimes substantial. The position of contractors to government institutions was uncertain, also. 'Offices of profit could not be defined exhaustively in advance, and neither, it seemed, could rules regulate the employment of ex-members' (p. 79). Members could, moreover, resign to accept positions in the civil service that had been promised to them when they were still in parliament. Between 1856 and 1890 about forty-five members of the Assembly (some 10 per cent of the total membership of the house in that period) accepted offices of profit of one sort or another from the Crown after leaving parliament.

Some members or ex-members accepted positions of a rather different kind – honorary positions, such as memberships on various committees which did not carry fees – but which were nevertheless sought after because they sometimes involved travelling and the payment of expenses, and always brought worth-while prestige.

Also in dispute were the ramifications of patronage for the quality of the public service. Knight (1961) suggests that in New South Wales, despite patronage, weight was also given to ability and qualifications – and the system did produce many able public servants. Loveday (1959) claims that men who entered the public service through political channels were no worse than other appointees. However, Caiden (1963) reports that a select committee in 1872 concluded that patronage had destroyed discipline in the civil service, and that applicants were of low calibre. Hawker (1971, ch. 5) similarly claims that patronage led to the recruitment of men without experience and of doubtful capacities at senior levels, which lowered the morale of long-serving officers and reduced the efficiency of the service.

As for its political role, although patronage was a valuable device for consolidating the strength of a ministry, it was not an unmixed blessing. In fact, ministers found it difficult to balance the various patronage claims against their rather limited resources, and increasingly tended to divest themselves of the bother.

Demands for reform also came from within the civil service itself, although public opinion was not greatly aroused. Newspapers of the time, such as the *Sydney Morning Herald*, opposed patronage, but admitted the right of a minister to consider his parliamentary interest and to give preference to his friends provided that the public was equally well served. It was not felt strongly that political appointments had prejudiced either the administration or the services it gave; all that was demanded was that patronage be confined to those persons who had evinced their fitness for office. It was felt that patronage was common to all political systems, and could not be abolished. If, in the absence of parties, government stability had to be secured by the use of patronage then that was the price that had to be paid (Loveday, 1959; Caiden, 1963).

However, because of pressures from ministries and from within the service itself, the Civil Service Act of 1884 provided for qualifying entrance examinations and a part-time Civil Service Board to arrange and supervise them. This was only a feeble attempt, since the Act applied to fewer than half of the public servants; even where it did apply, selection was not necessarily in order of merit (Knight, 1961). As Knight points out, a minister could choose any qualified applicant – so, unless a successful examinee could command some influence as well, it was quite possible that he would never be selected. Also, under section 31 of the Act, ministers could make temporary appointments without reference to the Civil Service Board;[1] this was an avenue for continuing ministerial patronage. From 1887 to 1893 no fewer than 1,544 temporary appointments were made over which the Board had no control.

The patronage exercised at the time by senior officials was almost as substantial as that of ministers. In 1894 the strength of the civil service[2] was 11,583, of whom 46 per cent were appointed by senior officials. Patronage, Knight reports, was apparently an important factor in promotion as well. For the bulk of the service, seniority was the ruling factor in promotion, but there were enough politically inspired promotions to cause considerable dissatisfaction among public servants.

The Civil Service Board set up in 1884 thus had little power as a controlling agency. With restricted jurisdiction and no real independence, there was little it could accomplish. In sum, the 1884 Act failed to achieve its purpose of excluding political influence from the public administration in New South Wales.

Queensland

The situation was not much different in Queensland. Caiden's (1963) analysis shows that in 1859, just before Queensland's separation from New South Wales, the system of patronage was not yet entrenched. Regulations enacted at the beginning of the 1860s provided for competitive examinations, so that appointments might go to people with individual merit rather than to those with political connections. Nevertheless, patronage became one of the prime sources of appointment to higher posts (see also Morrison, 1960). The Civil Service Act, which extended these regulations, did not achieve much; it was repealed in 1869, whereupon the practice of patronage continued unhampered.

In 1889, a Royal Commission reported that political influence was pervasive in making civil service appointments. In consequence, a new Civil Service Act was passed providing for a full-time Civil Service Board to overhaul the service and to see to it that appointments were made by merit. However, the Board was not beyond political influence itself, and did not achieve much success in ridding the service of such influence; it was abolished in 1901.

Victoria

Neither did Victoria differ greatly from the other States. General and administrative histories of this State all speak of the public service in the 1860s in most unflattering terms. It was reported that political appointments were rife. Although an extensive Civil Service Act of 1862 provided for the recruitment of large sectors of the service by qualifying examinations, and for advancement by merit, certain classes of officials were exempt from these requirements. Serle (1971, ch. 1) points out that there were loopholes in the Act, and ministers habitually appointed their sympathizers as supernumeraries to whom classification did not apply, and promoted them at whim. In any case, the Act was so largely circumvented that it became meaningless within a decade.

It became almost impossible to enter the service without help of a political patron; by 1883 there were at least twice as many supernumeraries as those who had entered in the standard manner. Clerks, policemen or railwaymen were appointed for no other reason than that they were friends, relatives or parliamentary supporters of the ministry of the day. Members of parliament were pestered by constant requests for patronage. The demand for secure public positions was enormous, for in the area of manual labour at least, most employment was temporary (see also Wettenhall, 1973).

Toward the end of the 1870s and in the 1880s, pressure mounted to remove the civil service from the sphere of politics, and to end the system of 'utilizing state patronage for the purpose of serving private ends and rewarding the blind attachment of political followers' (The *Age*, 27 July 1879, quoted by Caiden, 1963). The conditions of the railway department, where patronage was at its worst, alarmed the public the most. A series of railway accidents was attributed to the subordination of safety to political machinations over personnel and public opinion demanded that the management of the railways be placed in the hands of qualified and efficient men. A Civil Service Association was formed specifically to press public demands for reform.

In response, the Public Service Act of 1883 provided for a full-time Public Service Board to ensure appointments and promotions by merit and to eliminate patronage. Gradually, however, this Act, too, came to be ignored. Towards the turn of the century, the public

151

service of Victoria was still riddled with corruption, favouritism and political influence.

The smaller States

The smaller States – South Australia, Western Australia and Tasmania – were critical of the system prevailing in the other States, but did not improve on it much. The Tasmanian public service was no exception; in the main, Caiden (1963) claims, patronage determined appointments. As in other States, public opinion was uninterested unless stirred by public scandal, and the politicians enjoyed freedom in appointments as long as they were not embarrassed by public allegations of corruption. The Civil Service Act of 1900 provided for a Civil Service Board to administer examinations. Although it brought some semblance of order into the service, it did not greatly improve the situation as far as political appointments were concerned.

In South Australia, regulations issued in 1853 provided for a Board to examine candidates for the public service. Additional regulations issued in 1854 provided for the political neutrality of public servants. However, with the advent of responsible government, successive ministries ignored these regulations. In 1862, the government passed a special Act to validate the appointments it had made, and thereafter political patronage proceeded to entrench itself. The Civil Service Act of 1874 provided for appointment to permanent positions by examination, and for promotion by merit. But it left control of appointments in the hands of the government; thus it wrought little change in the political system, which apparently was maintained until the beginning of the twentieth century. In Western Australia, too, appointments were under ministerial control at that time – a practice that resulted in a long period of patronage which was not terminated until the beginning of the twentieth century (Crowley, 1960).

The age of reforms

Eventually the British administrative reforms had their echoes in Australia, and there was a vague search after alternative procedures. Towards the end of the century political influence came to be regarded as detrimental to the efficiency and morale of the public service and there developed the general belief in the necessity of separating recruitment and administration from political control. Although there were some lags between precept and practice, the States eventually moved towards a system of public service commissions (and later boards) to fashion the structure of the public service and act as watchdogs for the neutrality of appointments (Bland, 1944, Introduction; Wiltshire, 1974, ch. 11).

The new system was not introduced in the various States all at once. Knight (1961) reports that at the beginning of the 1890s, the system of political appointments in New South Wales came under strong attack and some far-reaching reforms were introduced. The Royal Commission on the Public Service in 1895 recommended the appointment of a Public Service Board, completely independent of political control, to be vested with powers of recruitment as well as general control over departmental organization. Accordingly, the Public Service Act of 1895 (re-enacted in 1902) provided such independent board control over the public service and especially over recruitment; it succeeded in eliminating party politics from a large section of the public administration. There is some evidence of contemporaries to support this analysis: the Webbs noted in their *Australian Diary of 1898* (1965, p. 30):

> It is surprising with such a franchise and complete public apathy that there is so little corruption in the American sense – selling franchises, taking bribes, removals from office and political appointments there is absolutely none at all.

However, as Bland (1932) shows, the Public Service Act of 1895 did not apply to certain corporate bodies such as the railways. Subsequently, several new departments were established and placed outside the control of the Public Service Board; in 1900 an increasing number of statutory corporations were created with exemptions from the Public Service Act, so that eventually over 70 per cent of the State's employees (many of them wage-earning employees) were beyond its control. Even within the public service proper, Bland claims, there were employees over whom the powers of the Board were only vaguely defined. Thus, various fields in the public service once more turned into hunting-grounds for politicians and members of parliament, who became employment brokers for their constituents. In their effort to live up to this role, the members plagued the ministers, who themselves were anxious to secure the members' co-operation. 'In this sense,' Bland (1932, p. 37) complained, 'political influence is all pervading.'

Nevertheless, Parker (1960), who wrote almost thirty years later, maintains that the practices of recruitment and promotion did not revert to pre-1895 standards. The very existence of the 1895 Act set a standard which was not easy to disregard. Politicians were now also willing to surrender patronage because, with the growth of the service, it had become too bothersome. So routine patronage had fallen into the hands of independent agencies who, on the whole, were also too busy to bother with it.

At the same time he agrees that a wide field of political appointments has opened to the governing boards. Most of the Board members have been specifically exempted from the provisions of the Public Service Act (even though their staff have not been) and this field has been fully exploited. Since 1941, Parker writes, there have been dozens of government appointments of men with no qualifications other than political, to corporations ranging from the Maritime Services Board down to local water boards and hospital boards. However, he emphasizes that these statutory offices constitute the only area in which political appointments still persist in New South Wales. Contrary to the American practice, there is no rotation of public servants following electoral victory (or defeat), and no group of public servants has aligned itself with a political party.

In Queensland, we learn from Morrison (1960), the beginning of a modern public service came in 1919; however, it was not until 1932 that an effort was made to close the door against patronage appointments. It was provided that all admissions to the public service must be recommended by the public service commissioner. Thereafter, entrance into the service was according to results of examinations.

The extent of party influence upon the present-day public service in Queensland is hard to assess. Crown employees are compelled to join a union, and the Public Service Union is affiliated to the Labor Party. However, no figures are available on the proportion of active Labor supporters in this union.

In Western Australia, the authority to make salaried appointments under the Public Service Act has been vested since 1904 in a public service commissioner. The establishment of this office clearly marked a change from ministerial to commissioner control of public servants, and ended the long period of political patronage (Crowley, 1960).

When the Commonwealth public service was created after federation in 1901, it strove for political neutrality from the beginning. The principles of the 1895 Act of New South Wales were incorporated into the Commonwealth Public Service Act of 1902. To avoid political influence, recruitment was by competitive examinations under the control of the Public Service Board, which served in the Commonwealth (as in the States) as the major mechanism against patronage.

Encel (1970, ch. 13) points out that promotion, too, has come to be, to a much greater extent than before, by objective criteria. In the Commonwealth, permanent heads of departments are in charge of promotions, but since 1945 such promotions may be appealed against by officers in the public service who believe they are better qualified. Promotions are provisional until any such appeals have been heard by an appeals committee that includes a staff representative. In the Commonwealth service, 21.9 per cent of provisional promotions were appealed against in 1970. In the States, the Public Service Board is the promoting authority, but its formal role varies. The departmental head may do the recommending with an appeal to the Board; the Board itself may nominate, with an appeal to some special tribunal, or there may be another variant of this procedure.

Political neutrality: the situation today

Does all this mean that the present Australian public service is politically neutral – that is, free from partisan consideration – both in appointment and promotions and in the shaping of its policies? Observers agree that the above procedures ensure that both appointments and promotions are generally made on criteria of merit more than in many other bureaucracies. Heads of departments and other powerful bureaucrats are still motivated to promote those loyal to themselves in order to solidify their power. But the appeals system adopted in the Commonwealth public service certainly imparts a certain caution to promoting authorities, and leads to greater objectivity than would otherwise be the case. The Public Service Board system adopted by the States is also designed to maximize objectivity. Observers further agree that great pains are taken to remove partisan-political interference (see, for instance, Caiden, 1967, ch. 2, and Wiltshire, 1974, ch. 11).

Spann (1973, p. 590) concurs that, as a rule, politicians cannot use posts in the administration as political rewards, and that political patronage 'is not a serious problem in Australia, though there are a few cases, especially on statutory boards of "political" appointments to administrative jobs'. Public officials, once recruited, are permanent; this means that a new party in power does not, on the whole, ease its passasge by introducing its supporters into the public service. Nevertheless it is recognized that a few of the very top public servants, such as heads of departments and private secretaries to ministers, have frequently been appointed through political influence (see, as an illustration, Wiltshire, 1974, ch. 11).

It has been reported, for instance, that the former Liberal government made some political appointments to diplomatic posts; and when Labor came into power in 1972, it made what the *Sydney Morning Herald* (22 November 1976) termed 'blatant' political appointments by introducing three former private secretaries to Mr Whitlam as permanent heads of government departments. This, perhaps, is the reason why many influential people in Australia feel that the public service is becoming more politicized. In a research project on the Australian elite conducted by Dr John Higley of the Australian National University, respondents[3] were asked about the political neutrality of the public service; 72 per cent of these respondents felt that this neutrality was decreasing.

However, in fact, the dimensions of political appointments are very modest indeed compared with what takes place in Israel (see below). Even so, the practice caused an uproar and determined opposition on the part of the professional bureaucrats – who, backed up by powerful public service unions, were intent on preserving their domain from political intrusion.

These appointments have also antagonized public opinion. As the *Sydney Morning Herald* (22 November 1976) put it: 'Legislation to control such a situation has obviously become necessary.' And, in fact, legislation has been introduced according to which an incoming government will be allowed to choose department heads from outside the professional public service, but such appointments will not be permanent, being limited to a maximum of five years. Such legislation is obviously a compromise; even so, it will severely circumscribe political appointments. At any rate our concern is not with the future, but the past – and it is clear that the bulk of public service appointments have been by merit rather than political considerations.

The Australian system of administration also implies a division between bureaucratic and political careers; no one may combine the two. At the same time the lines drawn between the public service and political activity are not as strict as they are in Britain. Officers may stand for election but have to step down temporarily to do so. Public servants may hold political offices at local government levels, but permission for such activity may be withheld if the duties of the political office encroach upon official duties. Since 1903, officers in the Commonwealth have been allowed to take part in political activities under certain conditions; in consequence, fears have arisen that this would be only a short step from a politicized public service. When public servants are politically active, it was felt, they may form political connections which may subsequently assist in their promotions. In practice, however, the political activities of Commonwealth officers have had little impact on the pattern of neutrality. Not many officials have availed themselves of their political rights, and the great majority of these have not been members of the administrative elite (Caiden, 1967, ch. 16). Moreover, officers who have been politically active (and provided they have not let this activity interfere with their administrative work) have usually not been penalized with the advent of an opposing government.

In line with this general pattern of neutrality, incumbent

governments have not been able to utilize the public service for their own political purposes to anything like the same extent as has occurred in the United States. With approaching elections, ministers may expect their departments to issue publications presenting the department's achievements in a favourable light. But they certainly cannot get public servants to work for them at elections, neither can they utilize the tax authority for political purposes as has been done in the United States (see chapter 8). In fact, the taxation department is a separate statutory authority, insulated from the rest of the bureaucracy and, therefore, relatively immune to political pressures.[4]

It would be fruitless to suppose that public servants, even if not active in politics or utilized for political purposes, are devoid of values or political persuasions. It would also be incorrect to suppose that the administration's policies which they help to shape and implement have no political implications. But a deliberate attempt is made to abstain from political partisanship. Although the bureaucracy has a potentially powerful political influence, it exercises self-restraint which prevents it from exploiting this influence in the service of partisan interests. Instead, it usually extends its loyalty to the prevailing regime, whatever its political composition (Caiden, 1967, chs 2 and 3).

When Labor came into power in 1972 after more than twenty years of Liberal (i.e. Conservative) rule, it was not surprisingly suspicious of the administration and, in fact, some difficulties in co-operation may have developed. But these were probably due to public servants' habits of thought more than to their political commitments. In any event, Spann (1973) asserts that these problems were not great, and that on the whole the Labor governments have found it easy to work with officials inherited from their non-Labor predecessors. From this it may be concluded that the retained officials did not hold partisan anti-Labor commitments – at least as far as the shaping of their official policies was concerned. In the matter of policy, then, no less than in appointments and promotions, the Australian public administration has been largely free from partisan intrusion.

Like its British counterpart, therefore, it has been viewed as approaching Weber's ideal-type model of bureaucracy. Yet this does not mean that it is considered to be flawless; in fact, to the extent that it approaches the Weberian model it may be open to all the criticisms that have been levelled at such structures (see, for instance, Merton, 1957b). However, political partisanship is not one of them.

It has been argued that, in some ways, a politically neutral bureaucracy falls short of a politically committed one. For instance, it has been claimed that public servants who share the political convictions of their ministers will be much more enthusiastic and adept in implementing their policies. It has also been claimed that at present senior officials are insensitive to the objectives of the government and inclined to resist, at least passively, when these objectives conflict with their own assessment of the public interest (Coombs et al., 1976, ch. 2). It has further been alleged that people of intelligence and imagination usually have firm political opinions, and that such people will steer clear of occupations which discourage personal self-expression (Wiltshire, 1974, ch. 11).

It has by no means been established, though, that the level of intelligence in the public service has been lowered by this factor (if it exists) to a greater extent than it has been raised by recruitment by merit. In any case it is not my purpose to offer a general evaluation of the two patterns of administration – the 'politocracy' vs. the 'meritocracy' – but merely to point out the connections between these patterns and electoral manipulation of material inducements.

The politicized administration and material inducements

In Australia, as in Britain, the period of political influence over the bureaucracy coincided with the period in which electoral manipulation included material inducements; the gradual elimination of political influence over the bureaucracy roughly coincided with the elimination of such manipulation (see chapter 4). This parallelism (which is characteristic of other countries as well) demonstrates that the two practices are closely related. It was pointed out in chapter 6 that, in general, there may be a threefold relationship between politicization of the bureaucracy and the political manipulation of material inducements: in the first place, some of the material inducements offered in return for political support are usually administrative appointments (patronage). To this extent, the two variables are partly co-terminous. Second, a politicized bureaucracy may supply the resources for the allocation of other benefits in return for political support (the spoils system). Third, the politicized bureaucracy and the employment of material inducements for political purposes both emanate from a common elite culture which condones (or conversely condemns) both.

In Australia the first type of connection was evident throughout the latter part of the nineteenth century, but the second one was not, as no real spoils system seems to have developed. The third connection seems to be the most significant; the funds utilized for the treating and cash-bribing of voters mostly did not emanate from the public administration but rather from the private pockets of wealthy politicians (see chapter 4). Yet this practice, too, declined at approximately the same time as the public administration was de-politicized. It must be concluded, then, that this is due to the common ethical framework of both patterns. As long as the prevailing codes of ethics among the elites condoned the allocation of administrative posts by political criteria, they also accepted the allocation of other pecuniary rewards by such criteria; as soon as the first of these practices came to be considered as illegitimate, the second was no longer seen as legitimate either.

The broader framework

The ethics of neutrality and objectivity

The source of the de-politicization of the Australian bureaucracy is thus to be sought in the evolvement of certain notions of propriety among those who shaped the bureaucracy: the political and the administrative elites. Once established, a system of political neutrality in the bureaucracy is, to a certain extent, self-perpetuating. Just as a politically committed bureaucracy serves the vested interests of politicians, a politically neutral bureaucracy serves the vested interests of professional bureaucrats. These professionals want to keep their power from being usurped by politicians – just as in another system, politicians are jealous of their power in utilizing the bureaucracy for political purposes. But these vested interests cannot explain how and why the system evolved in the first place, and why, in Australia (in contrast to America, for instance) the vested interests of bureaucrats override those of politicians. Only the evolving norms of political neutrality which both elites held in common can supply that explanation.

It seems clear that legislation was a factor as well, but legislation was initially, blatantly ineffective. Only when legislation came to be embedded in the appropriate codes of professional ethics could it be efficacious. Once established and institutionalized, observers agree, such oral codes and traditions have done more to maintain the system than has formal legislation. 'There are no manuals or textbooks, no notices on the wall about correct behaviour. Yet the oral law is transmitted from person to person, and irrespective of the written law, everybody is expected to obey the higher natural law of tradition, custom and expectation . . . which is a firm link, binding career public servants to their trade' (Caiden, 1967, p. 382). 'The written law falls short, and in-service penalties, such as bars to promotion, ostracism, and so forth . . . may be more effective sanctions than those provided by law" (p. 383; see also Wiltshire, 1974, ch. 2).

Spann (1973) offers a similar analysis. The principle of political neutrality is not fully defined in statutes and regulations, neither could it be effectively enforced by outside sanctions, since there are too many subtle ways of evading them. Rather, it is part of a code of conduct to which public servants are socialized and which is reinforced by self-selection. This code is part of the Australian 'spirit of bureaucracy', part of the general Australian style of thinking about the world, part of those implied understandings that form the basis of the Australian culture.

Moreover, in the civil service code of ethics, political neutrality is closey connected to a general trend toward objectivity. Wiltshire, for instance, maintains that the foremost consideration in the introduction of political neutrality has been the desire to ensure equal treatment of all citizens by public servants. One of the basic Australian norms is that 'public servants do not discriminate in favour of, or against, any citizen or group of citizens for reasons other than those laid down by law' (Wiltshire, 1974, p. 170; see also Caiden, 1967, p. 390). While it is hard to accept the notion that favouritism never occurs, greater efforts are clearly made to eliminate such occurrences, than is the case in most other countries. In Spann's words (1973, p. 586): 'The desire to avoid charges of favouritism and inconsistency is very strong in government. It accounts for much of its heavy reliance on rules and precedents and its so-called "red tape".' This is, of course, far removed from the political culture prevailing in the Israeli bureaucracy for instance. In this country too, charges of red tape have been levelled at the public administration – but so far, no one has claimed that this is due to a marked tendency to rule out favouritism (see the next chapter).

Norms calling for political neutrality and for the elimination of favouritism, also referred to as the tendency to objectivity, or the 'spirit of bureaucracy', are not contained merely in the Australian bureaucracy itself; they branch out into other institutional areas as well. This is what Encel (1970, ch. 5) has termed the 'bureaucratic ascendency'. Davies (1964) (as quoted by Encel) goes as far as to claim that the characteristic talent which Australians possess is their talent for bureaucracy, and that this gift is exercised on a massive scale not only in the bureaucracy proper, but also in various other spheres of government, in the economy and in various other institutions.

The arbitral principle

This stress on codes of neutrality and objectivity may also be seen as a tendency in the Australian governmental system, towards universalism, towards separating the allocation of resources from particularist (political and personal) interests. In line with this, Parker

160

(1968) shows a widespread Australian tendency to transmute power conflicts into arbitration processes. Instead of allowing allocative decisions to depend merely on the relative power of competing interest groups, the system seeks adjudication by committees, boards, tribunals and similar quasi-judicial bodies that – presumably – have no stakes in the outcomes of these struggles.

Frequently, judges or retiring public servants are appointed to head such bodies; they are not directly involved, and are considered to be politically independent. While it is recognized that these people hold political views and cannot possibly represent the embodiment of objectivity, they are considered to be as close to objectivity as is humanly possible. The arbitral principle and the tendency to put allocative decisions outside the scope of political and personal influence undoubtedly had its imperfections.[5] But it has apparently been carried further in Australia than in any other country (with the possible exception of New Zealand). Encel (1970, p. 246) writes:

> there is no real counterpart to the remarkable scope of the arbitral principle in Australia, and the extent to which its operation supersedes both the discretionary powers of high officials and the authority of a central controlling agency . . .

In the same vein Parker (1968, p. 27) writes:

> I am not here saying that all these attempts to substitute arbitral institutions for a free play of power are unique in Australia; only that they have been carried further here than in most other societies. I am not saying that they wholly succeed in neutralizing the relevant conflicts of interest or in supplanting the arbitrament of power. But I would claim that they appreciably reduce (or at any rate modify) the role of [political] power in this society . . . Let us make all allowances for the possibility of certain diluted pressures being applied to those bureaucratic institutions . . . The fact remains that, to an appreciable degree, their allocative function takes the form of independent analysis and reasoning, and to this extent displaces the trail of power that would otherwise engage the embattled interests . . .

The Australian arbitration system operates in a wide range of spheres. In the industrial field, compulsory arbitration by quasi-judicial tribunals has replaced collective bargaining as the main means of determining wages and salaries.[6] The Industrial Assistance Commission in charge of tariffs and duties is meant to extricate this sphere from political manipulation.[7] Another example is the Fox Commission on the mining and exporting of uranium, which recently submitted its recommendations to the government.

Within the political apparatus itself there is the redistribution of constituency boundaries (at intervals provided by statute). In most electoral systems this redistribution has been entrusted to statutory commissions which include a public servant and a judicial officer. While this device may not have eliminated bias, it has doubtlessly cut it down.[8] The distribution of special financial assistance among the needier State governments is, by convention, according to the recommendations of a politically independent Commonwealth Grants Commission which, since 1933, has superseded the previous process of bargaining between the governments concerned (see Parker, 1968). An Administrative Appeals Tribunal has also recently emerged (under the presidency of a judge) as an important intermediary between the public, politicians and special interests. Many policy decisions and actions by the bureaucracy stand in danger of reversal by this Tribunal. The implications of the Tribunal's work are beginning to percolate through the bureaucracy and the business of the Tribunal is mounting rapidly.[9]

Several more instances of this type could be cited; I would like to conclude, however, with the recent changes in the administration of broadcasting. At the time of the Whitlam government, plans were being made to replace the existent Broadcasting Control Board with two bodies. One would be quasi-judicial, to consider applications for licences (the aim being to extricate the government from political pressures in this matter). The second would advise on technical matters and planning proposals. The Fraser government decided on a similar division of functions; it also decided to reshape the Australian Broadcasting Commission.

Recently it has been claimed that there is a government conspiracy to pack the newly shaped Broadcasting Commission with government supporters in order to destroy its independence. It is apparently a widespread belief that there is some political interference in the Commission. On this allegation, the *Sydney Morning Herald* (10 November 1976) had this to say:

> This is wild talk, considering that the government has not yet announced the membership of the new Commission. Even then, such charges will be unconvincing until the new body can be seen, in its performance, to be the government's puppet. If that were to become clear, then who doubts that public outrage would quickly compel the government to think again?

It is hard to imagine a similar paragraph in an Israeli newspaper.

Structural differentiation

The arbitral principle – basically an unusually pervasive attempt to separate allocation of resources from party politics – is further connected with a tendency toward differentiation between party politics and the non-partisan spheres of the institutions of government, in particular the judiciary, the police and the military. The judiciary, for one, has been non-political from the very beginning.[10] Up to the 1850s judiciary appointments were determined from London and judges were therefore independent not only of local politics but of the local judiciary as well. Later on, there were no elections of judges as in the United States, and appointments, on the whole, were not political either. While one can point to certain phenomena such as moving attorneys to the bench, this did not leave any flavour of political overtones.

After the establishment of the Commonwealth, chief justices were men who had previously been politicians and even cabinet ministers, but it was expected that politicians would sever their political ties upon being appointed to the bench. In 1931 some Labor government judicial appointments were criticized, especially the appointment of politicians to the High Court. This was on account of the fact that most lawyers are usually Conservatives. Appointment of Conservatives to the bench go unnoticed, whereas appointments of differently-minded people stand out and are therefore criticized as 'political'. In any event, despite judges' ideological affinities, one cannot point to political decisions or verdicts. As there is no Bill of rights, judges can hardly project their political ideologies into their decisions, such decisions being based strictly on legal precedent.

The Australian police force has – at times – been charged with corruption such as payoffs by non-violent but illegal operators. Sometimes the party that was out of office would attack this, but things would not be changed basically when it itself came to office. Sometimes such corruption had some indirect political connotations as when police payoffs gave working-class people a chance of illegal gambling (whereas middle-class people could gamble in the more expensive legal establishments). But it is difficult to point to long-term trends of this nature. Attempts have been made by politicians to gain control of the police, but these have been actively and successfully resisted.[11]

There is also a religious aspect to this. The police force used to be divided between Protestant and Catholic groups; at certain times – e.g., after the First World War – the Labor Party supporters were disproportionately Catholic. So there was a faction in the police force that was sympathetic to Labor and another that was not. However, by the 1930s, these phenomena were becoming diluted; the issue was revived in the 1950s and 1960s, but nothing definite was established.

No explicit political slant is evident in the military, either. Until the First World War, senior officers were appointed from Britain and the policies were part of a wider imperial system – so no local politics were involved. Later on (and at present), officers have been selected by competitive examinations and not by political criteria. Most of them are not Labor sympathizers and tend to vote for Labor's opponents. But this is not because they have been deliberately selected in this manner; rather, going into the army is a matter of family (and geographical) tradition: many recruits come from well-to-do rural families and especially from Queensland where a relatively greater proportion of the population is rural. There are a number of senior officers who, upon retirement, have become politically active. Some have stood for parliament for the coalition parties – but there are also a few who have stood for the Labor Party. In any case there is no political activity by officers in active service, so the armed forces may be regarded as exempt from party politics.

In sum, the de-politicization of the Australian bureaucracy may be explained by the development of certain elite codes of ethics, specifically the notions of neutrality and objectivity. These codes have been employed not only in the administration proper but in various governmental and other institutional spheres as expressed in the pervasive arbitral principle; they have also been closely connected with tendencies to differentiate between political and non-political aspects of the institutions of government. But where does this stress on neutrality and objectivity, the pervasiveness of the arbitral principle, stem from?

The origins of the system

The Australian bureaucracy and institutions of government have been modelled on the British ones, accepting their ethics, their basic organizational principles and styles of work (although some differences have prevailed). As the British institutionalized the principle of differentiation between party-political and non-political spheres of government, so did the Australians. As the British gradually eliminated politicization in the public service and adopted the principle of political neutrality, so did the Australians. Thus, it may be said that the British political and administrative traditions became part of the Australian heritage.

However, it seems that the principle of neutrality and objectivity has been carried even further in Australia than it has in Britain, at least as far as the arbitral principle is concerned. Parker (1968) offers an interesting suggestion about the origin of this principle: that it is to be found among earlier, undisguised contests of power –

the nineteenth-century struggles among convicts or ex-convicts, free settlers, wealthy squatters, small farmers, shearers, importers, manufacturers and the like. A feature of these struggles in Australia, noted by many historians, has been the absence of any traditional elite to claim impartiality – and hence the prevalence of mutual distrust. Even today, it is claimed, this distrust has not disappeared and hence conflicts are potentially more disruptive. It is this which, according to Parker, has created the Australian passion for the outsider, the 'independent' statutory institution, to settle such conflicts.

If this interpretation is correct, a curious paradox emerges: in Australia, mutual distrust led to the institutionalization of the principles of neutrality and objectivity. Conversely in Israel, where strong collective commitments and cohesiveness furnished the conditions for extensive mutual trust, such principles of neutrality and objectivity were not institutionalized and this, presumably, led to a basic distrust of the machinations of the system. These developments will be our topic in the next chapter.

10 Administrative power in Israel: the persistence of political pervasiveness

Israel supplies an almost perfect example of a party-politicized civil service whose character explains the pervasiveness of material electoral inducements.

The politically involved bureaucracy

This politicization had its roots in the Yishuv era (as did electoral manipulation). Shapiro (1975) made a major contribution to our understanding of that era by showing how party-political and administrative roles came to intermesh to such an extent that they were practically indistinguishable.

At the head of the Histadrut[1] and its affiliated institutions stood party (especially Ahdut Ha-Avoda)[2] representatives, in elected political roles. Most of these persons, as well as those elected to high positions within the parties themselves, did not receive any remuneration in their capacity as party representatives since the party did not have the funds to pay their salaries. Consequently, the politicians found paying jobs in the growing Histadrut administration, so they held elected and appointed jobs at the same time.[3]

These two facets reinforced each other: people were appointed to administrative posts in the Histadrut as rewards for their political adherence, and their administrative work was geared to satisfy the demands of their political bosses (who happened to be their Histadrut superiors as well). At the same time, the connections they established through their administrative work helped to enhance their political careers. This means that many decisions in the Histadrut administration were based on party-political considerations.

This pattern was established not only in the Histadrut, but in the entire political system of the Yishuv – including the national institutions of self-government.[4] As Medding (1972, ch. 11) points out,

166

these institutions had no career civil service, and no system of entry based upon formal qualifications and objective achievements. Party-political considerations prevailed, and appointments were made by the party key – that is, all parties that co-operated with the national institutions were allocated jobs according to their electoral size.

This intermingling of political and administrative posts, and the consequent interference of political bodies and political considerations in administrative activity, came to be a custom which has been largely perpetuated in the present-day Israeli bureaucracy. With the establishment of the state in 1948, the civil service expanded greatly to man the newly created government departments as well as those relinquished by the Mandatory authorities. The new state's public service was no less politicized than was its predecessor in the Yishuv, since the parties were called upon to fill the new positions. As Medding reports, the bulk of the decisive appointments, and certainly those above the middle levels, were party appointments, following upon the traditions of the Jewish Agency[5] and the Histadrut. Whole ministries soon became staffed with party faithfuls.

Mapai (formerly Ahdut Ha-Avoda and later the ILP)[6] as the dominant party, had the most important key ministries and the largest reservoir of members from which to draw its officials, and it took full advantage of the situation. According to Medding (1972, p. 139), Golda Meir complained to the Mapai Central Committee in 1949 that

> the Tel-Aviv branch are completely involved in whether yet another member can be got into the governmental administrative apparatus . . . The Tel-Aviv branch struggles for this, and the most important thing as far as it is concerned, is how many members will get into this ministry or that.

Not only appointments, but working procedures too, were politicized. With the establishment of the state, a great proportion of the posts in the state administration was filled by persons who had previously held posts in the Histadrut and in the Yishuv's national institutions. By the end of the 1950s these people were in most of the senior posts in the government administration (Globerson, 1970, p. 53). Not surprisingly, they perpetuated the work patterns to which they had become accustomed in the Yishuv era. These included loyalty to an informal structure headed by the party leaders, and precedence for party goals over state policies.

Eventually, Eisenstadt (1967, ch. 9) writes, there were efforts to professionalize the public service – for instance, by on-the-job training and by increasing the percentage of university graduates.

167

Also, Medding (1972, ch. 11) notes, the new civil service regulations called for appointment by merit, public announcements of openings, and the use of independent experts and representatives of the public in choosing candidates for appointment. Civil servants were not allowed to serve on the executive bodies of political parties, to stand for political office, to campaign publicly on behalf of political parties and so forth.

But these regulations did not eradicate politicization in the civil service. For one thing, the hiring regulations applied only to new appointments; they had little effect on political appointments made earlier. The top posts were also left as political appointments which the ministers could fill almost at their discretion. In fact 31 per cent of the senior appointments throughout the years 1960–6 were not made after a public announcement of a vacancy (Globerson, 1970, p. 57). Even when there was such an announcement, writes Medding (p. 237),

> party considerations were still important in encouraging candidates to apply, in drawing up the precise qualifications and experience being sought so as to fit a party candidate already in mind . . . and in deciding between otherwise evenly matched candidates. But it also seems to be true that if the person preferred for party reasons was manifestly less qualified than another candidate, the latter was more likely to get the job. The effect in many cases then was one of negative screening, that is, the choice was made between a number of suitably qualified candidates all of the right party affiliation.

Promotions, too, were still based on the political criterion of service to the party, rather than on the objective criteria of talent, efficiency and initiative alone.

Moreover the regulation forbidding civil servants to engage in major political activity was not always heeded. According to a study conducted in the late 1960s, more than half of the senior civil servants were active in political affairs, and the higher the rank of the public servant, the greater was his tendency to engage in party activity (Globerson, 1970, p. 140). Finally, Akzin and Dror (1966) demonstrate that Israeli politicians continued to take a more active role in determining administrative policy than do those in most Western countries. As a result, the autonomy of the administration was still severely restricted. Thus, de-politicization has been slow and only partly effective, and by the end of the 1960s and the beginning of the 1970s the penetration of parties – especially the ILP and its coalition partners – into Israel's major bureaucratic structures had not been eliminated. As Eisenstadt (1967, ch. 9) saw it, several of the ministerial departments were still maintained as the feudal estates of political parties, and the civil service was still a major arena of political struggle.

While political influence in the government administration was at least somewhat restrained, politicization of the bureaucracy still reigned supreme in the Histadrut and the Jewish Agency. Medding's analysis (1972, ch. 11) shows that even at the end of the 1960s and the beginning of the 1970s, party control of the Histadrut administration was regarded as entirely legitimate. It was understood and accepted that the various Histadrut departments were to be staffed by key party personnel – which put control of practically all of them in the hands of the ILP. The Jewish Agency, which still looks after immigration and settlement, was even more political in the development of its administrative apparatus. The fact that it too was staffed on the basis of party privilege was frankly acknowledged, and it still retained a high degree of politicization well into the 1970s.

Apparently, no fundamental change in these patterns is to be expected with the advent to office of the right-wing Likud, following the most recent election. When still in opposition, this party had advocated greater stress on statehood over partisanship, and therefore the de-politicization of the public service. Accordingly, when it took office, the new government retained the bulk of the previous senior public servants, making only few political appointments. Recently, however, the party's leaders have privately criticized the government for being 'imprisoned' by the public servants inherited from its Labour predecessors, these being persons who allegedly oppose and undermine its policy. They did not demand the dismissal of such (tenured) officials but they insisted on increasing party representation through the filling of vacancies. Indeed they went so far as to establish a committee in charge of spotting such vacancies and pressuring the government into filling them with party faithfuls.[7]

The politicized administration and material inducements

In the Yishuv era, the politicization of the major administrative structures has led these to finance the party machines, thus strengthening especially the major Labour Party Ahdut Ha-Avoda (later Mapai). Similarly, after independence, the partisan penetration into Israel's major administrative structures has strengthened the (erstwhile) coalition parties, each of which has been in charge of one or more ministries; it has strengthened especially Mapai (later the ILP), which has been in charge of the largest number and the most powerful ministries. It has done so, among other things, by enabling coalition parties (and especially the ILP) to use posts in the administration itself as direct inducements or rewards for political support.

The political character of the bureaucracies has also enabled parties to obtain large sums of money from the government beyond those provided by law. For instance, Shapiro (1977, ch. 6) shows that the 1974–5 coalition agreement included secret provisions for financial support of the coalition parties, such as credit and loans on easy terms for party-controlled economic concerns. Such provisions could hardly be implemented by a politically neutral bureaucracy.

Furthermore, party-committed public servants have allocated various resources and benefits on which many private economic concerns are greatly dependent (see chapter 5). It is not surprising, then, that many of these public and private companies have shown a solicitous concern for the party's welfare and have donated large sums for various party-sponsored projects. These donations, in turn, have increased the party's ability to pass out financial benefits to potential party supporters.

The politicization of non-government bureaucracies such as the Histadrut and the Jewish Agency means that some of these bodies' funds have been diverted to the parties in proportion to their electoral strength. Substantial parts of the resources that flow into Israel from the World Zionist Organization (United Jewish Appeal) through the Jewish Agency have been allocated to the parties for their various 'constructive' projects – and what could be more constructive than the gaining of political support?

Since the ILP has controlled the administrations of the Histadrut and the Jewish Agency, for a long time it has had control over their resources as well – and it has not been uncommon for large sums to be transferred to the party in secret, in addition to the ones allocated by the political key (see Medding, 1972, p. 243). It was recently revealed that Histadrut-affiliated concerns donated hundreds of millions of pounds – directly or indirectly – to the ILP.[8]

As a consequence, Israeli parties (until the last election – especially the Labour Party) have been quite affluent in comparison with other democratic parties in the Western world. Until lately, they have not been required to reveal their financial transactions for public scrutiny. Hence there was nothing to prevent them from using their large resources to build up extensive party machines, to pay salaries to large numbers of functionaries (whose political support was automatically assured) and to hand out benefits to large numbers of supporters.

The Elections and Party Finance Acts of 1969 and 1973 were designed to end this situation. They provided for state financing of the parties, prohibiting donations to parties from corporations and associations in Israel, and ruled that parties seeking state aid must submit their financial transactions to the state comptroller. However, these Acts did not specify any punishment for illegal activities – so it seems safe to assume that they have been transgressed (or at least circumvented), and that the previous situation has not undergone substantial change.

Furthermore, the government (and the Histadrut) control a wide array of resources and benefits which go directly to citizens, such as certain types of housing, employment and welfare benefits (see chapter 5). The fact that the allocation of these resources is frequently in the hands of party-committed public servants explains why it too is frequently used to gain political support.

This is evident, for instance, in the area of immigrant absorption. After independence, the process of channelling mass immigration was in the hands of the Jewish Agency, where the party key was in operation, but eventually an attempt was made to transfer the various functions of immigrant absorption to state agencies. However, since the state bureaucracy was also politicized, and was frequently manned by party-committed public servants, absorption activities remained indirectly under party control. It was this politicization of the administration of immigrant absorption that made it possible for the parties to reward the faithful and the would-be faithful among the new immigrants with employment, housing and welfare, and thus to put pressure on them for political support.

In this manner the politicized bureaucracy has supplied the resources for the allocation of material benefits in exchange for votes. The two patterns are interrelated, however, not only because the one furnishes the financial basis for the other, but also because they are embedded in a common normative framework which quasi-legitimizes both.

The broader framework

The ethics of particularism

This framework is characterized by the partial subjugation of universalist, objective criteria by particularlist ones, as expressed in the reluctant (or willing) acceptance on part of the ruling elites (and the public as well) of political and personal favouritism alike. The penetration of politics into the administration and the allocation of favours on political grounds could become so widely institutionalized because it was seen as natural by the Yishuv's founding fathers and their successors and not actively resisted by the public. The adverse consequences of this pattern for the democratic process were not consciously pondered or, if they were, were considered as a minor evil. Only much later, after the establishment of the state, did second thoughts arise and even then political penetration was still accepted by the (Labour) leadership if not as fully legitimate, at least as semi-legitimate.[9] It is for this reason that regulations proscribing such penetration and providing for the hiring and advancement of public servants by non-partisan criteria remained largely on paper, while informally political criteria still prevailed.

The same normative ambivalence is also apparent with regard to favouritism on personal grounds. Israel's laws and regulations are designed to provide equal treatment of all citizens by the authorities. However, personal considerations frequently affect the relationships between public servants and their clients. This practice, known popularly as *proteksia*[10] (i.e., favouritism), is not necessarily engaged in by public servants of their own free will. Elsewhere (Etzioni-Halevy, 1975) I have shown that an official in a position of even minor authority is subject to severe cross-pressure. On the one hand, he is frequently plagued by friends and relatives who seek favours by invoking norms of friendship and family solidarity; such norms are so strongly entrenched in Israeli society that it is difficult for an official to extricate himself from such pressures. On the other hand, he is censured by colleagues or superiors who condemn such favours by invoking organizational norms and regulations – even though they themselves may be subject to similar cross-pressures on other occasions.

This ambivalence is also reflected among the public, where *proteksia* is widely condemned, yet widely sought and accepted. According to a study by Danet (1971),[11] most respondents disapproved of *proteksia*, yet a majority of those who had needed it and had had the opportunity to use it admitted actually having done so.

The regulations provide that citizens may appeal against a lack of impartiality to the judiciary or to an ombudsman. However, favouritism is difficult to prove. Unless civil servants and the public are also socialized, and accept as part of their role definitions a severe professional ethic of impartiality, and a culture in which the restraint of personal considerations is expected as a matter of course, there is little that formal regulations or an ombudsman can accomplish – and *proteksia* is likely to persist.

Thus, Israel's elite as well as popular political culture is characterized by the erosion of boundaries between administrative considerations and political considerations, and between political considerations and personal considerations; between the benefit of the state and the benefit of the party, and between the benefit of the party and the benefit of individuals. Favouritism for personal or family reasons becomes intermeshed with favouritism on political grounds, which reinforces the system and the interlocking patterns become more firmly entrenched. The lack of self-restraint on the part of the elites in the passing out of political and personal favours is thus based on a normative framework in which particularism is not severely held in check in areas where, by law and regulations, universalist criteria alone should have prevailed.

Political pervasiveness

This in turn is closely related to a wider framework characterized by a fusion of party-political and non-political considerations and by the pervasiveness of political considerations in all walks of life. In somewhat over-simplified terms it may be said that the differen-tiation between the party-political and non-political aspects of the institutions of government which Huntington (1968) holds to be part of modernization has not greatly advanced in Israel. While Huntington perceived such a fusion in the United States polity as well, it is clearly more emphasized, far-reaching and persistent in Israel.

In this respect the Israeli system stands in marked contrast to the Australian one. While political considerations have been clearly circumscribed and legal-bureaucratic criteria have gained ascen-dancy over political ones in Australia, it has been the other way around in Israel. Just as observers of the Australian scene speak of a 'bureaucratic ascendancy', so observers of the Israeli scene speak of a 'political ascendancy', not only in the bureaucratic sphere but also in a wide array of other institutional spheres which in Western societies are usually more politically neutral.[12]

This pattern dates back to the Yishuv era when social life was highly politicized and a great part of it took place in the framework of political movements. As Eistenstadt (1974) emphasizes, one of the major features of Yishuv society was that it emerged not as a homogeneous community, but as a collection of ideologically committed movements – and the leadership of each was convinced that it and only it had the right answers to the problems of the Jewish people. All these movements either originated as political parties in the Zionist Movement or else eventually formed themselves into parties. Other social bodies which were not themselves political parties were related to them. There were few bodies that were not affiliated in one way or another with parties.

Political affiliation with these movements and parties also carried great weight in the life of the individual, both in self-identification and in informal social relations. The political movements aimed to envelop their members in a network of party-directed activities and relationships that would reinforce their ideological commitment. Consequently, informal social relations took place to a surprisingly large extent within political sectors; tensions between leaders and even between members of diverse political movements were quite high at times.

The establishment of the state was accompanied by some de-politicization of informal social relations and formal social structures, but in some spheres a high degree of politicization still persists. Social networks are no longer demarcated to their previous extent by political affiliation, but rather more by socio-economic boundaries. While self-defence in the Yishuv had been undertaken by politically affiliated underground military organizations[13] and headed by politically affiliated commanders, these were disbanded and replaced by the Armed Forces of the State of Israel.[14]

Also in the Yishuv era three 'streams' in education had developed – each of which had been affiliated with a major political movement: the Labour stream (affiliated with the labour movement), the general stream (affiliated with the various centre-right-wing 'Citizens Groups') and the religious stream (affiliated with religious parties). In 1953, the Labour and general streams were abolished and incorporated into a state-controlled educational system, while the religious stream was maintained – under state control – as a separate entity. Thus, the politicization of education was diminished, but not eliminated; although the formal ties of education to political parties were severed, some informal influence was maintained. The religious sector in education continues to enjoy a marked degree of autonomy, and the National Religious Party has retained a great deal of influence over it.[15]

Even the Labour stream, although no longer an autonomous sector of education, did not disappear completely. Its remnants are apparent in the Kibbutz Movements affiliated with the various Labour Parties. These movements retained their own education departments in charge of teacher-training and teaching appointments in kibbutz schools; consequently,' kibbutz schools have maintained their socialist-ideological character.

Party-political affiliation was maintained to an even greater extent in the public health services. The major service – Kupat Holim Klatit – is in the hands of the Histadrut, and thus is a major tool for enhancing the Labour Party's power. Medding (1972, p. 235) quotes a former secretary-general of the Histadrut as declaring that if the British Labour Party had been in charge of such a health service, it would not have gone out of power. It is not surprising, therefore, that the new ruling party, the right-wing Likud, is doing all that lies in its power to restructure the health services. In a similar vein, the police are subjugated to political authorities in

Israel even more than in the United States, and political considerations pervade what would have been purely professional police
decisions in many other Western societies.

Political control of the economy was another basic feature of the
Yishuv, and the pattern has been maintained in Israel. In the
pre-state era, the nucleus of this control was in the Histadrut, which
owned some of the country's largest and most powerful economic
concerns. Many of the managerial positions in these concerns were
in the hands of politically appointed personnel. Not surprisingly,
then, the companies served socio-political goals to a greater extent
than purely economic goals – and their managements came to be
evaluated and rewarded on this basis.

With the advent of statehood, the public sector of the economy –
which has been mainly under the auspices of the Histadrut – was
reinforced by the government sector. Perpetuating the Histadrut
tradition, the government sector of the economy has been controlled largely by politically appointed personnel, and its policy has
been shaped largely by political considerations rather than by
considerations of economic efficiency ·and profitability. Consequently, many publicly controlled economic enterprises came to be
a burden on the public purse.

The pervasiveness of political penetration is manifested not only
in the public sector of the economy but also in the government's
indirect control over the private sector. Right from the beginning,
in the Yishuv era, the political (Labour) leaders made extensive
efforts to extend their influence over the private sector, although
this influence was necessarily of a more indirect nature. These
efforts were later continued by the Israeli government in which
Labour continued to dominate. Government intervention in the
private sector of the economy implied that this sector too was highly
politicized, and the free play of market forces severely limited. As
Eisenstadt (1967, ch. 6) pointed out, in the public sector, political
considerations have shaped economic policy from within; in the
private sector, similar considerations have been superimposed on
the market from without.

In Australia, as in Israel, the state is active in the economy – but
the patterns of intervention are different. In Australia, the potentially politicizing effects of such intervention are offset, at least to
some extent, by various objectivizing devices which make decisions
more independent of partisan political control (see chapter 9). In
fact, the role of the state in the Australian economy is conceived in a
different manner. As Encel (1970, p. 205) put it:

> state intervention, whether of a regulatory or operating
> character tends to be detached as much as possible from the

175

central apparatus of government, either by dealing with demands in a quasi-judicial or non-political manner (e.g., arbitration tribunals, the Tariff Board and frequent Royal Commissions) or by diffusing responsibility among a number of quasi-independent organs with claims to authority in their own spheres.

Such detachment of state intervention from political criteria is not to be found in Israel. The new right-wing government has recently introduced some changes in economic policy but, as far as can be judged at this time, de-politicization of the economy is not one of them.

The origins of political pervasiveness

How can such political pervasiveness be accounted for? Part of the answer lies in the absence of a unified state framework in the Yishuv era, and part in the character of the Yishuv's ideology, and the source from which it originated.

The political movements, organizations and parties that developed in the Yishuv were not contained within the structure of a state which could have caused them to tailor their activities to fit its needs. The British Mandatory Government was considered to be something external – to be coped with as well as possible, but not to be accepted as part of the indigenous social framework. On its part, the Mandatory Government adopted a policy of minimum interference in the Yishuv society. Consequently, the political movements were little hampered by external constraints, and it was possible for them to undertake activities in fields rarely undertaken by political parties in other countries (see Medding, 1972, ch. 11).

Also, in the absence of a commonly accepted state framework, the Jewish community relied on an internal political authority (composed of two bodies which came to be known as the national institutions). Although this political centre enjoyed a fair degree of autonomy, it had, in the phrasing of Horowitz and Lissak (1971), authority without sovereignty. Lacking the ultimate force of sanctions available to a sovereign state, the national institutions had to base their authority on voluntary recognition by the various political bodies (which included the parties, the Histadrut and some independent labour organizations) and by the community at large.

To elicit the co-operation of these political bodies, the national institutions were obliged to cede several functions to them – thereby turning them into what Horowitz and Lissak refer to as political sub-centres. It is this situation, in part, which gave rise to the fusion of politics with other institutional spheres and to the marked politicization of all facets of social life. It enabled the various political organizations to organize immigration, settlement, health, welfare, and a host of other economic, social and cultural services – which, in turn, enabled these same organizations to hand out a variety of benefits to the public in return for political support.

The central authority also had to provide the financial resources for the functions which it had relinquished. These resources (supplied by the World Zionist Organization) flowed through the national institutions to the various political bodies – by the party key – in return for voluntary co-operation and support. Money was not the only resource so allocated. Since they were so dependent on the parties, the national institutions were also obliged to allocate posts in their own administrations – again by the party key.

Thus the lack of the solid, common framework of a sovereign state weakened the Yishuv's national authority, enabling the various political bodies to encroach upon it, and this resulted in a marked politicization of the system. This, however, explains only the emergence of politicization, not its persistence. Once established, this politicization was maintained in a large part after statehood, even though the fragmented political and administrative system had by that time been replaced by a powerful and highly centralized one. To understand this persistence, one must take into account another source of the politicization: the dominant ideology advocated by the elites (and generally accepted by the public), and the political culture from which it originated.

The basic ideology of the Yishuv was collectivist Zionism. This held that the major effort of the Yishuv should focus on realizing a common goal, and that this collective effort took priority over individual goals of self-advancement, a higher standard of living and the like. The collectivist nature of the Zionist ideals was reinforced by the socialist ideology of the labour movement which was collectivist as well; as the labour movement gained dominance, the socialist ideology came to be the Yishuv's dominant ideology.[16] As the primacy of collective goals was widely recognized, it was also recognized that the implementation of such goals naturally should be in the hands of the Yishuv's leadership – that is, its political elite.

In addition, the ideology of socialism to which the Labour leaders actively adhered held that the collective (as represented by the state – or, lacking that, by its political organization) should own the means of production, and should play a major role in organizing and controlling all facets of socio-economic life. This ideology thus furnished the rationale for the political control of both administrative and economic activities; a direct line thus leads from collectivism to political ascendancy.

The primacy of collectivism, in turn, may be explained in part by the Yishuv's *raison d'être* and the nature of the Zionist movement

177

which brought it into being. In contrast to other countries of immigration, such as the United States and Australia, the Jewish community in Palestine was created in order to realize the declared national goal of the Jewish people. This common goal gave thrust to the collective effort to settle the poor and under-developed country in which but meagre prospects for individual prosperity existed. Hence, this common goal also imprinted its marks on the trends of thought in the emerging community.

The primacy of collectivism in its socialist form may be explained in part by the cultural background of the Yishuv. Israel, the United States and Australia were at one time in their history, dominated by British political institutions. In colonial America and Australia these were accepted as part of the indigenous political culture and as models for political and administrative patterns; in Israel's pre-state society, on the other hand, they were regarded largely as alien forces. The political culture from which Israel's nation-builders originated and on which they drew in devising the nation's emerging political structures was the Russian one.[17]

The leaders who founded the socio-political frameworks and shaped the evolving patterns of social life had mostly emigrated from Russia, where they had learned their basic political techniques. As Shapiro (1975) extensively demonstrates, they reached Palestine (at the beginning of the twentieth century) when they were mostly in their twenties and had already experienced several years of political activity in socialist and Zionist organizations. Thus they were greatly under the influence of Russian political culture, many elements of which they endeavoured to import. The pre-communist Russian *Weltanschauung* was collectivist, and this principle was widely accepted by the various anti-Tsarist groups, and later by the Soviet regime.

The collectivist socialist principle, as noted, called for the political leaders to control the administration and the economy. One of the major aims of the communist leaders was to gain control of these structures, and this control serves as the backbone of the Soviet regime to this day. In Soviet Russia, therefore, the roles of the bureaucrat and the politician intermesh; the resulting role is that of a 'bureaucratic-politician', and not an electoral politician as in the United States (see Brzezinski and Huntington, 1964).

While Israel's founders did not accept the Soviet one-party system,[18] they did adopt the Russian concept of pervasive political control and the fusion of political, administrative and economic roles which this control implied. Their success in getting the public to accept these patterns goes back to the fact that, in those early years, most of the rank-and-file had also been reared in Russia and shared their leaders' political culture. Even those groups that were not fully committed to socialism accepted the primacy of collective goals over individual benefits, and hence of political organizations over economic ones.

Thus the ideological and political backgrounds of the founding fathers of the Yishuv at least partly explain the emergence of the politician as bureaucrat (or the bureaucrat as politician) and the fusion, in turn, largely explains the amassment of economic resources in the hands of political or semi-political organizations; the branching out of these organizations into socio-economic activities such as housing, banking and health services; and the concentration of resources in the hands of a politically committed public service. It also explains the appearance of strong party machines that were financed, and whose personnel were paid, by that public service. And, hence, it finally explains the exchange of various benefits for political support.

The fusion of administration and politics flourished and was resilient also because it served the vested interests of the ruling politicians, intent on enhancing their power in the evolving society. The veteran leadership had no difficulty in initiating successive generations of political leaders into the same patterns, as their vested interests were also served by them. But vested interests alone could not account for the persistence of the political-administrative fusion, had this pattern not had ideological backing, and had it not been part of the basic political culture to which the elite had been socialized, to which the public was receptive and to which it was further socialized by the elite.

Thus we conclude that the exchange of material benefits for electoral support had little to do with a lack of ideological commitment on the part of the public, as one would suppose on the basis of Scott's theory (see chapter 6). On the contrary we saw (chapters 5 and 6) that the Israeli public, especially in the Yishuv era, was highly committed ideologically. In fact, it was the extensive commitment to the collectivist socialist ideology that gave thrust and legitimation to this development; the political culture and background of the founding fathers explains, in part, the adoption of this ideology.

Conclusion

The foregoing country-by-country review of bureaucracies and their settings was designed to give empirical substance to the posited connection[1] between the political manipulation of material inducements[2] and the politicization of administrative power structures (politocracy). To recapitulate, then, it has been established that material inducements and politocracy were prevalent at one time in each of the four countries, and that both subsequently diminished. But in Britain and in Australia this dual decline came about much earlier and was much more extensive as compared to the United States, and especially to Israel, where both material inducements and politocracy still persist, at least to some extent.[3]

In turn, the differences between the countries in the depoliticization of the bureaucracy were traced back to codes of ethics developed by political and administrative elites: in England and in Australia the elites developed fairly unequivocal (though not necessarily formally explicated) codes of propriety proscribing party-political considerations in administrative action. In the United States and Israel the elites' notions of propriety remained ambiguous. These developments can now be considered in the light of the theoretical concerns with which this analysis began.

Political manipulation and theories of political participation

One such concern was with the relationship between political manipulation *of* the public and political participation *by* the public. It will be recalled that two antithetical views have been presented with regard to this participation. Some observers consider that, with modernization and after, broader strata have gradually been drawn into the political process and have made an increasing impact on it. Others feel the opposite to have been the case as the 'masses' have become more politically impotent and apathetic.

180

Successive development of representative institutions, gradual extension of the franchise and increasing electoral participation in Western countries on the face of it support the first rather than the second theory. The latter, however, is based on the argument that manipulation of the public by the elites renders increasing democratic participation meaningless.

Which of the two theories is supported by the developments traced in the present study? In each of the countries studied at least one form of political manipulation evolved with the development of representative democratic institutions themselves: in pre-democratic societies, or where deferential voting under the sponsorship of traditional patrons prevailed, the need to manipulate the public by material inducements did not arise. Only with the extension of the franchise and the gradual emancipation of rank-and-file voters from their traditional patrons did the practice become prevalent. Hence it has been claimed that the evolvement of this type of manipulation may be taken to indicate that the public's participation and importance in the political process has in fact been growing.

The employment of material inducements in elections, however, is in itself elite-centred to a considerable extent. It does involve rank-and-file participation, but this is the kind of participation in which the public is activated by the elites rather than being active on its own accord. For a minor consideration, rank-and-file citizens are induced to act so as to enhance the power of the elites and to promote ends and purposes that have little to do with their own welfare and interests. Therefore this is a passive kind of participation and it is doubtful whether it allows the public any more influence on the political process than did the previous pattern of deferential voting.

This is so, among other things, because the manipulation of material inducements is contingent upon the manipulators having access to large-scale pecuniary resources. So this manipulation enhances the political advantage of the financially well-endowed political bodies that usually are also the well-established ones, of the ones closest to the existing centres of power over the ones that attempt to make new inroads into the political system. Holding an election campaign is in itself an expensive endevour. So unless the state finances the election expenses of all contestants on a completely egalitarian basis, the well-established political bodies are at an advantage in any case. But the employment of material inducements in the political process greatly enhances this advantage. Specially advantaged are long-standing ruling or incumbent parties that have a leverage over the state's administration and are capable of utilizing its resources – as has been the case in Israel, for instance, for many years. Well-established political bodies (including long-term incumbent parties) have a stake in the maintenance of the *status quo*. Thus the employment of material inducements distorts the democratic process not only because it entails a passive electorate induced to promote interests that are not its own, but also because it lends additional advantage to the advantaged, and works for the perpetuation of the prevailing socio-political regime.

In spite of all this, the data lend greater support to the optimistic theory. For while the initial development of democratic institutions was largely invalidated by political manipulation of material inducements, the *further* development of democratic institutions, and especially the further extension of the franchise, was accompanied by a decline (or a partial decline) of this practice. It must be concluded that, in recent times, at any rate, the quantitative extension of public participation in politics was, in fact, related to a qualitative increase in its significance as well.

Paradoxically, however, the same findings which strengthen the optimistic view of increasing rank-and-file political participation also lend support to the elitist view. They do so by showing that the decline in political manipulation of material inducements and the consequent increase in the significance of public political participation were initiated by the ruling elites rather than having been achieved by an ideologically conscious rank-and-file public. This does not mean that public opinion was insignificant. But mostly it followed the lead of elite initiative and where it did not, it was not greatly effective.

Political manipulation, and theories of domination

This, in turn, brings us to our next theoretical concern: the model of social domination which could most profitably serve as a framework for this analysis. Two – it will be recalled – are prominent in contemporary social thought: the Marxist class model which stresses economic power and the elite model which stresses political power. A study of political manipulation by means of material inducements could, in principle, have found its place within either of the two traditions. In fact, however, the second model (with some modifications) has been adopted as the more appropriate. The study's major perspective has been that (in line with the Marxist view) political and economic power are closely inter-related, but that (contrary to the Marxist view) political power is not necessarily subservient to economic power (either immediately or ultimately); that it is more likely to serve autonomous interests. In other words, it is held that political power is not necessarily exercised as a function of class objectives, but rather more often as a function of autonomous elite objectives – and that class objectives frequently even become subservient to elite objectives, without the process ultimately being reversed, as some Marxists would claim.

These propositions have been referred to as perspectives rather than hypotheses because they (as well as their Marxist counter-propositions) are on such a high level of abstraction that they hardly lend themselves to straightforward empirical testing and verification. Nevertheless, it seemed that the patterns of manipulation of material inducements, the conditions under which it thrived and the conditions under which it declined could best be understood in terms of these, rather than in terms of the Marxist perspectives.

The close interrelation of political power and economic power is attested to by the manner in which they are jointly employed in political manipulation through material inducements: political elites use their control over economic resources to enhance their political power. In turn, they may use their political power to enhance their material resources, which once more may be used to augment their political power. But this interconnectedness of political power and economic power does not necessarily lend itself to a class model interpretation.

According to the class model one would have expected manipulation through material inducements to flourish most continuously, to show the most resilience where it clearly benefited the economically dominant classes (the owners of the means of production and the expropriators of economic surplus) and to be most easily eliminated where it clearly did not serve the interests of these classes. Yet this was hardly the case. This is not to say that the economically dominant classes were invariably the innocent and passive victims of the ruling elites' conspiracies; wherever possible, they tried to make the most of material inducements. But they generally did not gain the upper hand in this particular power struggle. The practice of extending material inducements in return for political support was resilient not where it served the vested interests of the upper classes, but where it served the vested interests of the political elites.

In nineteenth-century Britain, the landed aristocracy and to a lesser extent the wealthy bourgeoisie (and their representatives) had a virtual monopoly over central elite positions. In nineteenth-century Australia the social basis of political power was broader, but here, too, the economically advantaged almost totally monopolized political power. The continued use of material inducements could have entrenched these advantaged classes in political power and permanently excluded the labouring classes. Yet Britain was the country in which material inducements declined earlier and more completely than in any of the other countries studied and Australia followed closely behind. Concomitant with this decline was the increase in the political power of labour and the consequent loss of the political monopoly of the economically dominant classes.

On the other hand, the countries in which material inducements persisted much longer did not have a common pattern as far as class domination over the political process is concerned. In the United States those higher in socio-economic status had a clear advantage in elite participation, but in Israel the political elite was drawn almost exclusively from the labour camp for almost half a century. Yet material inducements flourished more extensively and longer there than in any of the other countries studied.

Moreover, nineteenth-century America and nineteenth-century Australia resembled each other in that both had political elites monopolized by the economically advantaged, but, in both, the elites were not monopolized by the dominant classes proper to the same extent as they were in Britain. Yet Australia resembled Britain (not America) in the early and virtual elimination of material inducements. Thus what explains the difference between the countries where material inducements were eradicated fairly early and the countries in which they persisted much longer and, to some extent, up to the present is neither the class-connectedness of the political elites nor the class interests which these inducements served. Rather, it is the evolution of well-structured conglomerations of political power that came to be in charge of the material resources used for political manipulation.

In nineteenth-century Britain, resources came mainly from private members of the upper classes, and only to a smaller extent from the public administration. Although party organizations developed, they did not take over the main financial burden of political manipulation. With the extension of the franchise and the growth of the electorate to unprecedented dimensions, private resources (even of the wealthy) no longer sufficed for effective electoral manipulation. As the expenses involved in such manipulation soared and became an increasing burden on candidates and their sponsors, the pressure mounted to eliminate the practice. In nineteenth-century Australia, too, a substantial part of electoral manipulation was privately financed by wealthy elite members. Since the practice never reached the dimensions reached in Britain, it was subdued with relative ease not long after its eradication in Britain.

In the United states and in Israel, on the other hand, much greater strongholds of political power evolved in the form of political machines,[4] and most of the resources for manipulation accrued from, or were channelled through, these machines. The funds were thus both extensive and freely available for political purposes. Since the personnel of the machines were not privately burdened with the expenses of manipultion and at the same time greatly benefited from the manipulation, they developed strong vested interests in its persistence. The practice was therefore much more difficult to eradicate in these countries.

Two basic patterns thus developed. One was exemplified by Britain (and to a lesser extent by Australia), where material inducements derived mostly from private resources and served the interests of the wealthy; here the practice of handing out such inducements declined much earlier and much more thoroughly. The other pattern was that exemplified by the United States and Israel, where material benefits were handed out mainly by (and served the interests of) political machines; here the practice was maintained much longer, and even then was only partly eliminated.

It seems, then, that the machines were a crucial element – if not in the emergence of this type of political manipulation, then at least in its persistence. Could it have been that the machines themselves (deliberately or unwittingly) served the interests of the capitalist classes? And if so, does not the crucial role of the machines in the persistence of material inducements vindicate the class model rather than the elite model?

This certainly was not the case in Israel. Not only was the ruling elite which controlled these machines drawn largely from the labour camp, but (and in line with labour's ideology) a lion's share of the means of production were (and still are) publicly owned. The means of production thus came under the control of the ruling elite by virtue of its political power, rather than under the control of an economic class by virtue of its property rights. To the extent that the economic surplus accruing from these means of production was used by political machines for political manipulation, it clearly served the ruling elite rather than the capitalist class. Neither can the ruling elite be said to have disproportionately represented the interests of the capitalist class (or what passed for one in Israel); the latter was greatly dependent on the powerful ruling elite and therefore subservient to it, rather than the other way around.

In the United States, Mills (1959) has posited a close affinity between the political elite and the magnates of capitalism. The analysis in chapter 3 has lent further support to this conception. But it is by no means a foregone conclusion (and Mills did not claim it to be) that the former unilaterally serves the interests of the latter. Indeed, much of the material cited in the present study shows that the American machines gave preferential treatment only to those members of the capitalist classes who were willing to support them both financially and politically. The ruling elites thus exploited the

185

dominant classes no less (and probably even more) than they served them. The party machines survived as long as they did not because they served class interests, but because they were conglomerations of political power with great financial resources at their disposal – and because these resources could be used for electoral manipulation and to solidify the machines' vested interests at one and the same time.

Does this imply, then, that material inducements have persisted where political elites have been able to amass large scale financial resources, and that political machines have played such a crucial role in this persistence because they served as the tools for amassing the resources? It would certainly seem to be so at first sight, but a closer look casts some doubt on this conception.

Clearly the ruling elites of all contemporary societies have control over relatively large financial resources. Hence the difference between the countries was not so much in the scale of the resources available to the elites but in the manner in which the resources could be used. In the United States and in Israel – with the aid of machines – such resources could be used for party-political purposes. In Britain and Australia, where no substantial machines of the relevant type developed, such resources ceased to be available for political manipulation precisely when (because of the growing electorate) they were most direly needed. The political machines, then, were crucial not in the amassing of resources but in their deployment.

But why is it that political machines of this type developed in the United States and in Israel and not in Britain or in Australia? The foregoing analysis shows that where party machines did develop, they drew most of their resources from the public administration. Hence, such machines could flourish only where the administration was thoroughly politicized and thus made its resources available on a partisan basis.

Initially, to be sure, the public administration was politicized at least to some extent in all four countries. But in Britain and Australia this politicization was not carried far enough to allow for the provision of large-scale resources that would have been necessary for the evolvement of substantial political machines. Moreover, in these countries, politicization in the administration declined precisely at a time when party-political machines would have been essential to sustain electoral manipulation.

In contrast, in the other two countries, the politicization of the bureaucracy was maintained much longer and, when it declined, it did so only partially. Consequently, the resources made available by the bureaucracy for political purposes sufficed to give rise to and sustain political machines engaged in political corruption; and these

186

patterns could be maintained up to much later points in time and partly up to the present.

Political manipulation, administrative power and normative restraints

The earlier and more complete de-politicization of the administration in Britain and Australia (as compared to the United States and Israel) in turn may be seen as part of a wider process of differentiation between the political and non-political aspects of the institutions of government. This long-term process of differentiation which, following Huntington (1968), may be seen as part of modernization progressed in Britain and Australia but was arrested to a certain extent in America and even more so in Israel. In Britain and in Australia this differentiation took the form of the political neutralization of various governmental structures such as the judiciary, the military and the police (besides that of the administration itself), and the limitation of partisan politics to the cabinet, the parliament and political parties.

Such a differentiation of structure was closely interrelated with the development of normative frameworks, i.e., certain clear-cut codes of ethics or role definitions among the British and Australian elites. Like the process of differentiation with which it was interrelated, the evolution of such role definitions took place over extended periods of time. But once developed – and adopted – these codes restrained the elites from utilizing the respective structures of which they had charge for party-political purposes. Observers of both Britain and Australia emphasize the importance of the evolution of such unequivocal codes of propriety in the de-politicization of these countries' administrative structures and see them as outweighing the importance of appropriate written regulations and legislative acts.

Not so in the United States and Israel. In these countries the elites' notions of propriety have remained ambiguous and hence have not served to restrain those elites from utilizing various governmental structures for party-political purposes. The Nixon administration could still attempt to utilize the Internal Revenue Service to embarrass political enemies. And if the attempt was not as successful as expected, this was allegedly not because Nixon's staff of public servants refused to co-operate or because the Internal Revenue Service resisted political pressures and regarded them as unethical, but because it had a greater commitment to the rival party. In Israel (contrary to regulations but with the tacit agreement of all involved), not only a large part of the administration but major economic concerns, some educational structures and even

187

the health services still have their policies shaped to a large extent by party-political guidelines.

It has been argued (see Introduction) that where a process of differentiation has taken place between party-political and non-political structures, and where the appropriate elite notions of propriety have developed, this may also be viewed as a differentiation between areas where the elites are guided by particularist criteria of action and spheres where universalist criteria alone are activated. Where the political neutralization of some governmental structures has taken place this may also be seen as one of circumscription or limitation of elite particularism which – before modernization – had been much more pervasive. Conversely, the imperfect differentiation between political and non-political aspects of the institutions of government and the persistence of ambiguous elite ethics may also be regarded as a continuous penetration of particularist criteria where, by formal regulations and standards, objective criteria of universalism alone are deemed to be relevant.

The present argument that started out with an elite frame of reference is thus coming to its conclusion with the aid of normative concepts advocated by the structural-functional (Parsonian) school. The employment of these concepts – long disparaged for their alleged inability to deal with power and interest structures – is meant to show that they are actually quite appropriate for this purpose and that they contribute to the understanding of the patterning of such structures. It is meant to show not only that the analysis of norms and values can be integrated with the analysis of power and interests, but, indeed, that one can hardly be understood without the other.

More specifically the employment of the ostensibly out-dated pattern-variables in this context may serve to explain some phenomena pertaining to power structures which otherwise would seem perplexing: the politicization of the bureaucracy and material inducements in the electoral process flourished and declined simultaneously even where (as was the case in nineteenth-century Britain) most resources for such inducements did *not* derive from the bureaucracy. The explanation seems to lie in the general emphasis on universalism vs. particularism in the codes of ethics prevailing among the elites. Where such codes tacitly countenanced particularlist criteria of action in the bureaucracy (irrespective of formal laws and regulations), they ccuntenanced such criteria in the electoral process as well. But where such codes restrained particularist criteria of action, they came to be considered as illegitimate in both areas simultaneously.[5]

The employment of these concepts would also help to explain

188

why in Israel, where the politicization of the bureaucracy is most persistent, observers have also found extensive employment of favouritism in the same structure. Conversely, in Australia, where political neutralization of the bureaucracy has proceeded to great lengths – much greater efforts are made to ban favouritism from bureaucratic action:[6] where particularism based on political grounds is condoned, there is a greater tendency to condone particularism based on family and personal ties as well, and vice versa.

Finally, the employment of the pattern variables as an analytical tool helps to clarify the role of two power structures – that of political parties *vis-à-vis* that of the public administration – in Western-style democracies. In many Western countries, political parties have tended to present themselves as the chief pillars of democracy and to base their claims for large-scale, public pecuniary support on this image. In a way, the foregoing historical analysis has lent additional substance to this (basically correct) claim by showing that the development of political parties (for instance in nineteenth-century Australia) made the employment of material inducements less crucial for the attainment of parliamentary majorities and thus facilitated the unfolding of an unbiased democratic process.

On the other hand, however, the analysis has also shown that the over-development of political parties (no less than their under-development) is apt to jeopardize the democratic process. Where administrative structures have been pervaded by party-political considerations – that is by particularist criteria which legitimately prevail in political parties – this has resulted in political manipulation in which material inducements were employed. It is only where the state's major administrative power structures have been activated chiefly on the basis of universalist criteria of action, and where political parties have thus been severely circumscribed, that an unbiased democratic process has evolved. Severe restraint of particularist criteria in state bureaucracies, which may also be seen as a severe restraint on the pervasiveness of political parties, is thus a basic prerequisite of democracy.

This is not to say that the limitation of particularism as expressed in the political neutralization of the bureaucracy is necessarily an unmixed blessing. It may be argued that politically neutral administrative elites lack commitment to the government's policies. They may not, therefore, do their utmost to make these policies work, and may be even less inclined to employ their own initiative in order to enhance the government's success. This deficiency may be specially decisive in developing countries. As Armstrong (1973) points out, accelerated economic development requires an interventionist role definition on the part of the administrative elite.

Such a role definition, in turn, is based on both administrative responsiveness to government policies and independent initiative on part of the officials themselves. Although it has not been proved to be correct, it may be claimed with some degree of plausibility that such a role definition requires political commitment rather than political neutrality on the part of the administrative elite.

But while political commitment of the administrative elite may conceivably contribute to a country's economic development, it is most unlikely to help that country along the road to democracy. This, perhaps, would help explain why, in developing countries, bureaucracies are usually politically committed, rather than politically neutral. On the other hand, it would also help explain why such countries mostly have not adopted the democratic pattern or, if they have, have not been very successful in its implementation.

Normative restraints and the curbing of elite power

Many observers – of both the Marxist and the elitist persuasion – would claim that it makes little difference whether or not a country adopts the democratic pattern, since the advantage of the dominant classes or elites over the exploited classes or the masses is maintained in any event. It could be argued, however, that it is the degree of the advantage which counts. In this sense, both the Marxist and the elitist model seem to have overshot their mark, albeit in opposite directions. The Marxist model envisages the abolition of the ruling class and the advent of a classless society in the future. The elite model does not incorporate an equivalent belief in the eventual abolition of the ruling elites and holds that society always was and always will be divided into those who dominate and those who are dominated, the elites and the masses.

Whether the more optimistic or the more pessimistic view is adopted, in either case this does not mean that all forms of inequality or domination – as long as they exist – are equivalent. With regard to the political sphere, for instance, it is evident that some elites are more despotic than others, some are more humane than others and some are easier to dislodge than others. Therefore, whether or not one accepts the view that domination can eventually be *abolished*, it is important that in the meantime it can quite definitely be *restricted*. Neither the Marxist nor the elitist model has paid sufficient attention to the manner in which such restrictions come about or may be brought about.

Manipulation of the public is one major way by which elites enhance their power, and the extension of material benefits in return for political support is one major form of such manipulation.

190

The elimination of material inducements (at least material inducements to individuals) from the political process in some Western democracies is therefore one way of restricting the power of the elites by making them more accountable to the public for their actions, by making public participation in the political arena more efficacious or, in other words, by enhancing the democratic process.

It is important to incorporate into the analysis of political domination a conception of the normative codes which, once adopted by the elites and institutionalized into governmental structures, make it exceedingly difficult (or perhaps even impossible) for the elites to engage in this type of manipulation. Such norms or rules of the game are – as the analysis has shown – among the most effective restraints on elite power. They will not bring about the utopia of a classless or an eliteless society, but they are important in making life in an elite-dominated society more tolerable.

Notes

Introduction

1 Although, according to this view, the state apparatus has a certain degree of autonomy *vis-à-vis* the various factions of the ruling class that are jockeying for power, ultimately it utilizes that autonomy in the interests of the ruling class as a whole.

2 An exception is C. W. Mills's analysis of the power elite. This has been admitted into the racial camp, perhaps because Mills included the holders of economic power in his ruling group.

3 The Marxist argument is that elite activity, designed to fortify its own rule, also solidifies a certain socio-economic regime, and thereby willy-nilly serves the class that is advantaged by that regime. It is not surprising, of course, that Marxists have not admitted the reverse to be equally true: a capitalist class, by solidifying the economic *status quo*, entrenches the political regime as well, and thereby serves the interests of the ruling elite. This study will show that ruling elites have in fact deliberately manipulated capitalist classes with this purpose in mind.

4 See, for instance, Althusser (1969 and 1977); Baran and Sweezy (1967); Connell (1977); Miliband (1973); Poulantzas (1973 and 1975).

5 Perhaps Pareto's model is an exception.

6 For a concise overview of the development of this idea in Western thought, see Partridge (1971) and Pitkin (1965, 1966).

7 On the distinction between symbolic and non-symbolic manipulation see Etzioni-Halevy (1977, ch. 5).

8 This should become clear below when actual manipulation is discussed.

9 The political machine has been defined as 'a party organization that depends crucially upon inducements that are both specific and material' (Banfield and Wilson, 1963, p. 115). Nevertheless, I prefer to define the topic under study as concern with material inducements in return for electoral support, rather than concern with political machines – for several reasons. In the first place, the literature does not always use the term 'machine' in strict accordance with the above definition, and some analyses refer to a political machine simply as a party organization even when no mention is made of material inducements. Second, material

inducements are sometimes given when no political machine exists. Third, I am concerned with inducements as such, and with the structure of the organization offering these inducements only to the extent that it explains such inducements.

10 On the distinction between the political realm in general and party politics, see also chapter 7.

1 The development of elections

1 The main sources for this chapter are: Allen (1964); Butler and Cornford (1969); Converse (1972); Hogan (1945); Hughes (1968); Huntington (1968); Key (1964); Lane (1959); Leonard (1968, ch. 3); Loveday, Martin and Parker (eds), 1977 and Penniman (1962).

2 Leaving aside referenda which are not as widely institutionalized.

3 On this argument see for instance Milbrath (1965) and DiPalma (1970), p. 208.

4 Elections fulfil this symbolic function in any case. But in one-party systems this is their only function.

5 New South Wales introduced it in 1858; by 1859 five States had the ballot; Western Australia followed in 1877.

6 Israel, as a latecomer to the political scene, adopted the secret ballot right from the first election in the pre-state era (1920).

7 A few States were slower in giving up their property requirements. Virginia, for instance, persisted until 1850, and North Carolina until 1856.

8 Although innocuous remnants of tax-paying requirements remained in various jurisdictions even into the twentieth century.

9 Delaware, North Carolina, Pennsylvania, Rhode Island.

10 Wyoming, Colorado, Idaho and Utah.

11 For details on these and other discriminatory laws, see Penniman (1962), p. 16.

12 The United States preceded only Switzerland, which did not grant women the vote until 1971. Aborigines in Australia began voting only in the 1960s but the numbers and the percentage of Aborigines in the Australian population are rather small so that they cannot be referred to as a 'major' population group.

13 Except for Western Australia which became self-governing in 1890.

14 The Australian literature speaks of universal manhood suffrage – despite the fact that Aborigines were not included.

15 The reconstruction of the Jewish community in Palestine began at the end of the nineteenth century, when the country was under Turkish (Ottoman) rule. But the development of the political system gained impetus after the First World War, when the country became a British mandate.

16 Yishuv literally 'settlement'.

17 However, Orthodox Jews were opposed to women's voting; as a compromise, separate voting booths were set up for orthodox and non-orthodox voters. Also, in some municipal elections, women did not gain the vote until the early 1940s.

18 For instance in Belgium, manhood suffrage was introduced in 1893,

universal suffrage came in 1948; in Canada, suffrage for all men was introduced in 1917, universal suffrage in 1920; in Denmark manhood suffrage was adopted in 1901, universal suffrage in 1915; in France, manhood suffrage was granted in 1848, but voting took place in an authoritarian environment which was not abolished until 1875; universal suffrage was adopted in 1944; in the Netherlands all men were ensuffraged in 1917 and universal suffrage followed in 1919; in Norway almost all men got the vote in 1898, women in 1913, but universal suffrage came only in 1919 when persons on public assistance were given the vote as well; in Sweden manhood suffrage was introduced in 1909, universal suffrage in 1921. Finally, Switzerland was a pioneer by granting manhood suffrage as early as 1848, but universal suffrage was not obtained until 1971 (source: Mackie and Rose, 1974).

19 For instance, in Belgium, in 1971, voting turnout was 91.5 per cent; in Canada in 1972 the percentage was 77.2; in Denmark in 1971 – 87.2; in Finland in 1972 – 81.4; in France, in 1968 – 80.0; in the Netherlands, in 1972 – 83.5; in New Zealand in 1972 – 89.9; in Norway in 1969 – 83.8; in Sweden in 1970 – 88.3, and only in Switzerland in 1971 was voting turnout lower than in the United States – with 56.8 per cent of the electorate turning up at the polls, (possibly because of the new enfranchisement of women).

20 The trend of voter turnout in Israel resembles those of Britain and the United States. After an initial turnout of 77 per cent in 1920, there was a slump that persisted for several decades. With the establishment of the state in 1948, there was a recovery; since then, the turnout has been around 80 per cent. However, since Israel was a latecomer to the political scene, the developments there do not seem relevant to an understanding of the general voting trends in Western democracies.

21 Although this increase has lagged behind the potential created by the extension of the franchise.

22 The Survey Research Center on the University of Michigan has repeatedly included four items on political efficacy; three of them show a decreasing sense of efficacy. In 1952, around 65 per cent of the respondents (a cross section of the American population) disagreed with the statement that 'Public officials don't care much what people like me think'; in 1968, 60 per cent disagreed. In 1952, 66 per cent disagreed with the statement that 'People like me don't have any say about what the government does'; in 1968, 60 per cent disagreed. In 1952, 29 per cent disagreed with the statement that 'Politics and government are so complicated that persons like me can't really understand what's going on'; in 1968, only 19 per cent disagreed. On the other hand, in 1952 less than 17 per cent disagreed with the statement that 'Voting is the only way in which people can have a say about how the government runs things'; in 1968 almost 42 per cent disagreed.

2 Political manipulation of material inducements in Britain

1 The same may also be said of Ireland until the rise of the National Party which had neither the money nor the need to appeal to the electors by

venal practices. In Scotland, where populous constituencies were all newly created, no tradition of bribery developed and corruption was almost unknown.

2 For a definition of such machines see Introduction, n. 9. On the characteristics of such machines see next chapter.

3 This point will be further elaborated in chapter 7.

4 On the neo-feudal factory deference which developed between employees and bosses in the northern factory towns in the later nineteenth century see Joice (1975).

5 On one such reported instance of treating see Taylor (1972, p. 50).

6 This does not mean that absolute justice to all is done in British elections. According to Butler and Rose (1960, ch. 3) there remains a bias in the electoral system which means that the Labour Party needs about 400,000 more votes than the conservatives to get a given number of seats. To acquire equal numbers of seats, the Conservatives need 45.9 per cent and Labour −47.3 per cent of the votes cast (assuming the vote for the Liberals and minor parties remains constant). However, this type of electoral bias is not our concern in the present analysis.

7 This part of the chapter is based mainly on analyses by McKenzie (1958, ch. 18), O'Leary (1962), Gwyn (1962) and King (1970).

8 There was a reforming element within the church which spoke out against corruption but even this movement was not very active in its anti-corruption campaign. A more active opposition to corruption was taken around the middle of the century by the Christian Socialist Movement. But with all their efforts the reformers did not exert a very large influence while the greater part of the church did not back them.

9 It has been claimed that in some places the lower classes and especially the working class were not simply the passive objects of upper-class manipulation. Foster (1974) in a detailed study of some industrial towns makes the point that the working class in effect ran the town of Oldham in the 1820–40 period. Though denied the vote, working-class radicals used their and their followers' buying power to induce merchants and shopkeepers (who possessed the franchise) to vote as directed. But this was clearly the exception rather than the rule.

10 Some of these reforms will be discussed in chapter 7.

11 In 1874, 1885 and 1892 – the Labour candidates elected to parliament numbered 2, 10 and 15 respectively.

3 Political manipulation of material inducements in the United States

1 For a more extensive discussion of patronage in the United States, see chapter 8.

2 The article was previously published in 1905.

3 Besides, even a 2 per cent minority of purchasable votes (or even less) could have tipped the balance if the distribution of the party vote among the non-venal voters was pretty even.

4 In 1968, a Republican won the governorship; in 1972, the winner was an independent Democrat who had no ties to Daley.

5 Democratic activists tend to be of somewhat lower socio-economic

    status than their Republican counterparts, but they too, are of disproportionately high social background.

6 The 513 men who between 1789 and 1953 occupied the following positions: president, vice-president, speaker of the House of Representatives, cabinet member and Supreme Court justice.

4 Political manipulation of material inducements in Australia

1 The study of material inducements in the electoral process in Australia is hampered by fragmentary evidence – even more so than in other countries. There is little systematic data to go on. Whatever evidence does exist is either illustrative or else imparted in passing, and therefore is couched in the most general terms, which makes quantification practically impossible. It is only when the fragments of information are pieced together that certain patterns and trends emerge.

2 By Dr Bruce Mitchell of the University of New England, in a private conversation.

3 By Ms Eileen Price of the University of New England, in a private conversation.

4 In New South Wales, for instance, the first (restricted) election took place in 1842 and the ballot was introduced in 1858; in Victoria, the first election was held in 1843 and the ballot was adopted thirteen years later.

5 See, for instance, in Dickey (1969), a letter from William Windeyer to Henry Parkes of 22 September 1868 (p. 19); a letter from the Parramatta District Hospital to H. Taylor, member of the Legislative Assembly of NSW, of 17 April 1890 (pp. 30–1); and a letter from H. C. Brown to Henry Parkes of March 1872 (p. 27).

6 From James Brunker to Henry Parkes, 17 August 1863 (pp. 35–6). See also James Brunker to Henry Parkes, 3 August 1863 (p. 34).

7 From Stephen Scholey to Henry Parkes, 14 February 1872 (p. 39).

8 Eventually this law was abolished as it was felt that it was no longer necessary to keep public houses closed on election day to prevent treating.

9 Queensland separated from New South Wales in 1859.

10 By the 1871–2 Election Act, voters had to have written permission to vote.

11 *Argus*, 11 December 1855, as cited by Scott (1920).

12 I did not succeed in obtaining pertinent data on South Australia and Western Australia. However, there is no reason to suppose that the situation there was fundamentally different from what it was in the other States, or that developments followed a different path.

13 The same treasurer was also accused of another form of electoral corruption. This was the Dalley electorate scandal of 1927 in which a Royal Commissioner declared that the sitting member had been enticed with a bribe of several thousand pounds to resign the seat in his favour (Kennedy, 1978).

14 See *House of Representative Debates*, 25 November 1931.

15 This point was made by Dr Don Rawson of the Australian National University in a private conversation.

16 This is not to say that *other* electoral manipulations are not being employed in Australia. Some political scientists assert that one form has been and still is widespread in Australia: namely the manipulation of electoral boundaries (gerrymandering). Not all political scientists, however, accept this conclusion. Mr Malcolm MacKerras of the Royal Military College, Duntroon, has pointed out to me that he has followed elections closely for several years, but could not find evidence for such manipulation.

It is commonly agreed that there is a weighting of electoral boundaries in favour of rural areas over urban ones. But whether this may be subsumed under the heading of electoral manipulation is another question. It is considered as such by some observers, since it violates the principle of one vote, one value – but others see it as a legitimate overrepresentation for a section of the population which contributes disproportionately to the Australian economy while at the same time being negligible in numbers.

17 This point was made by Dr Peter Loveday of the Australian National University in a private conversation.

18 By Ms Eileen Price, Dr Bruce Mitchell and Professor John Nalson of the University of New England, and Dr Colin Hughes of the Australian National University, in private conversations.

19 As in America, all these practices are more common on the local rather than on State or federal levels. But local authorities have little power or money except from federal sources, so there is not much that local politicians can hand out.

20 However, it must be taken into account that the Australian parties do not have to spend money on getting voters to the polls, as voting is compulsory by law. Apparently, some part of other countries' electoral expenses are due to the 'getting the turnout' aspect of a campaign.

5 Political manipulation of material inducements in Israel

1 See chapter 1, n. 16.

2 This authority was composed of two bodies known as the national institutions. One was the elected assembly and its executive body, the National Council; it was concerned primarily with culture, education, health and welfare. More important and more powerful, however, was the Zionist Executive (later the Jewish Agency Executive), the local representative of the World Zionist Organization. It was elected by the World Zionist Congress, and was in charge of finance (including the mobilization of capital from abroad), immigration and settlement, labour, industry and defence. It also represented the interests of the Jewish community before the Mandatory Government.

3 Ahdut Ha-Avoda: literally 'Unity of Labour'.

4 See Yuval Elizur 'Where did the millions come from and where did they go?' *Ma-Ariv*, 18 February 1977 (*Ma-Ariv* is Israel's most widely read newspaper).

5 Mapai: literally 'Land of Israel's Workers' Party'.

6 Gush: literally 'bloc'.

7 In 1948, Israel had 758,700 Jewish inhabitants; in 1958, the number had grown to 1,810,200. This means that within ten years the population had more than doubled.

8 The Jewish Agency Executive had come to be one of the two bodies comprising the national institutions in the pre-state era (see note 2 above). With the replacement of the national institutions by the Israeli government, the Jewish Agency was retained to mobilize financial aid from Jews abroad and to deal with immigration and settlement. With the massive influx of immigrants, these functions were expanded.

9 An extremist communist party. Rakah: literally 'New Communist List'.

10 See Ran Kislev 'The political aspect of the Koenig document' *Ha-Aretz*, 10 September 1976. (*Ha-Aretz* is Israel's elite newspaper.)

11 For instance, a *Ma-Ariv* reader claimed that he had personally witnessed the bribery of voters in several elections, including the 1973 election (*Ma-Ariv*, 10 March 1977). It has also been alleged that some activists of a new party (Dash) had paid the membership fees of thousands of Druze, Arab and Jewish citizens, with the further intent of bribing them to vote for the activists in the forthcoming intra-party election. Subsequently, large numbers of membership applications were rejected by the party on these grounds (see *Ha-Aretz*, 4 March 1977). (I did not find a record of treating having been employed.)

12 It has been alleged that the 'Tasmanian Dodge' has been employed in this country as well.

13 See Yuval Elizar 'Where did the millions come from and where did they go?'. *Ma-Ariv*, 18 February 1977.

14 Subsequent immigration was on a much smaller scale.

15 *Ha-Aretz* 12 and 19 November 1976.

16 Previously, in 1973, the elections were carried out in a smaller forum (the party centre); before that, the candidate was selected by top party leaders and functionaries.

17 See Amnon Barzilai, 'A home-made shock bomb', *Ha-Aretz*, 18 February 1977.

18 Likud: literally 'Cohesion'.

19 The Israel Institute of Applied Social Research (IIASR) under the directorship of Professor Louis Guttman, in conjunction with the Communications Institute of the Hebrew University headed by Professor Elihu Katz, has been carrying out periodic surveys on a cross-section of the urban Jewish population of Israel (which comprises about 90 per cent of the Jewish population) since the Six-Day War in 1967. These surveys included questions on support of the government until 1975, when they were discontinued (or at least ceased to appear in the Institute's Research Reports).

20 This assumption, of course, is not entirely accurate, since only about 80 per cent of the public usually votes, and surveys cover only the urban population. But since the urban population is the great majority in Israel, the voting public and the sample population seem to overlap sufficiently to justify this assumption as a rough approximation.

21 This subject is discussed in Etzioni-Halevy (1977).

6 Political manipulation of material inducements

1 It should be remembered that material inducements only to families and individuals are taken into account.
2 Of the Jews from Russia reaching the United States throughout the years 1901–6, 63 per cent were industrial workers and artisans and 25 per cent were engaged in personal services (see Rubinow, 1907).
3 It must be taken into account that considerable numbers left again. Nevertheless, it has been estimated that by mid-1973 immigrants made up about 30 per cent of the male Australian population aged 20 to 44 and about 26 per cent of females in that age group (Baldock, 1978, pp. 64–5).
4 GNP may be considered as a fair indicator of a country's general standard of affluence, especially in the more affluent countries where the population is above the minimum subsistence level. Obviously, all countries studied belong to this category.
5 An income of $3,000 per family of four or $1,000 *per capita* per annum was used as the poverty threshold.
6 The poverty threshold for a non-farm family of four in 1976 was an annual income of less than £5,815. The data on poverty in America have been compiled from the following sources: Bagdikian (1964, ch. 13); Masterman, ed. (1969, pp. 19–35); *Current Population Reports*, Series P60, no. 107 (September 1977).
7 The poverty line was drawn at a monthly *per capita* income of IL 140.
8 The measure of poverty adopted was the standard of living by which people were entitled to the assistance of the National Assistance Board.
9 The dividing line was drawn at A$33 a week for a household of four.
10 The dividing line was drawn at A$62.70 per week for a household of four.
11 The question of the relative quality of education in the respective countries cannot be enlarged on in this context.
12 This point will be more systematically elaborated in the conclusion to this study.
13 It is questionable whether it can explain even these developments. As Heidenheimer himself points out, nineteenth-century France did have a strong central bureaucracy prior to the development of effective organs of mass participation. And yet electoral manipulation composed of both intimidation and material inducements was rife during the third empire (see Zeldin, 1970).
14 A politicized bureaucracy is infiltrated by partisan-political criteria of action, which indicates the pervasiveness (or overpervasiveness) of political parties. However, this pervasiveness does not necessarily detract from the power of the administration. Thus, I would concur with Heidenheimer's theory to the extent that it pertains to the pervasiveness of political parties (see Conclusion), but not to the extent that it pertains to administrative power.
15 For an explanation of these terms, see Introduction.

7 Administrative power in Britain

1 These points were made by Professor R. F. V. Heuston of the University of Dublin in a seminar at the Australian National University on 11 August 1977.

8 Administrative power in the United States

1 A non-partisan nominating commission submits a list of candidates to the governor, who must make his appointments from this list. After one year in office, the judges go before the people at the next general election to secure approval for their continuation.
2 The commissioners are elected officials who serve as the legislature of the city, with each commissioner also heading a public agency.
3 The manager, a professional public administrator, selects the most capable individual available to be the chief of police.

9 Administrative power in Australia

1 The Act provided that temporary employment should cease after two years, but this stipulation proved to be a dead letter.
2 Excluding teachers, the military and post office employees.
3 The sample included 370 members of various sections of the Australian elite, such as politicians, academics and senior public servants (see Higley, Deacon and Smart (1979)).
4 These points were made by Dr Colin Hughes of the Australian National University in a private conversation.
5 It is not argued, for instance, that there is no corruption in Australia. But it is held that the dimensions of corruption are clearly more restricted than they are in the US or in Israel.
6 Admittedly, this system does not prevent numerous strikes – which, of course, are basically power struggles.
7 Although its recommendations are sometimes modified by the government.
8 Recently a federal minister was suspended following allegations that he had sought to influence the Electoral Commission in the last redistribution in Queensland, and a Royal Commission has been appointed to inquire into these allegations. This minister was subsequently cleared by the Commission and reinstated, but another federal minister was dismissed following the Royal Commission's conclusion that he had influenced the Electoral Commission with regard to the naming of an electorate. The Prime Minister himself encountered strong criticism because of allegations that he had known of the minister's action. Violation of the neutrality of electoral commissions is thus considered as a severe deviation from proper conduct.
9 See Bruce Juddery, 'New body may prove to be an important stimulant to government thinking', *Canberra Times*, 31 December 1977.
10 These points were made by Dr Colin Hughes of the Australian National University in a private conversation.

11 There were some allegations that, in New South Wales, illegal establishments have been allowed to operate in exchange for contributions to the
party in office; but no evidence for this has been uncovered.

10 Administrative power in Israel

1 The federation of Labour unions, which established its own economic
concerns, health service, etc., and was also a political organization ruled
by the various Labour parties (see chapter 5).
2 On the dominant position of the Ahdut Ha-Avoda party in the
Histadrut, see also chapter 5.
3 According to data presented by Shapiro (1975, p. 213), some 50 per cent
of the Ahdut Ha-Avoda party activists held paid positions in the
Histadrut administration.
4 On this institution, see chapter 5.
5 The Jewish Agency Executive came to be one of the two organizations
composing the national institutions; see chapter 5.
6 It will be recalled that Mapai was created through a merger of Ahdut
Ha-Avoda with another Labour party; see chapter 5.
7 See Dan Margalit, 'The lobby', Ha-Aretz, 27 April 1978.
8 See for instance Joel Marcus, 'With a settled mind and an iron hand',
Ha-Aretz, 16 February 1977, and Yuval Elizur, 'Where did the millions
come from and where did they go?', Ma-Ariv, 18 February 1977.
9 On this concept see Etzioni-Halevy (1975).
10 Proteksia: literally 'protection'.
11 On a cross-section of Israel's adult Jewish urban population (comprising
about 90 per cent of the Jewish population of Israel).
12 The Australian pattern of neutralizing political influence by setting up
semi-judicial bodies to allocate resources has not reached similar
dimensions in Israel. While some boards and commissions have been
created, their influence is neither as intensive nor as extensive as it is in
Australia. Some of them also fulfil rather different functions from those
they fulfil in Australia. On this, see Etzioni-Halevy (1977, ch. 6).
13 The Haganah (the major military organization) was formally under the
auspicies of the national institutions, but was actually under the
influence of the labour movement (as was its affiliate the Palmah); Etzel,
another military organization, was affiliated with the Revisionist
Movement.
14 This is not to say that the Israeli defence forces are entirely free of
political influence, but merely that they are less politicized than the
underground organizations were in the Yishuv era.
15 This was ensured by the establishment of a council in charge of religious
education, which is still composed chiefly of persons sponsored or
approved by the National Religious Party.
16 Counter ideologies proposed by the centre-rightist 'Citizens' Groups'
were far less attractive and less widely accepted by the public.
17 Only the judiciary was to some extent created on the British
model.
18 Many left Russia before or shortly after the establishment of the

communist regime, when the one-party system was not yet strongly entrenched.

Conclusion

1 See Introduction and chapter 6.
2 It will be recalled that material inducements on the micro-level only are being dealt with.
3 This is not to detract from the major (and rather self-evident) dissimilarities between America the superpower and the minute state of Israel in almost every other respect.
4 The term is used here in accordance with the definition presented in the Introduction.
5 It should be emphasized that the differences are matters of degree rather than absolutes (see Introduction).
6 The complete elimination of favouritism is not to be expected anywhere.

Bibliography

ABEL-SMITH, B. and TOWNSEND, P. (1965), *The Poor and the Poorest,* Occasional Papers on Social Administration, no. 17, London, Bell.

AKZIN, B. and DROR, Y. (1966), *National Planning in Israel*, Jerusalem, College for Administration (Hebrew).

ALEXANDER, H. E. (1976), *Financing Politics*, Washington, Congressional Quarterly Press.

ALLEN, A. J. (1964), *The English Voter*, London, English Universities Press.

ALMOND, G. and VERBA, S. (1965), *The Civic Culture*, Boston, Little Brown.

ALTHUSSER, L. (1969), *For Marx* (trans. B. Brewster), London, Allen Lane.

ALTHUSSER, L. (1977), *Lenin and Philosophy and Other Essays*, 2nd edn (trans. B. Brewster), London, New Left Books.

ARMSTRONG, J. A. (1973), *The European Administrative Elite*, Princeton University Press.

ARON, R. (1950), 'Social structure and the ruling class', *British Journal of Sociology*, 1, part 1, pp. 1–16; part 2, pp. 126–43.

ARONOFF, M. J. (1972), 'Party center and local branch relationship: the Israeli Labor Party', in Arian, A. (ed.), *The Elections in Israel, 1969*, Jerusalem, Academic Press, pp. 152–83.

AUSTIN, A. G., ed. (1965), *The Webbs' Australian Diary, 1898*, Melbourne, Pitman.

BAGDIKIAN, B. H. (1964), *In the Midst of Plenty*, Boston, Beacon Press.

BAGWELL, P. S. and MINGAY, G. E. (1970), *Britain and America 1850–1939*, London, Routledge & Kegan Paul.

BALDOCK, C. V. (1978), *Australia and Social Change Theory*, Sydney, Ian Novak.

BANFIELD, E. C. and WILSON, J. Q. (1963), *City Politics*, Harvard University Press.

BARAN, P. A. and SWEEZY, P. M. (1967), *Monopoly Capital*, New York, Monthly Press Review.

BARKAI, C. (1964), 'The public sector, the Histadrut sector and the private

203

sector in the Israeli economy', Jerusalem, Falk Project, sixth report (Hebrew).

BELL, D. (1960), *The End of Ideology*, Chicago, Free Press.

BENT, A. E. (1974), *The Politics of Law Enforcement*, Lexington, Heath.

BERLE, A. A. Jr (1962), 'Elected judges or appointed?', in Scigliano, R. (ed.), *The Courts*, Boston, Little Brown, pp. 97–103.

BERNAYS, C. A. (n.d.), *Queensland Politics During Sixty Years (1859–1919)*, Brisbane, Government Printer.

BIRCH, A. H. (1973), *The British System of Government*, rev. edn, London, Allen & Unwin.

BLAND, F. A. (1932), 'The spoils system in the public service', *Australian Quarterly*, 4, pp. 34–43.

BLAND, F. A., ed. (1944), *Government in Australia*, 2nd edn, Sydney, Government Printer.

BRIDGES, E. (1971), 'Portrait of a profession', in Chapman, R. A. and Dunsire, A. (eds), *Style in Administration*, pp. 44–60.

BRINTON, C. (1959), *The Anatomy of Revolution*, New York, Vintage Books.

BRZEZINSKY, Z. and HUNTINGTON, S. P. (1964), *Political Power U.S.A./U.S.S.R.*, London, Chatto & Windus.

BUTLER, D. E. and CORNFORD, J. (1969), 'United Kingdom', in Rokkan, S. and Meyriat, J. (eds), *International Guide to Electoral Statistics*, The Hague, Mouton, pp. 330–51.

BUTLER, D. E. and FREEMAN, J. (1968), *British Political Facts*, 2nd edn, London, Macmillan.

BUTLER, D. E. and PINTO-DUSCHINSKY, M. (1971), *The British General Election of 1970*, London, Macmillan.

BUTLER, D. E. and ROSE, R. (1960), *The British General Election of 1959*, London, Macmillan.

BYRT, W. J. and CREAN, F. (1972), *Government and Politics in Australia*, New York, McGraw-Hill.

CAIDEN, G. E. (1963), 'The study of Australian administrative history', Department of Political Science, Research School of Social Sciences, Canberra, Australian National University (mimeo).

CAIDEN G. E. (1967), *The Commonwealth Bureaucracy*, Melbourne University Press.

CHAPMAN, R. A. and DUNSIRE, A., eds (1971), *Style in Administration*, London, Allen & Unwin.

CHASE, H. W. (1972), *Federal Judges: The Appointment Process*, University of Minnesota Press.

CHRISTOPH, J. B. (1975), 'High civil servants and the politics of consensualism in Great Britain', in Doyan, M. (ed.), *The Mandarins of Western Europe*, New York, Wiley, pp. 25–62.

CLARK, C. I. (1947), *The Parliament of Tasmania: an Historical Sketch*, Tasmania, Government Printer.

COHEN, E. *et al.* (1962), *Research on Absorption of Immigrants in Development Towns: a Summary Report*, Jerusalem, Hebrew University (Hebrew).

CONNELL, R. W. (1977), *Ruling Class, Ruling Culture*, Cambridge University Press.

CONVERSE, P. E. (1972), 'Change in the American electorate', in Campbell, A. and Converse, P. E. (eds), *The Human Meaning of Social Change*, New York, Russell Sage Foundation, pp. 263–338.

COOMBS, H. C. *et al.* (1976), *Royal Commission on Australian Government Administration Report*, Canberra, Australian Government Publishing Service.

CRAIG, F. W. S. (1976), *British Electoral Facts 1885–1975*, 3rd edn, London, Macmillan.

CRAIG, F. W. S. (1977), *British Parliamentary Election Results 1832–1885*, London, Macmillan.

CRISP, L. F. (1965), *Australian National Government*, Melbourne, Longmans.

CROWLEY, F. K. (1960), 'The government of Western Australia', in Davis, S. R. (ed.), *The Government of the Australian States*, London, Longmans, pp. 405–78.

DANET, BRENDA (1971), 'Confrontation with bureaucracy', Jerusalem, Communications Institute, Hebrew University and the Israel Institute of Applied Social Research (mimeo, Hebrew).

DAVIES, A. F. (1964), *Australian Democracy*, 2nd edn, London, Longmans Green.

DAVIS, S. R. (1960), 'Diversity in unity' in Davis, S. R. (ed.), *The Government of the Australian States*, London, Longmans, pp. 557–713.

DESHEN, S. A. (1970), *Immigrant Voters in Israel: Parties and Congregations in a Local Election Campaign*, Manchester University Press.

DESHEN, S. A. (1972), 'The business of ethnicity is finished? The ethnic factor in a local election campaign', in Arian, A. (ed.), *The Elections in Israel, 1969*, Jerusalem, Academic Press, pp. 278–302.

DEVINE, D. J. (1972), *The Political Culture of the United States*, Boston, Little Brown.

DICKEY, B., ed. (1969), *Politics in New South Wales, 1856–1900*, Melbourne, Cassell.

DIPALMA, G. (1970), *Apathy and Participation*, New York, Free Press.

DYE, T. R. and ZEIGLER, L. (1975), *The Irony of Democracy*, 3rd edn, North Scituate, Mass., Duxbury Press.

EDELMAN, M. J. (1964), *The Symbolic Uses of Politics*, University of Illinois Press.

EDELMAN, M. J. (1971), *Politics as Symbolic Action*, New York, Academic Press.

EIDENBERG, E. and RIGERT, J. (1971), 'The police and politics', in Hann, H. (ed.), *Police in Urban Society*, Beverly Hills, Sage Publications, pp. 291–305.

EISENSTADT, S. N. (1966), *Modernization, Protest and Change*, Englewood Cliffs, N.J., Prentice-Hall.

EISENSTADT, S. N. (1967), *Israeli Society*, London, Weidenfeld & Nicolson.

205

EISENSTADT, S. N. (1974), *Change and Continuity in Israeli Society*, New York, Humanities Press, in collaboration with Am Oved of Tel-Aviv (Hebrew).

EMY, H. V. (1974), *The Politics of Australian Democracy*, Melbourne, Macmillan.

ENCEL, S. (1970), *Equality and Authority*, Melbourne, Cheshire.

EPSTEIN, L. D. (1967), *Political Parties in Western Democracies*, London, Pall Mall Press.

ETZIONI-HALEVY, E. (1975), 'Some patterns of semi-deviance on the Israeli social scene', *Social Problems*, 22, pp. 356–67.

ETZIONI-HALEVY, E. (1977), *Political Culture in Israel*, New York Praeger.

EVANS, E. A. (1962), 'Political influences in the selection of federal judges', in Scigliano, R. (ed.), *The Courts*, Boston, Little Brown, pp. 65–9.

FERGUSON, J. H. and McHENRY, D. E. (1950), *The American Federal Government*, New York, McGraw-Hill.

FIELD, G. L. and HIGLEY, J. (1973), 'Elites and non-elites: the possibilities and their side effects', Andover, N.H., Warner Modular Publications, no. 13, pp. 1–38.

FIELD, G. L. and HIGLEY, J. (1978), 'Imperfectly unified elites: the cases of Italy and France', in Tomasson, R. (ed.), *Comparative Studies in Sociology*, New York, JAI Books, pp. 295–317.

FINER, S. E. (1952), 'Patronage and the public service: Jeffersonian bureaucracy and the British tradition', *Public Administration*, 30, pp. 329–60.

FISH, C. R. (1900), 'Removal of officials by the president of the United States', *Annual Report of the American Historical Association for the Year 1899*, Washington, D.C., Govt Printing Office, vol. 1, pp. 67–86.

FORBES, A. J. de B. (1956), 'The South Australian electoral system', *Australian Quarterly*, 28, pp. 47–51.

FOSTER, J. (1974), *Class Struggle in the Industrial Revolution*, London, Weidenfeld & Nicolson.

FREDMAN, L. E. (1968), *The Australian Ballot: the Story of an American Reform*, Michigan State University Press.

GLOBERSON, A. (1970), *The Administrative Elite in the Government Civil Service in Israel*, Tel-Aviv, Hamidrasha Leminhal (Hebrew).

GORNI, Y. (1970), 'Changes in the social and political structure of the Second Aliya in the years 1909–1940', *Zionism*, 2, pp. 47–99(Hebrew).

GORNI, Y. (1973), *Ahdut Ha-Avoda 1919–1930*, Tel-Aviv University Press and Hotsa'at Hakibbutz Hameuhad (Hebrew).

GOSNELL, H. F. (1937), *Machine Politics: Chicago Model*, University of Chicago Press.

GREAT BRITAIN, CENTRAL STATISTICAL OFFICE, *Annual Abstract of Statistics*, nos 47–8 (1885–1900); no. 67 (1906–20); no. 70 (1911–25); no. 82 (1913, 1924–37); no. 88 (1935–50); no. 113 (1976); no. 114 (1977).

GREEN, F. C. ed. (n.d.), *Tasmania: a Century of Responsible Government 1856–1956*, Hobart, Government Printer.

GREENSTEIN, F. I. (1966), 'The changing pattern of urban party politics', in Herzberg, D. G. and Pomper, G. M. (eds), *American Party Politics*, New York, Holt, Rinehart & Winston, pp. 253–63.

GUTTSMAN, W. L. (1963), *The British Political Elite*, London, MacGibbon & Kee.

GWYN, W. B. (1962), *Democracy and the Cost of Politics in Britain*, London, Athlone Press.

HAWKER, G. N. (1971), *The Parliament of New South Wales 1856–1965*, Ultimo, N.S.W., Government Printer.

HEARD, A. (1960), *The Costs of Democracy*, University of North Carolina Press.

HEIDENHEIMER, A. J. ed. (1970), *Political Corruption: Readings in Comparative Analysis*, New York, Holt, Rinehart & Winston.

HENDERSON, R. F. (1969), 'The dimensions of poverty in Australia', in Masterman, G. G. (ed.), *Poverty in Australia*, Sydney, Angus & Robertson, pp. 71–83.

HENDERSON, R. F. (1975), Chairman, Commission of Inquiry into Poverty, *Poverty in Australia: an Outline*, Canberra, Australian Government Publishing Service.

HIGLEY, J., DEACON, D. and SMART, D. (1979), *Elites in Australia*, London, Routledge & Kegan Paul.

HIGLEY, J., FIELD, G. L. and GRØHOLT, K. (1976), *Elite Structure and Ideology*, Columbia University Press.

HOGAN, J. (1945), *Election and Representation*, Oxford, Cork University Press.

HORNE, D. (1971), *The Lucky Country*, Harmondsworth, Penguin.

HOROWITZ, D. and LISSAK, M. (1971), 'Authority without sovereignty', in Lissak, M. and Gutman, E. (eds), *Political Institutions and Processes in Israel*, Jerusalem, Akademon.

HUGHES, C. A. (1968), 'Compulsory voting', in C. A. Hughes (ed.), *Readings in Australian Government*, University of Queensland Press, ch. 16.

HUNTINGTON, S. P. (1968), *Political Order in Changing Societies*, Yale University Press.

INTERNATIONAL INSTITUTE FOR STRATEGIC STUDIES (1977), *The Miliary Balance: 1977–78*, London.

JENKS, E. (1891), *The Government of Victoria*, London, Macmillan.

JOYCE, P. (1975), 'The factory politics of Lancashire in the later 19th century', *Historical Journal*, 18, pp. 525–53.

JUPP, J. (1964), *Australian Party Politics*, Melbourne University Press.

KENNEDY, K. H. (1978), *The Mungana Affair*, University of Queensland Press.

KEY, V. O. Jr (1964), *Politics, Parties and Pressure Groups*, 5th edn, New York, Crowell.

KING, J. P. (1970), 'Socioeconomic development and the incidence of English corrupt campaign practices', in Heidenheimer, A. J. (ed.), *Political Corruption: Readings in Comparative Analysis*, pp. 379–90.

KNIGHT, K. (1961), 'Patronage and the 1894 Royal Commission of Inquiry into the N.S.W. Public Service', *Australian Journal of Politics and History*, 7, pp. 166–85.

KUZNETS, S. (1966), *Modern Economic Growth*, Yale University Press.

LACK, C., ed. (n.d.), *Three Decades of Queensland Political History: 1929–1960*, Brisbane, Government Printer.

LANE, R. E. (1959), *Political Life: Why People Get Involved in Politics*, Chicago, Free Press.

LASKI, H. (1945), *Parliamentary Government in England*, London, Allen & Unwin.

LEONARD, R. L. (1968), *Elections in Britain*, London, Van Nostrand.

LIPPMAN, W. (1961), *Public Opinion*, New York, Macmillan.

LLOYD, T. (1968), *The General Election of 1880*, Oxford University Press.

LOVEDAY, P. (1959), 'Patronage and politics in New South Wales 1856–1870', *Public Administration* (Sydney), 18, pp. 341–58.

LOVEDAY, P. and MARTIN, A. W. (1966), *Parliament, Factions and Parties: The First Thirty Years of Responsible Government in New South Wales 1856–1889*, Melbourne University Press.

LOVEDAY, P., MARTIN, A. W. and PARKER, R. S. (eds) (1977), *The Emergence of the Australian Party System*, Sydney, Hale & Iremonger.

LUKAS, A. J. (1976), *Nightmare*, New York, Viking Press.

McCALLUM, R. B. and READMAN, A. (1964), *The British General Election of 1945*, London, Frank Cass.

McCOOK, J. J. (1892), 'The alarming proportion of venal votes', *Forum*, 14.

McKENZIE, W. J. M. (1958), *Free Elections*, London, Allen & Unwin.

MacKERRAS, M. H. (1975), *Elections 1975*, London, Angus & Robertson.

MACKIE, T. T. and ROSE, R. (1974), *The International Almanac of Electoral History*, London, Macmillan.

MARCUSE, H. (1964), *One-Dimensional Man*, London, Sphere Books.

MARTIN, A. W. (1958), 'Henry Parkes and electoral manipulation, 1872–82', *Historical Studies*, *ANZ*, 8, pp. 268–80.

MASTERMAN, G. G. ed. (1969), *Poverty in Australia*, Sydney, Angus & Robertson.

MEDDING, P. Y. (1972), *Mapai in Israel*, Cambridge University Press.

MERTON, R. K. (1957a), 'Manifest and latent functions', in *Social Theory and Social Structure*, rev. edn, New York, Free Press, pp. 19–84.

MERTON, R. K. (1957b), 'Bureaucratic structure and personality', in *Social Theory and Social Structure*, rev. edn, New York, Free Press, pp. 195–206.

MICHELS, R. (1949), *Political Parties*, Chicago, Free Press.

MILBRATH, L. W. (1965), *Political Participation: How and Why Do People Get Involved in Politics?* Chicago, Rand McNally.

MILIBAND, R. (1973), *The State in Capitalist Society*, London, Quartet Books.

MILLER, J. D. and JINKS, B. (1971), *Australian Government and Politics*, 4th edn, London, Duckworth.

MILLS, C. W. (1959), *The Power Elite*, New York, Oxford University Press.

MILLS, J. E. (1942), 'The composition of the first Victorian parliament 1856–1881', *Historical Studies ANZ*, 2, pp. 25–39.

MORLAN, R. L. (1949), 'City politics: free style', *National Municipal Review*, 38, pp. 485–90.

MORRISON, A. A. (1950), 'Politics in early Queensland', *Royal Historical Society of Queensland Journal*, 4, pp. 293–312.

MORRISON, A. A. (1951), 'Religion and politics in Queensland (to 1881)', *Royal Historical Society of Queensland Journal*, 4, pp. 455–70.

MORRISON, A. A. (1952), 'The town "liberal" and the squatter', *Royal Historical Society of Queensland Journal*, 4, pp. 599–618.

MORRISON, A. A. (1953), 'Liberal Party organization before 1900', *Royal Historical Society of Queensland Journal*, 5, pp. 752–70.

MORRISON, A. A. (1960), 'The government of Queensland', in S. R. Davis (ed.), *The Government of the Australian States*, London, Longmans, pp. 249–332.

MORRISON, A. A. 1960–1), 'Some lesser members of parliament in Queensland', *Royal Historical Society of Queensland Journal*, 6, pp. 557–79.

MORRISON, A. A. (1966), 'Colonial society 1860–1890', *Queensland Heritage*, 1, pp. 21–30.

MOYNIHAN, D. P. and WILSON, J. Q. (1966), 'Patronage in New York State 1955–1959', in Herzberg, D. G. and Pomper, G. M. (eds), *American Party Politics*, New York, Holt, Rinehart & Winston, pp. 213–31.

MUELLER, C. (1973), *The Politics of Communication*, New York, Oxford University Press.

NAIRN, N. B. (1967), 'The political mastery of Sir Henry Parkes: New South Wales politics 1871–1891', *Journal of the Royal Australian Historical Society*, 53, pp. 1–53.

NEALE, R. S. (1967), 'H. S. Chapman and the Victorian ballot', *Historical Studies ANZ*, 12, pp. 506–21.

O'LEARY, C. (1962), *The Elimination of Corrupt Practices in British Elections 1868–1911*, Oxford, Clarendon Press.

PARKER, R. S. (1960), 'The government of New South Wales', in Davis, S. R. (ed.), *The Government of the Australian States*, London, Longmans, pp. 55–171.

PARKER, R. S. (1968), 'Power in Australia', in Hughes, C. A. (ed.), *Readings in Australian Government*, Queensland University Press, pp. 21–33.

PARRIS, H. (1969), *Constitutional Bureaucracy*, London, Allen & Unwin.

PARTRIDGE, P. H. (1971), *Consent and Consensus*, London, Macmillan.

PEARL, C. (1958), *Wild Men of Sydney*, London, W. H. Allen.

PENNIMAN, H. (1962), *The American Political Process*, Princeton, N.J., Van Nostrand.

PITKIN, H. (1965), 'Obligation and consent: I', *American Political Science Review*, 59, pp. 990–8.

PITKIN, H. (1966), 'Obligation and consent: II', *American Political Science Review*, 60, pp. 39–52.

POULANTZAS, N. (1973), *Political Power and Social Classes* (trans. T. O'Hagan), London, New Left Books.

POULANTZAS, N. (1975), *Classes in Contemporary Capitalism* (trans. D. Fernbach), London, New Left Books.

PRICE, C. A. and MARTIN, J., eds (1976), *Australian Immigration*, Canberra, Australian National University Press.

PUTNAM, R. D. (1976), *The Comparative Study of Political Elites*, Englewood Cliffs, N.J., Prentice-Hall.

QUAIFE, G. R. (1967), 'The history of the ballot in 1856', *Victorian Historical Magazine*, 38, pp. 144–58.

QUAIFE, G. R. (1969), 'Make us roads no matter how: a note on colonial politics', *Australian Journal of Politics and History*, 15, pp. 47–54.

REICHLEY, J. (1966), 'Reform and organization politics in Philadelphia', in Herzberg, D. G. and Pomper, G. M. (eds), *American Party Politics*, New York, Holt, Rinehart & Winston.

REID, R. L. (1960), 'The government of South Australia', in S. R. Davis (ed.), *The Government of the Australian States*, London, Longmans, pp. 333–404.

REYNOLDS, H. (1969), ' "Men of substance and deservedly good repute": the Tasmanian gentry 1856–1875', *Australian Journal of Politics and History*, 15, pp. 61–72.

ROURKE, F. E. (1970), 'Urbanism and the national party organizations', in Nelson, W. R. (ed.), *American Government and Political Change*, New York, Oxford University Press, pp. 182–95.

RUBINOW, I. M. (1907), 'Economic conditions of the Jews in Russia', *United States Bureau of Labor Bulletin*, Washington, no. 72, pp. 499–506.

SCHLESINGER, J. A. (1975), 'The primary goals of political parties: a clarification of positive theory', *American Political Science Review*, 69, pp. 840–9.

SCHUBERT, G. (1974), *Judicial Policy Making*, rev. edn, Chicago, Scott, Foresman.

SCOTT, E. (1920), 'The history of the Victorian ballot', *Victorian Historical Magazine*, 8, pp. 1–14.

SCOTT, J. C. (1973), *Comparative Political Corruption*, Englewood Cliffs, N.J., Prentice-Hall.

SERLE, G. (1963), *The Golden Age*, Melbourne University Press.

SERLE, G. (1971), *The Rush to be Rich: a History of the Colony of Victoria, 1883–1889*, Melbourne University Press.

SHAPIRO, Y. (1975), *The Organization of Power*, Tel-Aviv, Am Oved (Hebrew).

SHAPIRO, Y. (1977), *Democracy in Israel*, Ramat Gan, Massada.

SHILS, E. A. (1975), 'Center and periphery', in *Center and Periphery: Essays in Macrosociology*, University of Chicago Press, pp. 3–16.

SHONFIELD, A. (1971), 'Britain in the postwar world', pp. 399–419 in Chapman, R. A. and Dunsire, A. (eds), *Style in Administration*, London, Allen & Unwin.

SISSON, C. H. (1971), 'The politician as intruder', in Chapman, R. A. and Dunsire, A. (eds), *Style in Administration*, pp. 448–56.

SORAUF, F. J. (1956), 'State patronage in a rural county', *American Political Science Review*, 50, pp. 1046–56.

SORAUF, F. J. (1960), 'The silent revolution in patronage', *Public Administration Review*, 20, pp. 28–34.

SPANN, R. N. (1972), *The Public Bureaucracy in Australia*, AIPS Monographs, no. 8.

SPANN, R. N. (1973), 'Bureaucracy and the public service', in Mayer, H. and Nelson, H. (eds), *Australian Politics: a Third Reader*, Melbourne, Cheshire, pp. 579–612.

SPEED, J. G. (1970), 'The purchase of votes in New York City', in Heidenheimer, A. J. (ed.), *Political Corruption: Reading in Comparative Analysis*, pp. 422–6.

STEINBERG, A. (1972), *The Bosses*, New York, New American Library.

STUBB, J. (1966), *The Hidden People*, Melbourne, Cheshire.

TAYLOR, A. J. P. (1972), *Beaverbrook*, London, Hamish Hamilton.

TOWNSLEY, W. A. (1960), 'The government of Australia', in Davis, S. R. (ed.), *The Government of the Australian States*, London, Longmans, pp. 479–555.

TOWNSLEY, W. A. (n.d.), 'The electoral system and the constituencies', in Green, F. C. (ed.), *Tasmania: a Century of Responsible Government 1856–1956*, pp. 59–112.

U.S. BUREAU OF THE CENSUS (1975), *Historical Statistics of the United States: Colonial Times to 1970*, Washington, D.C.

U.S. BUREAU OF THE CENSUS (1977), *Statistical Abstract of the United States* (98th edn), Washington, D.C.

WATSON, L. (1973), 'The party machines', in Mayer, H. and Nelson, H. (eds), *Australian Politics: a Third Reader*, Melbourne, Cheshire, pp. 339–65.

WATSON, R. A. and DOWNING, R. G. (1969), *The Politics of the Bench and the Bar*, New York, Wiley.

WEBB, B. and S., *see* Austin, A. G.

WETTENHALL, R. L. (1973), 'The ministerial department: British origins and Australian adaptations', *Public Administration* (Sydney), 32, pp. 233–50.

WHITE, T. H. (1975), *Breach of Faith*, New York, Atheneum Publishers.

WILTSHIRE, K. (1974), *An Introduction to Australian Public Administration*, Melbourne, Cassell.

WOOD, R. C. (1966), 'The suburban boss', in Herzberg, D. G. and Pomper, G. M. (eds), *American Party Politics*, New York, Holt, Rinehart & Winston, pp. 272–7.

ZAMIR, R. (1964), *Beer Sheba: 1958/59, Social Processes in a Development Town*, Sociological Research, Notebook 5, Jerusalem, Hebrew University (Hebrew).

ZELDIN, T. (1970), 'How the government won the election under Napoleon III', in Heidenheimer, A. J. (ed.), *Political Corruption: Readings in Comparative Analysis*, pp. 373–8.

Index

56–60, 92, 94–100; legislation against, 38, 40–1, 43–8, 64, 79, 80–1, 83, 84, 106, 170–1; party finances, 38–9, 56, 69,100–1; public administration and, 119–21, 128–30, 140–1, 158–9; to public generally, 43; and reform movements, 58, 79; survival, US, 66–70; types, 10, 36, 37, 40–1, *40*, 54, *62*, 92, 98–9; and types of bureaucracy, 12, 14, 118; and welfare movement, 59
Medding, P. Y., 14, 93, 96–8, 100, 166–9, 170, 174, 176
media: conservatism, 9; as watchdogs, 9
Meir, Golda, 167
meritocracy, 12–13
Merton, R. K., 13, 54, 69, 157
Michels, R., 1, 4, 7
Miller, J. D. and Jinks, B., 73–4
Mills, C. W., 3, 5, 6–7, 34, 69, 137, 185
Mills, J. E., 81, 82
monarchy, 20–1, 123, 131–3
Morlan, R. L., 61
Morrison, A. A., 73, 79–80, 81, 150, 154
Moynihan, D. P. and Wilson, J. Q., 137, 140
Moynihan, Senator, 139
Mueller, C., 7, 9

Nairn, N. B., 76, 77, 79
Naples, kingdom of, 20
New Zealand, 161
Nixon, Richard M., 138–9, 140, 187
normative frameworks, *see* ethics, codes of

O'Leary, C., 42, *42*, 47, 51

Parker, R. S., 79, 83, 85, 109–10, 153–4, 160–2, 164
Parkes, Henry, 76, 77
parliamentary government, 20–2, 131–2
Parris, H., 123–4, 125, 129, 132
Parsons, 4, 15, 122, 188
Partridge, P. H., 7
party organization: Australia, 76, 79, 81, 84–5, 87–9, 90; Britain, 38–9, 49, 51–2; and capitalism, 69–70, 185; and democracy, 56, 189; Israel, 91–8, 103–4, 170; private contributions, 60, 66, 120, 140–1; and public administration, 54–5, 70, 77, 119–21, 135–6, 140–1, 170; United States, 39, 54–66, 69, 146

patronage: of candidates, 48–9, 67; decline, 129–30, 136–9, 149, 153; deferential voting, 22, 36, 37, 41, 49, 108; public office, 37, 55, 60, 119–21, 124–6, 128–30, 134–9, 147–52
Perkins, Patrick, 80
police: Australia, 163; Israel, 174–5; United States, 145–6
political manipulation: and economic domination, 1–3, 116–17, 182–7; and efficacy, 34; and electoral process, 4–5, 18; factors allowing, 107–22; growth, 7–8; and political participation, 180–2; secret ballot and, 22–4; symbolic and non-symbolic, 8–10
political participation: Britain, 29–33, *30*; efficacy, 5–8, 18, 19, 33–4, 90; elections as, 18; expansion, 18, 29–33, 90, 181; expectations, 34; and manipulation, 180–2; need for, 19; social factors influencing, 32, 47; United States, 29–33, *31*; working-class, 51–2
politocracy, 13, 180
popular representation, 20–2
poverty, 111–15
Powell, Adam Clayton, 64
power and conflict school, 3–4
Price, C. A. and Martin, J., 111
public: factors allowing manipulation of, 11, 35–6, 38, 49–51, 58, 92, 94–5; education, 115–16; ideological commitment, 107–10; immigration and disorganization, 110–11; poverty, 111–15
Putnam, R. D., 52, *68*

Quaife, G. R., 72, 74, 82

radical minorities, votes for, *see* franchise, extension
reforms, administrative, 124–8, 135, 136–7, 147, 150–2, 152–5, 167–8, 172
Reichley, J., 61–2
Reid, B. L., 84
religious attitudes to corruption, 46
representative assemblies, 20–2; Greek and Roman, 19; increase of power, 35
Robertson (Australian politician), 76
Rockefeller, John D. IV, 66
Roosevelt, Franklin D., 60
Rourke, F. E., 63
Russia, 178

Routledge Social Science Series

Routledge & Kegan Paul   London, Henley and Boston

39 Store Street, London WC1E 7DD
Broadway House, Newtown Road,
Henley-on-Thames, Oxon RG9 1EN
9 Park Street, Boston, Mass. 02108

Contents

*Authors wishing to submit manuscripts for any series in
this catalogue should send them to the Social Science Editor,
Routledge & Kegan Paul Ltd, 39 Store Street,
London WC1E 7DD*

● *Books so marked are available in paperback
All books are in Metric Demy 8vo format (216 × 138mm approx.)*

International Library of Sociology

General Editor John Rex

GENERAL SOCIOLOGY

Barnsley, J. H. The Social Reality of Ethics. *464 pp.*
Brown, Robert. Explanation in Social Science. *208 pp.*
● Rules and Laws in Sociology. *192 pp.*
Bruford, W. H. Chekhov and His Russia. *A Sociological Study. 244 pp.*
Burton, F. and **Carlen, P.** Official Discourse. *On Discourse Analysis, Government Publications, Ideology. About 140 pp.*
Cain, Maureen E. Society and the Policeman's Role. *326 pp.*
●**Fletcher, Colin.** Beneath the Surface. *An Account of Three Styles of Sociological Research. 221 pp.*
Gibson, Quentin. The Logic of Social Enquiry. *240 pp.*
Glucksmann, M. Structuralist Analysis in Contemporary Social Thought. *212 pp.*
Gurvitch, Georges. Sociology of Law. *Foreword by Roscoe Pound. 264 pp.*
Hinkle, R. Founding Theory of American Sociology 1883-1915. *About 350 pp.*
Homans, George C. Sentiments and Activities. *336 pp.*
Johnson, Harry M. Sociology: *a Systematic Introduction. Foreword by Robert K. Merton. 710 pp.*
●**Keat, Russell** and **Urry, John.** Social Theory as Science. *278 pp.*
Mannheim, Karl. Essays on Sociology and Social Psychology. *Edited by Paul Kecskemeti. With Editorial Note by Adolph Lowe. 344 pp.*
Martindale, Don. The Nature and Types of Sociological Theory. *292 pp.*
●**Maus, Heinz.** A Short History of Sociology. *234 pp.*
Myrdal, Gunnar. Value in Social Theory: *A Collection of Essays on Methodology. Edited by Paul Streeten. 332 pp.*
Ogburn, William F. and **Nimkoff, Meyer F.** A Handbook of Sociology. *Preface by Karl Mannheim. 656 pp. 46 figures. 35 tables.*
Parsons, Talcott, and **Smelser, Neil J.** Economy and Society: *A Study in the Integration of Economic and Social Theory. 362 pp.*
Podgórecki, Adam. Practical Social Sciences. *About 200 pp.*
Raffel, S. Matters of Fact. *A Sociological Inquiry. 152 pp.*
●**Rex, John.** (Ed.) Approaches to Sociology. *Contributions by Peter Abell,* Sociology and the Demystification of the Modern World. *282 pp.*
●**Rex, John** (Ed.) Approaches to Sociology. *Contributions by Peter Abell, Frank Bechhofer, Basil Bernstein, Ronald Fletcher, David Frisby, Miriam Glucksmann, Peter Lassman, Herminio Martins, John Rex, Roland Robertson, John Westergaard and Jock Young. 302 pp.*
Rigby, A. Alternative Realities. *352 pp.*
Roche, M. Phenomenology, Language and the Social Sciences. *374 pp.*
Sahay, A. Sociological Analysis. *220 pp.*

3

Strasser, Hermann. The Normative Structure of Sociology. *Conservative and Emancipatory Themes in Social Thought. About 340 pp.*
Strong, P. Ceremonial Order of the Clinic. *About 250 pp.*
Urry, John. Reference Groups and the Theory of Revolution. *244 pp.*
Weinberg, E. Development of Sociology in the Soviet Union. *173 pp.*

FOREIGN CLASSICS OF SOCIOLOGY

● **Gerth, H. H.** and **Mills, C. Wright.** From Max Weber: *Essays in Sociology. 502 pp.*
● **Tönnies, Ferdinand.** Community and Association. *(Gemeinschaft and Gesellschaft.) Translated and Supplemented by Charles P. Loomis. Foreword by Pitirim A. Sorokin. 334 pp.*

SOCIAL STRUCTURE

Andreski, Stanislav. Military Organization and Society. *Foreword by Professor A. R. Radcliffe-Brown. 226 pp. 1 folder.*
Carlton, Eric. Ideology and Social Order. *Foreword by Professor Philip Abrahams. About 320 pp.*
Coontz, Sydney H. Population Theories and the Economic Interpretation. *202 pp.*
Coser, Lewis. The Functions of Social Conflict. *204 pp.*
Dickie-Clark, H. F. Marginal Situation: *A Sociological Study of a Coloured Group. 240 pp. 11 tables.*
Giner, S. and **Archer, M. S.** (Eds.). Contemporary Europe. *Social Structures and Cultural Patterns. 336 pp.*
● **Glaser, Barney** and **Strauss, Anselm L.** Status Passage. *A Formal Theory. 212 pp.*
Glass, D. V. (Ed.) Social Mobility in Britain. *Contributions by J. Berent, T. Bottomore, R. C. Chambers, J. Floud, D. V. Glass, J. R. Hall, H. T. Himmelweit, R. K. Kelsall, F. M. Martin, C. A. Moser, R. Mukherjee, and W. Ziegel. 420 pp.*
Kelsall, R. K. Higher Civil Servants in Britain: *From 1870 to the Present Day. 268 pp. 31 tables.*
● **Lawton, Denis.** Social Class, Language and Education. *192 pp.*
McLeish, John. The Theory of Social Change: *Four Views Considered. 128 pp.*
● **Marsh, David C.** The Changing Social Structure of England and Wales, 1871-1961. *Revised edition. 288 pp.*
Menzies, Ken. Talcott Parsons and the Social Image of Man. *About 208 pp.*
● **Mouzelis, Nicos.** Organization and Bureaucracy. *An Analysis of Modern Theories. 240 pp.*
Ossowski, Stanislaw. Class Structure in the Social Consciousness. *210 pp.*
● **Podgórecki, Adam.** Law and Society. *302 pp.*
Renner, Karl. Institutions of Private Law and Their Social Functions. *Edited, with an Introduction and Notes, by O. Kahn-Freud. Translated by Agnes Schwarzschild. 316 pp.*

Rex, J. and **Tomlinson, S.** Colonial Immigrants in a British City. *A Class Analysis. 368 pp.*
Smooha, S. Israel: Pluralism and Conflict. *472 pp.*
Wesolowski, W. Class, Strata and Power. *Trans. and with Introduction by G. Kolankiewicz. 160 pp.*
Zureik, E. Palestinians in Israel. *A Study in Internal Colonialism. 264 pp.*

SOCIOLOGY AND POLITICS

Acton, T. A. Gypsy Politics and Social Change. *316 pp.*
Burton, F. Politics of Legitimacy. *Struggles in a Belfast Community. 250 pp.*
Etzioni-Halevy, E. Political Manipulation and Administrative Power. *A Comparative Study. About 200 pp.*
● **Hechter, Michael.** Internal Colonialism. *The Celtic Fringe in British National Development, 1536–1966. 380 pp.*
Kornhauser, William. The Politics of Mass Society. *272 pp. 20 tables.*
Korpi, W. The Working Class in Welfare Capitalism. *Work, Unions and Politics in Sweden. 472 pp.*
Kroes, R. Soldiers and Students. *A Study of Right- and Left-wing Students. 174 pp.*
Martin, Roderick. Sociology of Power. *About 272 pp.*
Myrdal, Gunnar. The Political Element in the Development of Economic Theory. *Translated from the German by Paul Streeten. 282 pp.*
Wong, S.-L. Sociology and Socialism in Contemporary China. *160 pp.*
Wootton, Graham. Workers, Unions and the State. *188 pp.*

CRIMINOLOGY

Ancel, Marc. Social Defence: *A Modern Approach to Criminal Problems. Foreword by Leon Radzinowicz. 240 pp.*
Athens, L. Violent Criminal Acts and Actors. *About 150 pp.*
Cain, Maureen E. Society and the Policeman's Role. *326 pp.*
Cloward, Richard A. and **Ohlin, Lloyd E.** Delinquency and Opportunity: *A Theory of Delinquent Gangs. 248 pp.*
Downes, David M. The Delinquent Solution. *A Study in Subcultural Theory. 296 pp.*
Friedlander, Kate. The Psycho-Analytical Approach to Juvenile Delinquency: *Theory, Case Studies, Treatment. 320 pp.*
Gleuck, Sheldon and **Eleanor.** Family Environment and Delinquency. *With the statistical assistance of Rose W. Kneznek. 340 pp.*
Lopez-Rey, Manuel. Crime. *An Analytical Appraisal. 288 pp.*
Mannheim, Hermann. Comparative Criminology: *a Text Book. Two volumes. 442 pp. and 380 pp.*
Morris, Terence. The Criminal Area: *A Study in Social Ecology. Foreword by Hermann Mannheim. 232 pp. 25 tables. 4 maps.*
Podgorecki, A. and **Łos, M.** *Multidimensional Sociology. About 380 pp.*
Rock, Paul. Making People Pay. *338 pp.*

● **Taylor, Ian, Walton, Paul,** and **Young, Jock.** The New Criminology. *For a Social Theory of Deviance. 325 pp.*
● **Taylor, Ian, Walton, Paul** and **Young, Jock.** (Eds) Critical Criminology. *268 pp.*

SOCIAL PSYCHOLOGY

Bagley, Christopher. The Social Psychology of the Epileptic Child. *320 pp.*
Brittan, Arthur. Meanings and Situations. *224 pp.*
Carroll, J. Break-Out from the Crystal Palace. *200 pp.*
● **Fleming, C. M.** Adolescence: Its Social Psychology. *With an Introduction to recent findings from the fields of Anthropology, Physiology, Medicine, Psychometrics and Sociometry. 288 pp.*
● The Social Psychology of Education: *An Introduction and Guide to Its Study. 136 pp.*
Linton, Ralph. The Cultural Background of Personality. *132 pp.*
● **Mayo, Elton.** The Social Problems of an Industrial Civilization. *With an Appendix on the Political Problem. 180 pp.*
Ottaway, A. K. C. Learning Through Group Experience. *176 pp.*
Plummer, Ken. Sexual Stigma. *An Interactionist Account. 254 pp.*
● **Rose, Arnold M.** (Ed.) Human Behaviour and Social Processes: *an Interactionist Approach. Contributions by Arnold M. Rose, Ralph H. Turner, Anselm Strauss, Everett C. Hughes, E. Franklin Frazier, Howard S. Becker et al. 696 pp.*
Smelser, Neil J. Theory of Collective Behaviour. *448 pp.*
Stephenson, Geoffrey M. The Development of Conscience. *128 pp.*
Young, Kimball. Handbook of Social Psychology. *658 pp. 16 figures. 10 tables.*

SOCIOLOGY OF THE FAMILY

Bell, Colin R. Middle Class Families: *Social and Geographical Mobility. 224 pp.*
Burton, Lindy. Vulnerable Children. *272 pp.*
Gavron, Hannah. The Captive Wife: *Conflicts of Household Mothers. 190 pp.*
George, Victor and **Wilding, Paul.** Motherless Families. *248 pp.*
Klein, Josephine. Samples from English Cultures.
 1. Three Preliminary Studies and Aspects of Adult Life in England. *447 pp.*
 2. Child-Rearing Practices and Index. *247 pp.*
Klein, Viola. The Feminine Character. *History of an Ideology. 244 pp.*
McWhinnie, Alexina M. Adopted Children. *How They Grow Up. 304 pp.*
● **Morgan, D. H. J.** Social Theory and the Family. *About 320 pp.*
● **Myrdal, Alva** and **Klein, Viola.** Women's Two Roles: *Home and Work. 238 pp. 27 tables.*

Parsons, Talcott and **Bales, Robert F.** Family: Socialization and Inter-action Process. *In collaboration with James Olds, Morris Zelditch and Philip E. Slater. 456 pp. 50 figures and tables.*

SOCIAL SERVICES

Bastide, Roger. The Sociology of Mental Disorder. *Translated from the French by Jean McNeil. 260 pp.*
Carlebach, Julius. Caring For Children in Trouble. *266 pp.*
George, Victor. Foster Care. *Theory and Practice. 234 pp.*
  Social Security: *Beveridge and After. 258 pp.*
George, V. and **Wilding, P.** Motherless Families. *248 pp.*
● **Goetschius, George W.** Working with Community Groups. *256 pp.*
Goetschius, George W. and **Tash, Joan.** Working with Unattached Youth. *416 pp.*
Heywood, Jean S. Children in Care. *The Development of the Service for the Deprived Child. Third revised edition. 284 pp.*
King, Roy D., Ranes, Norma V. and **Tizard, Jack.** Patterns of Residen-tial Care. *356 pp.*
Leigh, John. Young People and Leisure. *256 pp.*
● **Mays, John.** (Ed.) Penelope Hall's Social Services of England and Wales. *About 324 pp.*
Morris, Mary. Voluntary Work and the Welfare State. *300 pp.*
Nokes, P. L. The Professional Task in Welfare Practice. *152 pp.*
Timms, Noel. Psychiatric Social Work in Great Britain (1939-1962). *280 pp.*
● Social Casework: *Principles and Practice. 256 pp.*

SOCIOLOGY OF EDUCATION

Banks, Olive. Parity and Prestige in English Secondary Education: a Study in Educational Sociology. *272 pp.*
● **Blyth, W. A. L.** English Primary Education. *A Sociological Description.* 2. Background. *168 pp.*
Collier, K. G. The Social Purposes of Education: *Personal and Social Values in Education. 268 pp.*
Evans, K. M. Sociometry and Education. *158 pp.*
● **Ford, Julienne.** Social Class and the Comprehensive School. *192 pp.*
Foster, P. J. Education and Social Change in Ghana. *336 pp. 3 maps.*
Fraser, W. R. Education and Society in Modern France. *150 pp.*
Grace, Gerald R. Role Conflict and the Teacher. *150 pp.*
Hans, Nicholas. New Trends in Education in the Eighteenth Century. *278 pp. 19 tables.*
● Comparative Education: *A Study of Educational Factors and Tra-ditions. 360 pp.*
● **Hargreaves, David.** Interpersonal Relations and Education. *432 pp.*
● Social Relations in a Secondary School. *240 pp.*
School Organization and Pupil Involvement. *A Study of Secondary Schools.*

7

● **Mannheim, Karl** and **Stewart, W.A.C.** An Introduction to the Sociology of Education. *206 pp.*
● **Musgrove, F.** Youth and the Social Order. *176 pp.*
● **Ottaway, A. K. C.** Education and Society: An Introduction to the Sociology of Education. *With an Introduction by W. O. Lester Smith. 212 pp.*
  Peers, Robert. Adult Education: *A Comparative Study. Revised edition. 398 pp.*
  Stratta, Erica. The Education of Borstal Boys. *A Study of their Educational Experiences prior to, and during, Borstal Training. 256 pp.*
● **Taylor, P. H., Reid, W. A.** and **Holley, B. J.** The English Sixth Form. *A Case Study in Curriculum Research. 198 pp.*

SOCIOLOGY OF CULTURE

Eppel, E. M. and **M.** Adolescents and Morality: *A Study of some Moral Values and Dilemmas of Working Adolescents in the Context of a changing Climate of Opinion. Foreword by W. J. H. Sprott. 268 pp. 39 tables.*
● **Fromm, Erich.** The Fear of Freedom. *286 pp.*
●   The Sane Society. *400 pp.*
  Johnson, L. The Cultural Critics. *From Matthew Arnold to Raymond Williams. 233 pp.*
  Mannheim, Karl. Essays on the Sociology of Culture. *Edited by Ernst Mannheim in co-operation with Paul Kecskemeti. Editorial Note by Adolph Lowe. 280 pp.*
  Zijderfeld, A. C. On Clichés. *The Supersedure of Meaning by Function in Modernity. About 132 pp.*

SOCIOLOGY OF RELIGION

Argyle, Michael and **Beit-Hallahmi, Benjamin.** The Social Psychology of Religion. *About 256 pp.*
Glasner, Peter E. The Sociology of Secularisation. *A Critique of a Concept. About 180 pp.*
Hall, J. R. The Ways Out. *Utopian Communal Groups in an Age of Babylon. 280 pp.*
Ranson, S., Hinings, B. and **Bryman, A.** Clergy, Ministers and Priests. *216 pp.*
Stark, Werner. The Sociology of Religion. *A Study of Christendom.*
  Volume II. *Sectarian Religion. 368 pp.*
  Volume III. *The Universal Church. 464 pp.*
  Volume IV. *Types of Religious Man. 352 pp.*
  Volume V. *Types of Religious Culture. 464 pp.*
Turner, B. S. Weber and Islam. *216 pp.*
Watt, W. Montgomery. Islam and the Integration of Society. *320 pp.*

SOCIOLOGY OF ART AND LITERATURE

Jarvie, Ian C. Towards a Sociology of the Cinema. *A Comparative Essay on the Structure and Functioning of a Major Entertainment Industry. 405 pp.*

Rust, Frances S. Dance in Society. *An Analysis of the Relationships between the Social Dance and Society in England from the Middle Ages to the Present Day. 256 pp. 8 pp. of plates.*

Schücking, L. L. The Sociology of Literary Taste. *112 pp.*

Wolff, Janet. Hermeneutic Philosophy and the Sociology of Art. *150 pp.*

SOCIOLOGY OF KNOWLEDGE

Diesing, P. Patterns of Discovery in the Social Sciences. *262 pp.*

● **Douglas, J. D.** (Ed.) Understanding Everyday Life. *370 pp.*

Glasner, B. Essential Interactionism. *About 220 pp.*

● **Hamilton, P.** Knowledge and Social Structure. *174 pp.*

Jarvie, I. C. Concepts and Society. *232 pp.*

Mannheim, Karl. Essays on the Sociology of Knowledge. *Edited by Paul Kecskemeti. Editorial Note by Adolph Lowe. 353 pp.*

Remmling, Gunter W. The Sociology of Karl Mannheim. *With a Bibliographical Guide to the Sociology of Knowledge, Ideological Analysis, and Social Planning. 255 pp.*

Remmling, Gunter W. (Ed.) Towards the Sociology of Knowledge. *Origin and Development of a Sociological Thought Style. 463 pp.*

URBAN SOCIOLOGY

Aldridge, M. The British New Towns. *A Programme Without a Policy. About 250 pp.*

Ashworth, William. The Genesis of Modern British Town Planning: *A Study in Economic and Social History of the Nineteenth and Twentieth Centuries. 288 pp.*

Brittan, A. The Privatised World. *196 pp.*

Cullingworth, J. B. Housing Needs and Planning Policy: *A Restatement of the Problems of Housing Need and 'Overspill' in England and Wales. 232 pp. 44 tables. 8 maps.*

Dickinson, Robert E. City and Region: *A Geographical Interpretation. 608 pp. 125 figures.*
The West European City: *A Geographical Interpretation. 600 pp. 129 maps. 29 plates.*

Humphreys, Alexander J. New Dubliners: *Urbanization and the Irish Family. Foreword by George C. Homans. 304 pp.*

Jackson, Brian. Working Class Community: *Some General Notions raised by a Series of Studies in Northern England. 192 pp.*

● **Mann, P. H.** An Approach to Urban Sociology. *240 pp.*

Mellor, J. R. Urban Sociology in an Urbanized Society. *326 pp.*

Morris, R. N. and **Mogey, J.** The Sociology of Housing. *Studies at Berinsfield. 232 pp. 4 pp. plates.*

Rosser, C. and **Harris, C.** The Family and Social Change. *A Study of Family and Kinship in a South Wales Town. 352 pp. 8 maps.*
● **Stacey, Margaret, Batsone, Eric, Bell, Colin** and **Thurcott, Anne.** Power, Persistence and Change. *A Second Study of Banbury. 196 pp.*

RURAL SOCIOLOGY

Mayer, Adrian C. Peasants in the Pacific. *A Study of Fiji Indian Rural Society. 248 pp. 20 plates.*
Williams, W. M. The Sociology of an English Village: *Gosforth. 272 pp. 12 figures. 13 tables.*

SOCIOLOGY OF INDUSTRY AND DISTRIBUTION

Dunkerley, David. The Foreman. *Aspects of Task and Structure. 192 pp.*
Eldridge, J. E. T. Industrial Disputes. *Essays in the Sociology of Industrial Relations. 288 pp.*
Hollowell, Peter G. The Lorry Driver. *272 pp.*
● **Oxaal, I., Barnett, T.** and **Booth, D.** (Eds) Beyond the Sociology of Development. *Economy and Society in Latin America and Africa. 295 pp.*
Smelser, Neil J. Social Change in the Industrial Revolution: *An Application of Theory to the Lancashire Cotton Industry, 1770–1840. 468 pp. 12 figures. 14 tables.*
Watson, T. J. The Personnel Managers. *A Study in the Sociology of Work and Employment. 262 pp.*

ANTHROPOLOGY

Brandel-Syrier, Mia. Reeftown Elite. *A Study of Social Mobility in a Modern African Community on the Reef. 376 pp.*
Dickie-Clark, H. F. The Marginal Situation. *A Sociological Study of a Coloured Group. 236 pp.*
Dube, S. C. Indian Village. *Foreword by Morris Edward Opler. 276 pp. 4 plates.*
  India's Changing Villages: *Human Factors in Community Development. 260 pp. 8 plates. 1 map.*
Firth, Raymond. Malay Fishermen. *Their Peasant Economy. 420 pp. 17 pp. plates.*
Gulliver, P. H. Social Control in an African Society: a Study of the Arusha, Agricultural Masai of Northern Tanganyika. *320 pp. 8 plates. 10 figures.*
  Family Herds. *288 pp.*
Jarvie, Ian C. The Revolution in Anthropology. *268 pp.*
Little, Kenneth L. Mende of Sierra Leone. *308 pp. and folder.*
  Negroes in Britain. *With a New Introduction and Contemporary Study by Leonard Bloom. 320 pp.*

Madan, G. R. Western Sociologists on Indian Society. *Marx, Spencer, Weber, Durkheim, Pareto. 384 pp.*

Mayer, A. C. Peasants in the Pacific. *A Study of Fiji Indian Rural Society. 248 pp.*

Meer, Fatima. Race and Suicide in South Africa. *325 pp.*

Smith, Raymond T. The Negro Family in British Guiana: *Family Structure and Social Status in the Villages. With a Foreword by Meyer Fortes. 314 pp. 8 plates. 1 figure. 4 maps.*

SOCIOLOGY AND PHILOSOPHY

Barnsley, John H. The Social Reality of Ethics. *A Comparative Analysis of Moral Codes. 448 pp.*

Diesing, Paul. Patterns of Discovery in the Social Sciences. *362 pp.*

● **Douglas, Jack D.** (Ed.) Understanding Everyday Life. *Toward the Reconstruction of Sociological Knowledge. Contributions by Alan F. Blum, Aaron W. Cicourel, Norman K. Denzin, Jack D. Douglas, John Heeren, Peter McHugh, Peter K. Manning, Melvin Power, Matthew Speier, Roy Turner, D. Lawrence Wieder, Thomas P. Wilson and Don H. Zimmerman. 370 pp.*

Gorman, Robert A. The Dual Vision. *Alfred Schutz and the Myth of Phenomenological Social Science. About 300 pp.*

Jarvie, Ian C. Concepts and Society. *216 pp.*

Kilminster, R. Praxis and Method. *A Sociological Dialogue with Lukács, Gramsci and the early Frankfurt School. About 304 pp.*

● **Pelz, Werner.** The Scope of Understanding in Sociology. *Towards a More Radical Reorientation in the Social Humanistic Sciences. 283 pp.*

Roche, Maurice. Phenomenology, Language and the Social Sciences. *371 pp.*

Sahay, Arun. Sociological Analysis. *212 pp.*

Slater, P. Origin and Significance of the Frankfurt School. *A Marxist Perspective. About 192 pp.*

Spurling, L. Phenomenology and the Social World. *The Philosophy of Merleau-Ponty and its Relation to the Social Sciences. 222 pp.*

Wilson, H. T. The American Ideology. *Science, Technology and Organization as Modes of Rationality. 368 pp.*

International Library of Anthropology

General Editor   Adam Kuper

Ahmed, A. S. Millenium and Charisma Among Pathans. *A Critical Essay in Social Anthropology. 192 pp.*
Pukhtun Economy and Society. *About 360 pp.*

Brown, Paula. The Chimbu. *A Study of Change in the New Guinea Highlands. 151 pp.*
Foner, N. Jamaica Farewell. *200 pp.*
Gudeman, Stephen. Relationships, Residence and the Individual. *A Rural Panamanian Community. 288 pp. 11 plates, 5 figures, 2 maps, 10 tables.*
The Demise of a Rural Economy. *From Subsistence to Capitalism in a Latin American Village. 160 pp.*
Hamnett, Ian. Chieftainship and Legitimacy. *An Anthropological Study of Executive Law in Lesotho. 163 pp.*
Hanson, F. Allan. Meaning in Culture. *127 pp.*
Humphreys, S. C. Anthropology and the Greeks. *288 pp.*
Karp, I. Fields of Change Among the Iteso of Kenya. *140 pp.*
Lloyd, P. C. Power and Independence. *Urban Africans' Perception of Social Inequality. 264 pp.*
Parry, J. P. Caste and Kinship in Kangra. *352 pp. Illustrated.*
Pettigrew, Joyce. Robber Noblemen. *A Study of the Political System of the Sikh Jats. 284 pp.*
Street, Brian V. The Savage in Literature. *Representations of 'Primitive' Society in English Fiction, 1858–1920. 207 pp.*
Van Den Berghe, Pierre L. Power and Privilege at an African University. *278 pp.*

International Library of Social Policy

General Editor Kathleen Jones

Bayley, M. Mental Handicap and Community Care. *426 pp.*
Bottoms, A. E. and **McClean, J. D.** Defendants in the Criminal Process. *284 pp.*
Butler, J. R. Family Doctors and Public Policy. *208 pp.*
Davies, Martin. Prisoners of Society. *Attitudes and Aftercare. 204 pp.*
Gittus, Elizabeth. Flats, Families and the Under-Fives. *285 pp.*
Holman, Robert. Trading in Children. *A Study of Private Fostering. 355 pp.*
Jeffs, A. Young People and the Youth Service. *About 180 pp.*
Jones, Howard, and **Cornes, Paul.** Open Prisons. *288 pp.*
Jones, Kathleen. History of the Mental Health Service. *428 pp.*
Jones, Kathleen, with **Brown, John, Cunningham, W. J., Roberts, Julian** and **Williams, Peter.** Opening the Door. *A Study of New Policies for the Mentally Handicapped. 278 pp.*
Karn, Valerie. Retiring to the Seaside. *About 280 pp. 2 maps. Numerous tables.*
King, R. D. and **Elliot, K. W.** Albany: Birth of a Prison—End of an Era. *394 pp.*

12

Thomas, J. E. The English Prison Officer since 1850: *A Study in Conflict.* *258 pp.*

Walton, R. G. Women in Social Work. *303 pp.*

● **Woodward, J.** To Do the Sick No Harm. *A Study of the British Voluntary Hospital System to 1875. 234 pp.*

International Library of Welfare and Philosophy

General Editors Noel Timms and David Watson

● **McDermott, F. E.** (Ed.) Self-Determination in Social Work. *A Collection of Essays on Self-determination and Related Concepts by Philosophers and Social Work Theorists. Contributors: F. B. Biestek, S. Bernstein, A. Keith-Lucas, D. Sayer, H. H. Perelman, C. Whittington, R. F. Stalley, F. E. McDermott, I. Berlin, H. J. McCloskey, H. L. A. Hart, J. Wilson, A. I. Melden, S. I. Benn. 254 pp.*

● **Plant, Raymond.** Community and Ideology. *104 pp.*

Ragg, Nicholas M. People Not Cases. *A Philosophical Approach to Social Work. About 250 pp.*

● **Timms, Noel** and **Watson, David.** (Eds) Talking About Welfare. *Readings in Philosophy and Social Policy. Contributors: T. H. Marshall, R. B. Brandt, G. H. von Wright, K. Nielsen, M. Cranston, R. M. Titmuss, R. S. Downie, E. Telfer, D. Donnison, J. Benson, P. Leonard, A. Keith-Lucas, D. Walsh, I. T. Ramsey. 320 pp.*

● (Eds). Philosophy in Social Work. *250 pp.*

● **Weale, A.** Equality and Social Policy. *164 pp.*

Primary Socialization, Language and Education

General Editor Basil Bernstein

Adlam, Diana S., *with the assistance of Geoffrey Turner and Lesley Lineker.* Code in Context. *About 272 pp.*

Bernstein, Basil. Class, Codes and Control. *3 volumes.*

● 1. *Theoretical Studies Towards a Sociology of Language. 254 pp.*

2. *Applied Studies Towards a Sociology of Language. 377 pp.*

● 3. *Towards a Theory of Educational Transmission. 167 pp.*

Brandis, W. and **Bernstein, B.** Selection and Control. *176 pp.*

Brandis, Walter and **Henderson, Dorothy.** Social Class, Language and Communication. *288 pp.*

Cook-Gumperz, Jenny. Social Control and Socialization. *A Study of Class Differences in the Language of Maternal Control. 290 pp.*

● **Gahagan, D. M** and **G. A.** Talk Reform. *Exploration in Language for Infant School Children. 160 pp.*

Hawkins, P. R. Social Class, the Nominal Group and Verbal Strategies. *About 220 pp.*

Robinson, W. P. and **Rackstraw, Susan D. A.** A Question of Answers. *2 volumes. 192 pp. and 180 pp.*

Turner, Geoffrey J. and **Mohan, Bernard A.** A Linguistic Description and Computer Programme for Children's Speech. *208 pp.*

Reports of the Institute of Community Studies

Baker, J. The Neighbourhood Advice Centre. A Community Project in Camden. *320 pp.*

● **Cartwright, Ann.** Patients and their Doctors. *A Study of General Practice. 304 pp.*

Dench, Geoff. Maltese in London. *A Case-study in the Erosion of Ethnic Consciousness. 302 pp.*

Jackson, Brian and **Marsden, Dennis.** Education and the Working Class: *Some General Themes raised by a Study of 88 Working-class Children in a Northern Industrial City. 268 pp. 2 folders.*

Marris, Peter. The Experience of Higher Education. *232 pp. 27 tables.*

● Loss and Change. *192 pp.*

Marris, Peter and **Rein, Martin.** Dilemmas of Social Reform. *Poverty and Community Action in the United States. 256 pp.*

Marris, Peter and **Somerset, Anthony.** African Businessmen. *A Study of Entrepreneurship and Development in Keyna. 256 pp.*

Mills, Richard. Young Outsiders: *a Study in Alternative Communities. 216 pp.*

Runciman, W. G. Relative Deprivation and Social Justice. *A Study of Attitudes to Social Inequality in Twentieth-Century England. 352 pp.*

Willmott, Peter. Adolescent Boys in East London. *230 pp.*

Willmott, Peter and **Young, Michael.** Family and Class in a London Suburb. *202 pp. 47 tables.*

Young, Michael and **McGeeney, Patrick.** Learning Begins at Home. *A Study of a Junior School and its Parents. 128 pp.*

Young, Michael and **Willmott, Peter.** Family and Kinship in East London. *Foreword by Richard M. Titmuss. 252 pp. 39 tables.*

The Symmetrical Family. *410 pp.*

Reports of the Institute for Social Studies in Medical Care

Cartwright, Ann, Hockey, Lisbeth and **Anderson, John J.** Life Before Death. *310 pp.*

Dunnell, Karen and **Cartwright, Ann.** Medicine Takers, Prescribers and Hoarders. *190 pp.*

Farrell, C. My Mother Said. . . . *A Study of the Way Young People Learned About Sex and Birth Control. 200 pp.*

Medicine, Illness and Society

General Editor W. M. Williams

Hall, David J. Social Relations & Innovation. *Changing the State of Play in Hospitals. 232 pp.*

Hall, David J., and **Stacey, M.** (Eds) Beyond Separation. *234 pp.*

Robinson, David. The Process of Becoming Ill. *142 pp.*

Stacey, Margaret *et al.* Hospitals, Children and Their Families. *The Report of a Pilot Study. 202 pp.*

Stimson G. V. and **Webb, B.** Going to See the Doctor. *The Consultation Process in General Practice. 155 pp.*

Monographs in Social Theory

General Editor Arthur Brittan

● **Barnes, B.** Scientific Knowledge and Sociological Theory. *192 pp.*

Bauman, Zygmunt. Culture as Praxis. *204 pp.*

● **Dixon, Keith.** Sociological Theory. *Pretence and Possibility. 142 pp.*

Meltzer, B. N., Petras, J. W. and **Reynolds, L. T.** Symbolic Interactionism. *Genesis, Varieties and Criticisms. 144 pp.*

● **Smith, Anthony D.** The Concept of Social Change. *A Critique of the Functionalist Theory of Social Change. 208 pp.*

Routledge Social Science Journals

The British Journal of Sociology. *Editor – Angus Stewart; Associate Editor – Leslie Sklair. Vol. 1, No. 1 – March 1950 and Quarterly. Roy. 8vo. All back issues available. An international journal publishing original papers in the field of sociology and related areas.*

Community Work. *Edited by David Jones and Marjorie Mayo. 1973. Published annually.*
Economy and Society. *Vol. 1, No. 1. February 1972 and Quarterly. Metric Roy. 8vo. A journal for all social scientists covering sociology, philosophy, anthropology, economics and history. All back numbers available.*
Ethnic and Racial Studies. *Editor – John Stone. Vol. 1 – 1978. Published quarterly.*
Religion. Journal of Religion and Religions. *Chairman of Editorial Board, Ninian Smart. Vol. 1, No. 1, Spring 1971. A journal with an inter-disciplinary approach to the study of the phenomena of religion. All back numbers available.*
Sociology of Health and Illness. *A Journal of Medical Sociology. Editor – Alan Davies; Associate Editor – Ray Jobling. Vol. 1, Spring 1979. Published 3 times per annum.*
Year Book of Social Policy in Britain, The. *Edited by Kathleen Jones. 1971. Published annually.*

Social and Psychological Aspects of Medical Practice

Editor Trevor Silverstone

Lader, Malcolm. Psychophysiology of Mental Illness. *280 pp.*
● **Silverstone, Trevor** and **Turner, Paul.** Drug Treatment in Psychiatry. *Revised edition. 256 pp.*
Whiteley, J. S. and **Gordon, J.** Group Approaches in Psychiatry. *256 pp.*

Printed in Great Britain by
Lowe & Brydone Printers Limited, Thetford, Norfolk